The Journey of Caste in India

This book provides a comprehensive overview of caste in contemporary India. With contributions from scholars like Valerian Rodrigues, B.B. Mohanty, Surinder Jodhka, and Anand Teltumbde, it discusses wide-ranging themes like the trajectory of caste in post-independence India; Dalits and cultural identity; the paradox of being a Dalit woman; caste violence and social mobility; Ambedkar's quest for the right of social equality; social security for the inclusive development of Dalits; discrimination and exclusion of Dalits in education; and Dalit merit and institutional injustice, and presents an overview of the struggles for distributive justice in India.

This volume will be of importance to scholars and researchers of Dalit studies, social justice, exclusion studies, caste studies, affirmative action, political studies, sociology, social anthropology, and South Asian politics.

N. Sukumar teaches Political Science at Delhi University, India. His area of interest includes Indian Political Thought, Ambedkar and Dalit Bahujan Studies, Human Rights, and Social Exclusion. Currently, he is engaged in the study of caste discrimination in Indian universities and Dalit Citizenship. He is also a member/advisor for many professional bodies in many Central Universities and other institutions. For his research credit he owns one international project on "Dalits and Well Being" (Indo-Swiss ICSSR Research Project), two major research projects – one on "Student Politics in Central Universities" (funded by UGC), and the second one is on "Exclusion and Discrimination in Higher Education" (funded by the ICSSR) – one sponsored project on "University as a Sight of Exclusion" (funded by the ICSSR). He also conducted two research projects – one on "Panchayati Raj" and another on "Atrocities on Dalits" – in association with the Indian Institute of Dalit Studies, Delhi. He has published widely in research journals, blogs, etc., and has been involved in both national and international research studies on poverty and public institutions, migration, and caste-based atrocities. Apart from the classroom, he is also actively involved in grassroots people's struggles.

Paul D'Souza, after completing his PhD from Jawaharlal Nehru University, Delhi, India, served at various institutes in Gujarat engaged in social action and research at the grassroots. Since 2013 he has been with the Indian Social Institute, New Delhi, India, first as Research Director and then working as Head of the Department of Dalit Studies. Indian Social Institute, established in 1951 is a premier Centre for Research, Training and Action for Socio-Economic Development and Human Rights in India.

His areas of interest and engagement have been marginalisation and development and city and caste. He has engaged with a number of research projects: "Negotiating Citizenship in Urban Space: A Study of Delhi Resettlement Project" (funded by the ICSSR); "Discrimination and Exclusion in Education: A Study of the Children of Communities Engaged in 'Unclean Occupations'" (funded by the ICSSR); half-widows of Kashmir, the refugees of Afghanistan, etc. His current research engagement focuses on "Single Women and the Emerging Social Change among Tribals of Gujarat". He has a number of years of experience working at the grassroots with marginalised communities. He has published articles in various journals and has contributed chapters to several edited volumes.

The Journey of Caste in India

Voices from Margins

Edited by
N. Sukumar and Paul D'Souza

Routledge
Taylor & Francis Group

LONDON AND NEW YORK

Designed Cover Image: Getty Image

First published 2023
by Routledge
4 Park Square, Milton Park, Abingdon, Oxon OX14 4RN

and by Routledge
605 Third Avenue, New York, NY 10158

Routledge is an imprint of the Taylor & Francis Group, an informa business

British Library Cataloguing-in-Publication Data
A catalogue record for this book is available from the British Library

ISBN: 978-1-032-31977-3 (hbk)
ISBN: 978-1-032-32886-7 (pbk)
ISBN: 978-1-003-31717-3 (ebk)

DOI: 10.4324/9781003317173

Typeset in Sabon
by Deanta Global Publishing Services, Chennai, India

Contents

PART III
Caste Violence: Movements for Social Mobility   93

Contributors

Teena Anil is Assistant Professor working at the programme of Public Policy and Governance, School of Global Affairs, Dr. B.R. Ambedkar University Delhi. She teaches graduate, postgraduate, and PhD students. She graduated in Social Sciences and completed her postgraduation, MPhil, and PhD in sociology from JNU, New Delhi, India. Her interest of research centres around issues of marginality and urban governance, citizenship, gender, caste, and city space.

Selvaraj Arulnathan is currently serving as Vice-President of Loyola College, Vettavalam, Tamilnadu, India. He is a social researcher, trainer, and activist. He has worked as Director and Research Director of the Indian Social Institute, Bangalore, and Head of the Department of Dalit Studies, Indian Social Institute, Delhi, India. He has published books and articles on caste, gender, developmental discourse, rights of minorities, and Dalit identity. His latest research is on "Mapping the Socio-Economic Status of the Marginalized Communities in Northern Tamilnadu" which is in print.

Pradyumna Bag is a sociologist by training and specialises in rural and agrarian studies, Dalit and minority studies, sociology of education, and environmental sociology. He has been teaching in the Department of Sociology, Jamia Millia Islamia (JMI), New Delhi, India, since 2008. He has authored several articles in reputed journals and chapters in edited books. Currently, he is working on caste in rural and agrarian society, Dalit middle class, inequality in education, and agrarian distress.

K.S. Chalam is Ex-Member Union Public Service Commission and a well-known Political Economist, Educationist, and a Scholar of Dravidian Studies. Prof. K.S. Chalam is known throughout the country as the facilitator of the Academic Staff College concept and was likewise recognised for his Studies on Higher Education. He served as Vice-chancellor, Dravidian University, Kuppam Andhra Pradesh, India. He has published over 25 books and numerous research papers in reputed journals. His recent book was *Caste-based Reservations and Human Development in India*.

Subhadra Mitra Channa taught Anthropology at the University of Delhi, India. Her areas of interest are marginalisation and identity, gender, religion and cosmology, ecology, and landscapes. She has written about 50 scholarly papers and is the author/editor of eight books. She was the President of the Indian Anthropological Association and an editor of the *Indian Anthropologist*. Her most recent publications include *Gender in South Asia* (Cambridge University Press),; *The Inner and Outer Selves'* (Oxford University Press), the edited book *Life as a Dalit* (ed.) (Sage Publications), and *Gendering Material Culture* (ed.).

Paul D'Souza is an independent researcher at the Centre for Human Rights and People's Empowerment in Songadh, Gujarat, India. After completing his PhD at Jawaharlal Nehru University, Delhi, he was with the Indian Social Institute, New Delhi, India, first as Research Director and then as Head of the Department of Dalit Studies. His areas of interest and engagement have been marginalisation and development and city and caste. He has published articles in various journals and chapters in edited books.

Surinder S. Jodhka is Professor of Sociology at the Jawaharlal Nehru University and Fellow at the Centre de Sciences Humaines, New Delhi, India. He has published extensively, including *Caste* (OUP), *Caste in Contemporary India* (Routledge), and *Mapping the Elite: Power, Privilege and Inequality* (OUP, co-edited). He is the editor of the Routledge Book Series Religion and Citizenship.

Raj Kumar is Professor in the Department of English at Delhi University, India. His research areas include autobiographical studies, Dalit literature, Indian writing in English, Odia literature, and post-colonial studies. His book *Dalit Personal Narratives: Reading Caste, Nation and Identity* has been published by Orient BlackSwan, New Delhi, India, in 2010 and got reprinted in 2011, 2015, and 2017. His English translation of Akhila Naik's *Bheda*, the first Odia Dalit novel, is published by Oxford University Press, Delhi, India, in 2017. His book *Dalit Literature and Criticism* was published by Orient BlackSwan, New Delhi, in 2019.

Prakash Louis is Director of the Xavier Institute of Social Research and Coordinator of Bihar Migrant Hub, Patna, India. He was Executive Director of the Indian Social Institute, New Delhi, as well as Director of the Indian Social Institute, Bangalore, India. He was also South Asia Director of Jesuit Refugee Services. He was also the editor of *Social Action Journal*. Two of his major publications are *People Power: The Naxalite Movement in Central Bihar* and *Political Sociology of Dalit Assertion*.

Shailaja Menon teaches modern Indian history at the School of Liberal Studies, Ambedkar University, Delhi, India. Her research interests revolve around gender, urban studies, social exclusion, and marginality on which she has published in national and international journals. She has also conducted research projects on these themes.

P. Muthaiah formerly headed the Department of Political Science at Osmania University, India. He has worked on issues of caste, especially sub-caste politics in Andhra Pradesh. He is known for his scholarship and has widely published in various edited books and journals.

Ambrose Pinto was the Executive Director of the Indian Social Institute and the Editor of the Social Action from 1998 to 2001. He was Lecturer in Political Science at St. Joseph's College, Bangalore, and later Principal of St. Joseph's College, Bangalore, India, from 2003 to 2011. He has published extensively on Dalits and political issues, with many books and edited volumes to his credit. He was formerly Fellow of the Indian Institute of Advanced Studies, Shimla, India.

Valerian Rodrigues is an Indian political scientist. He is known for his influential work on Babasaheb Ambedkar. Rodrigues has made substantial contributions to the debate on the working of the Indian Parliament, constitutionalism in India, and agrarian politics in India. He has taught Political Science at the Department of Political Science at Mangalore University, Karnataka, and at the Centre for Political Studies at Jawaharlal Nehru University (JNU), New Delhi, India. He held the first Ambedkar Chair at the Ambedkar University Delhi and was Fellow of the Indian Institute of Advanced Studies, Shimla, India.

Karunakar Singh was Professor and Head at St. Andrew's College, Gorakhpur, India. He has also widely published on issues of caste.

N. Sukumar teaches Political Science at Delhi University, India. His area of interest includes Indian political thought, Ambedkar and Dalit Bahujan studies, human rights, and social exclusion. Currently, he is engaged with in the study of caste discrimination in Indian universities and on Dalit citizenship. Apart from the classroom, he is also actively involved in grassroots people's struggles.

Anand Teltumbde is a civil rights activist and scholar. He was Professor at the Indian Institute of Technology Kharagpur and later became Senior Professor at the Goa Institute of Management, India. He has written extensively about the caste system in India and has advocated for the rights of Dalits. Among his many books are *Dalits: Past, Present and Future* and *Mahad: The Making of the First Dalit Revolt*. His book *Republic of Caste* is a collection of essays that assesses the position of Dalits, including the relationship between caste and class.

Foreword

The academic world places an undue emphasis on newness – or so I have often thought. In the race to find every newer thing to say, or the struggle to say old things in new ways, we risk missing the staple truths of social life. That is why I am especially happy to have the privilege of writing a few words as a preamble to this worthy collection of writings on one of the perennial subjects of Indian social science, namely caste and its discontents.

The latest event that goes to prove that "the journey of caste in India" is unending is the Supreme Court's recent judgement upholding the 103rd Amendment to the Constitution through which reservation was provided to the "Economically Weaker Sections" (EWS). Although caste is conspicuous by its absence from both the text of the Act and the criteria prescribed for determining eligibility for inclusion in the EWS category, the new law is effectively about caste. In its intent – and, of course, in the public's perception – this is a move to provide reservations for the upper castes. This intention is signalled through the controversial exclusion from the EWS category of all groups already provided reservation, i.e., the Scheduled Tribes, Scheduled Castes, and the Other Backward Classes, even when the economic conditions of eligibility are met.

This judgement erases the distinction between economic disadvantage and caste-based discrimination and deprivation. While the state should no doubt assist the poor, reservation need not (and perhaps should not) be the form that this assistance takes. Reservation is a strong measure because it deliberately overrules the principle of equality, which is an indispensable founding principle of our republic. As such, reservation should be used sparingly and with care. Until now, both the courts and the state had employed this modality only for castes that had suffered sustained social discrimination and exclusion. By using the same modality for the economically weaker segments of the upper castes, the state is now signalling that it does not consider caste-based discrimination to be any different from the disadvantages caused by "economic weakness."

It is hardly surprising, therefore, that most commentators – regardless of whether they are for or against this law – are perceiving it as part of the ongoing struggles around caste and social justice. Just three decades separate EWS reservation from the tumult around the extension of reservation to the

OBCs. Compared to the dramatic and widespread protests by upper-caste youth at that time, there is no public opposition to EWS reservations today. Reservation has been the topic most readily associated with caste by most Indians, and the example of the EWS reservation shows how much the terrain of this topic has changed since the original idea took shape as a prelude to the formation of the Indian nation.

This collection of essays and reports from *Social Action*, the journal of the Indian Social Institute (ISI), New Delhi, provides an overview of the past two decades of change around the caste question. Despite the friendly jokes about its initials, the Indian Social Institute has been one of the leading organisations in the social justice and human rights fields. It has an inspiring record of steadfast commitment to constitutional advocacy on behalf of the oppressed and the voiceless. The ISI's journal *Social Action* successfully straddles the gap between scholarly writing and the more immediate concerns of activists engaged in grassroots campaigns.

This collection of essays, originally published in *Social Action* between 2000 and 2018, provides a valuable and wide-ranging compendium of aspects and perspectives on issues related to caste. It features some of our best social scientists and engaged scholars and activists and illuminates specific aspects of change in caste-based inequalities, discrimination, and violence and the responses they have provoked over the decades. The areas covered include culture and identity, rights and rights-based movements, regional contexts and conflicts, globalisation and its impact, and various forms and processes of caste discrimination in institutions.

This volume makes three valuable contributions. The first is that it brings together essays that were otherwise scattered across two decades' worth of issues of a journal. This provides a synergistic boost to each essay, which gains by its proximity to others with similar or contrasting concerns. It also serves as a reminder of issues, questions, and problems that have receded from public memory. The very nature of a periodical publication – it being a continuing series – encourages the community of readers to "move on." By arresting this movement in the form of a book, this collection allows the essays included here to stand still and resonate with the readers' own concerns.

The second notable contribution of this volume is that it serves as a reminder of how far we have come on the caste question, but also how far we still need to go. Change has been so rapid and comprehensive that it challenges our collective memory to retain an awareness of how things were and in what ways they have been transformed, but also how some aspects of caste are stubborn in their persistence. This is particularly noticeable, for example, in the accounts of past conflicts and campaigns which require to be revisited periodically to measure the extent and direction of social change. What do we learn about the present state of intra-Dalit inequalities by recounting the course of the Dandora movement? Does remembering the conflict in Talhan tell us something about caste dynamics in Punjab today? Does recalling the days of Bahujan ascendance in Uttar Pradesh offer any clues about its right-ward majoritarian turn today?

The third contribution of this volume is perhaps the most significant. By including divergent perspectives and viewpoints, the editors have rightly highlighted the range of views on caste questions. The commonsensical expectation that questions of discrimination, oppression, or domination are straightforward and simple is routinely contradicted by historical experience. For example, the last three decades have seen the rise to dominance of rights-based approaches to justice, but in the very first chapter of this book, these approaches are challenged. Another chapter counters the widespread belief that the "high growth" period of the post-liberalisation economy has benefited all, including Dalits. Yet another contribution engages with what it terms Ambedkar's "prevarications" on the question of culture. As these examples (and they are not the only ones) go to show, this volume showcases a diversity of views within the broad rubric of commitment to fighting caste injustice in all its forms.

The authors of the original contributions and the editors of this volume have fulfilled their responsibility by providing us with wide-ranging perspectives on the continual transformation as well as the continuing reproduction of caste inequalities. For this they deserve our appreciation and thanks. It is now up to us, the readers, to fulfil our share of responsibility by engaging actively and critically with this book, while accompanying it on its journey through the landscape of caste.

To the reader about to set out on this journey: Bon voyage!

Satish Deshpande
Delhi

Acknowledgements

The Journey of Caste in India: Voices from Margins is indeed a story of a long journey. This book is the result of several discussions among concerned scholars about linking grassroots research with academic engagement. This is indeed required for most institutions in the country which conduct rigorous research which seldom see the light of the day. For many decades, "Social Action" has reflected intense debates on multiple social concerns revolving around caste in contemporary India.

We are grateful to the Indian Social Institute, New Delhi, and the editor of the journal for granting us permission to include the pre-published research works of the scholars. The Indian Social Institute was established in 1951 in response to the challenges of nation-building and a new emerging social order in an independent India. *Social Action* – a UGC-approved social science journal – has been published continuously since 1951 by the institute, capturing the social dimensions of independent India.

The contributors to this volume are scholars who have published their works in *Social Action*. Together, they cover a wide range of disciplinary backgrounds and have worked on the question of caste. They are Ambrose Pinto, Valerian Rodrigues, Pradyumna Bag, Raj Kumar, Selvaraj Arulnathan, Subhadra Mitra Channa, P. Muthaiah, K.S. Chalam, Prakash Louis, Surinder Jodhka, Anand Teltumbde, Karunakar Singh, Paul D'Souza, Tina Anil, N. Sukumar, and Shailaja Menon. We are grateful to each one of them for enriching this volume with their scholarly work.

We take this opportunity to express our gratitude to the anonymous reviewers for their encouragement, suggestions, and comments that have helped improve the manuscript. We are extremely grateful to Prof. Satish Deshpande (Delhi School of Economics) for enhancing this volume and for writing the foreword to this volume.

As editors, we express our gratitude to the team at Routledge who encouraged this endeavour. The idea of this edited volume was shared with Dr. Shashank Sinha, Publishing Director, who willingly explored the possibilities of taking it to its logical conclusion. His colleagues, Ms. Antara Ray Chaudhury, Ms. Anvita Bajaj, and Ms. Angelin Joy, who professionally, yet gently, guided and helped us through various phases of the publication. We are also beholden to Mr. Narayanan Ramachandran, the Copy Editor-Deanta

Global for his meticulous copy-editing of the manuscript; Mr. Christu John for preparing the index and Mr. Gillian Steadman, Senior Production Editor-Routledge for taking the project forward for final publication

This book would not have been possible without the active support of our colleagues at the Indian Social Institute and at Delhi University. We are indeed grateful to Vidyasagar Sharma and Anjana Ranjith, research scholars at the University of Delhi and TISS Mumbai, respectively, for their unfailing assistance at every stage of preparing the manuscript. Dayal Singh, Satya Srinivasan, Anjana Das, John Kullu, Ruben Minj, and Shabib Anwar from the Indian Social Institute deserve our gratitude for their assistance in the library, their support in preparing the manuscript, and for their practical secretarial assistance that made things happen.

Finally, our heartfelt thanks to the people who actively helped to make this project a reality. We gratefully acknowledge Dr. Denzil Fernandez and Dr. Shailaja Menon, without whose help this book would not have been possible.

Introduction

Paul D'Souza and N. Sukumar

The Journey of Caste in India: Voices from Margins

The journey of caste in India has a long genesis ranging from the most banal to the most philosophical. A wide spectrum of scholars has attempted to understand, analyse, and deconstruct caste in multiple contexts. At different historical junctures, ideas of caste have undergone permutations. Caste, despite all opposition in different times, has remained a system of operation in everyday interactions of different social groups. Apart from social and economic reasons (see Habib 2000), there are clearly visible connections between caste and power. The dominant groups in every historical period, whether *Brahmins* and *Kshatriyas*, the power elites of pre-medieval era, or the Indo-Muslim rulers in the medieval period or British powers during colonial rule, kept the caste discourse going on in one form or the other for their vested interests. "Rulers changed, but the caste structuring of society continued to find recognition irrespective of such changes" (Chatterjee 2004).

Nicholas Dirks in fact argues that

> caste as we know it now, is a relatively modern phenomenon – the product of the encounter between India and British colonial rule. This is not to suggest that the British invented caste, but to show that it was on account of British domination that "caste" became a single term capable of expressing, organizing, and above all "systematizing" India's diverse forms of social identity, community, and organization. Colonialism made caste the central symbol of Indian society.
>
> (Dirks 2002: 5)

In modern democratic India the emergence of caste as a significant factor in our socio-political life needs to be seen from a historical perspective.

With the coming of modernity and development it was expected that the secular would triumph over the sacred; it was predicted that primordial ideas and identities of caste, region, and religion would be dissolute with the onward march of progress and development. "Yet defying all theoretical postulations, these identities have come to form some of the major loci of politics in the modern world" (Gooptu 1996: 221). In the course of rapid

DOI: 10.4324/9781003317173-1

urban transformation, the poor and the marginalised have invested caste and religion with new meaning and significance for their social and political action. Gupta encapsulates this reality while he says, "Caste has not changed, but the potentialities that were always there within this stratificatory system are now out in the open and in full view" (Gupta 2004: xix). Caste remains a significant factor shaping social identities and relations, affecting the life-chances of various sections in democratic India in many ways. A culmination was reached with the adoption of the Indian Constitution which provided a concrete blueprint to dismantle the caste apparatus. The existence of caste acted as a blockade to the realisation of *liberty, equality, justice, and fraternity as envisioned in the constitution*. Despite its numerous obituaries, caste continues to flash its hydra-headed nature provoking a fresh investigation into its myriad journeys.

A historical perspective (see Guru 2000) indicates that the traditional caste system entrusted the "untouchables" with service and excluded them from holding any worthwhile assets in land. The hierarchical social structure barred them from the more dignified occupations and bonded them to occupations which were considered defiling. They were confined to fixed boundaries, ghettoised in space at the outskirts. The religious sphere debarred them from entering the places of worship as they were considered polluting. They were kept away from education (knowledge system). The field of politics and entry into the power structure was not accessible to them. They were subjects only to have an attitude of supplication and subservience to their patrons. The exclusion and marginalisation of the subordinated caste communities at the bottom of the hierarchy continued for ages.

The caste-based discrimination, economic and political injustice, and exploitation gradually gave rise to strong organised movements among the lower castes led by Jyotirao Phule in Maharashtra, Ramaswamy Periyar in Tamil Nadu, Narayana Guru in Kerala, Achutanand in Uttar Pradesh, Mangoo Ram in Punjab, and many others throughout India. In multiple socio-cultural and political contexts, these movements provided a distinct identity to the lower castes and challenged the dominance of the higher castes. Similarly, the political mobilisation led by Ambedkar through the establishment of the All India Scheduled Castes Federation brought sharpness and intensity to their self-definition and consciousness (Mohanty 2002; Vivek 2002). Over the last three decades the question of caste has come back into Indian political and economic life, defining differently the significance of caste for social change in Indian society.

The concepts of justice and equity are asynchronous with caste and have been instrumental in deconstructing social hierarchies. Justice is primarily a problem of moral philosophy. Though a problem of moral philosophy, it does not shed its character of being a determinant of distributive action in society. This very truth gives it a political fervour. The concept of social justice is best understood as forming one part of the broader concept of justice in general. To comprehend it properly, we should begin by looking at justice as a whole, and then attempt to mark off that division of justice which we call social justice. The question of justice arises under two conditions: (a) In a scarcity situation – when goods, services, etc. are too scarce to satisfy all contestants; and (b) in an open society – where all allocation of various benefits is not tied to fixed status of various individuals, but they are free to demand a fair share on some reasonable ground.

This highlights why many scholars call justice a "distributive" political principle. Now, to look for a just definition of "justice" would be a futile job as justice is not something that can be exactly bound in the limit of words but something of a broad use, and this use of the term has had its own contextual relevance and ever dynamic character. Most of the liberal theories on justice are based on three principles: (a) the principle of rights, (b) the principle of merits, and (c) the principle of needs. In his classic study on the practice of untouchability in the 1970s in Gujarat, I.P. Desai observed that with the process of modernisation and development even in rural areas a new "public sphere" of social interaction had emerged where the practice of untouchability was quite low. The norm of caste and untouchability had begun to be violated in the economic or occupational sphere as well. This included seating arrangements in schools, travelling in buses and the postal services. However, when it came to traditional relations that included the domestic and religious life of the people, untouchability was highly practised. Untouchability continued to be a major disability for the lower castes as far as water facilities were concerned (Desai 1976).

A repeat of the study was done nearly 25 years later, when Ghanshyam Shah visited the villages of Gujarat again with a similar set of questions; he found that with the exception of admission of "untouchables" into temples and houses of upper castes as well as access to barbers' services, the practice of untouchability had declined in most areas of everyday life. It was in the "public sphere" which is directly managed by the state laws and which has a relatively non-traditional character like schools, postal services and elected *panchayats* that untouchability had considerably declined. However, as Shah notes,

> one would have expected by now, complete disappearance of untouchability in public transport and post offices as it was not widespread in 1971. But it has not happened. The proportion of the villages observing untouchability in these spheres has, in fact slightly increased.
>
> (Shah 2002: 145)

The above case study illustrates that untouchablility continues to manifest in multiple forms despite the interventions of modern institutions and their policy frameworks. The concept of social justice, however, has to be seen as a larger paradigm. It is here that we locate the issue of the redistribution-recognition debate (Fraser 2005) that is central to recent arguments on justice.

Today, however, we increasingly encounter a second type of social justice claim in the "politics of recognition". Here the goal, in its most plausible form, is a difference-friendly world, where assimilation to majority or dominant cultural norms is no longer the price of equal respect. Examples include exploitation (having the fruits of one's labour appropriated for the benefit of others); economic marginalisation (being confined to undesirable or poorly paid work or being denied access to income-generating labour altogether); and deprivation (being denied an adequate material standard of living). The politics of recognition, in contrast, targets injustices it understands as cultural, which it presumes to be rooted in social patterns of representation, interpretation, and communication. Examples include cultural domination (being subjected to patterns of interpretation and communication that are associated with another culture and are alien and/or hostile to one's own); non-recognition (being rendered invisible via the authoritative representational, communicative, and interpretative practices of one's culture); and disrespect (being routinely maligned or disparaged in stereotypic public cultural representations and/or in everyday life interactions) (Fraser 1996: 3–7).

Social justice concerns the distribution of benefits and burdens throughout including intangible benefits like self-respect and social recognition. The problem of social justice has arisen especially in the context of the welfare state where some subaltern studies group as "subalterns" were denied equal access to resources and self-respect which is inevitable in a caste-based society. The point is how the marginalisation of these groups has occurred. Partha Chatterjee (2006) argues that this is a historical construct arising due to the adoption of the western structure of political institutions that undermined the caste and community way of living that upheld greater moral order compared to state institutions. However, the notion of the "subaltern" is also highly contested.

Undeniably, there has been a lack of equality for "subalterns", and this has created enough space for movements to grow and demand their rights. Thus, these movements are fighting for social justice. As democracy cannot prosper for long if the voice of the "unheard" is not heard, it led to the creation of various institutions and the implementation of an assortment of policies to respond to calls for social justice. Since these institutions responded unequally, it led to the creation of more marginal groups within the marginalised. The process of globalisation also added to these woes. As a result, new movements arose. These movements were termed either "New Social Movements" or "Politics at the grassroots". The demand of these movements is creating new public spaces which Partha Chatterjee calls "Political Society" (see Bhattacharyya 2021). Thus, we see a short glimpse of the trajectory of struggles for distributive justice in India.

The past few decades have witnessed the broadening of the contours of political society with multiple demands. On the one hand, we have marginalised groups of Dalits, tribals, and minorities demanding their constitutional rights, caste-based panchayats, self-rule through gram-sabhas arguing for communitarian benefits, to the vociferous middle class–dominated civil society struggles against organised corruption. Deconstructing the modes of protest and discursive formations of these rainbow groups makes for fascinating analysis.

The present volume is divided into three parts: Part I-The Trajectory of Caste in Post-Independent India; Part II- Dalit Culture and Identity; and Part III-Caste Violence: Movements for Social Mobility. This book dwells on some of the most telling aspects of the trajectory of the struggle for distributive justice for creating public space of Dalits of India. In addition, the themes traverse through the historical journey of caste, mobilisation, and caste violence and the movements for justice, dignity, and emancipation.

Thematic Descriptions

Part I: The Trajectory of Caste in Post-Independent India

The emergence of independent India after a long-drawn struggle against colonialism, the drafting of the Constitution, and the birth of a socialist, democratic republic reflected the hopes and aspirations of the masses. If Nehru's Tryst with Destiny set the template for a new imagination, Ambedkar's caution in the Constituent Assembly about the necessity of social democracy along with political freedom focused on the structures of caste, gender, and class inequalities. The emancipatory potential of the Ambedkarite constitution was left untapped by a socio-political class who wished to perpetuate their hegemony. Seeking a new path for the upliftment of the marginalised people, Ambedkar converted to Buddhism, igniting a new sociocultural discourse. In theory, the state was supposed to promote the welfare of the citizens in all spheres of life, but the nexus between the ruling elite and the landed aristocracy continued its hold on power. In the long term, this nexus resulted in the failure of land reforms, Civil Rights Protection Act (specifically introduced to prevent caste atrocities), unemployment and poverty led to the emergence of social movements.

The report of the National Commission for Scheduled Castes and Scheduled Tribes (April 1990), in its sample survey of a number of states, found that untouchability prevailed in various forms in different places (see S.P. Srivastava 1997). The Ambedkar Centenary celebration committee of Chittoor District of Andhra Pradesh conducted an elaborate door-to-door survey in a *padayatra* to 249 villages to assess the prevalence of untouchability (ACCCR 1991). The study obtained similar findings to that of I.P. Desai. The study found out that along with other restrictions in at least 16 of the villages visited, members of Scheduled Castes were not allowed to walk with any type of footwear through streets used by non-Dalits.

Another study conducted in Karnataka in 1973–74 in 76 villages and 38 urban centres confirmed the widespread practice of untouchability. The magnitude of the problem was less severe in urban centres, but even in urban areas, for example, 15 per cent of the respondents were not allowed to draw water from public water sources (Parvathamma 1984). Ramesh Kamble's study of Dalit social experience in the urban setting of Mumbai shows that the social discrimination and economic exploitation they face have not changed even in a metropolis like Mumbai. Rather, it has assumed different forms (Kamble 2002).

Even among Dalit groups, those at the bottom of the caste hierarchy experience untouchability, and discrimination from those above in the Dalit category. Moffatt argues that even the untouchables, the bottom-most stratum of Hindu society, accept the cultural principles and concede the definition of purity and the caste system which defines them as the "archetype of impurity" (Moffat 1979). And what Desai had observed a quarter of a century ago still remains a social reality that "there is untouchability among the ex-untouchables themselves" (Desai 1976). Among Dalits the scavengers are the most oppressed and disadvantaged section of the population (Human Rights Watch 1999). There is evidence that manual scavengers are considered untouchable by other ex-untouchables (NCDHR 2000).

One significant such movement which has continued to hold sway over the people is the Dalit movement which has ebbed and flowed over the past few decades. Gradually, the movement led to the demand grew for political representation, identity consciousness, emergence of Dalit literature, the first generation of Dalits accessing education and employment started questioning the status quo. "In different parts of the country Dalit leaders in multiple spheres such as politics, academics, literature, culture, bureaucracy professions, and activists are asserting their constitutionally mandated rights as they were denied their space". For the first time, the 73rd Constitutional Amendment guaranteed seats for the SC/STs in the local bodies which ignited social tensions in the form of caste violence. As argued by Ambrose Pinto (2000),

> an activist Dalit group in Karnataka has declared the millennium as an "Ambedkar Era". Benefitting from modern education, contributed by the colonial masters and missionary endeavours, several Dalits have been able to articulate their aspirations through the liberation theology and a transformative philosophy for their freedom from the caste. Seeking to define their identity outside the casteist framework of Hinduism has had a liberative impact on their lives. For a group, that was for a very long time, defined by others, the struggles for liberation and freedom though began during the British rule, received an impetus in the early nineties as a result of the scholarship and hard work from their own community.

The chapters in this part focus on the question of reconciling equality and justice under the contours of the constitution, which sought to establish an egalitarian society. In Chapter 1, in his "Critique of Right-Based Policies on Justice" Ambrose Pinto raises pertinent questions as, what do we understand by justice and what should be the approach to the question of justice?

There is a view that while the state confers rights, the states have been unable to protect rights of the discriminated and marginalised. For example, the Constitution of India has abolished untouchability, but the practice continues. Manual scavenging is done away with by law; however, its practice is widely prevalent. Pinto presents an alternative of "an awakened community of people" where justice then can be obtained through struggles, assertions, and civil society movements where citizens play an important role. "Instead of looking towards laws or a legal framework we may have to go for a mobilizational approach to obtain justice from an oppressive state and society".

This also witnessed a heightened scholarly engagement with Ambedkar's interventions against the Brahmanical *weltanschauung* and attempts at sociocultural transformation. The identity issues amongst Dalits vis-à-vis sub-castes and the political appropriation of caste have also been dwelt upon. As argued by Valerian Rodrigues, in Chapter 2, the issue of cultural identity is a central question in the Dalit movement from its very inception. It has led to seeking different kinds of recognition by segments of Dalits at different times. They have sought recognition as first settlers, labouring masses, depressed classes, untouchables, Indians, Buddhists, and simply as human beings at different phases of the movement and in different parts of the country, although such claims need not necessarily be exclusive. Some of these identities were commendatory as they mapped out and laid claim to certain resources and orientations as constitutive of their identity. Others drew attention to disabilities and disadvantages and sought their removal to enable Dalits to become different or to bring about the desired state of affairs. Ambedkar's intervention in this movement was to prove decisive in shaping this search for belonging and recognition for significant sections of Dalits in large parts of the country. The debate is continued by Pradyumna Bag, who argues for a society based on the principles of *Maitree*, or fraternity, which will help to foster social democracy which is a prerequisite for political and economic democracy.

Part II: Dalit Culture and Identity

This part seeks to explain "Dalitness" as a distinct category vis-à-vis the Brahmanical life world. Over the last four decades the "Dalit" category has brought a new set of agenda from below to the discourse on the caste system in India. This possibility of coming together on a single platform under one identity has strengthened the collective power of Dalit communities. Raj Kumar briefly discusses the various Dalit-Bahujan social reformers who strived to provide an anti-caste utopia. Selvaraj Arulnathan attempts to draw parallels between the Dalit experiences and the black movement for claiming equal rights in the United States. He notes that the present struggle for the practical realisation of civil and human rights is a new dimension of contemporary, emancipatory aspirations. To the extent that it stops being a mere phase of confrontation between governments and ideological camps, and achieves the character of a mass movement, it will contribute essentially to the abolition of present-day barriers to human freedom and social justice. In the entire debate on rights and social transformation, where do we locate Dalit women? It is also essential to focus on the social psychology of exclusion when the Dalits and dominant castes occupy the opposite ends of the spectrum. Subhadra Mitra Channa brings out this dimension in Chapter 6 while arguing about the paradoxes which encompass Dalit women. She analyses the beliefs and values which are taken for granted and reproduced through a set of practices embodied in the day-to-day existence of a people, which, taken together, reproduce the very conditions of existence, especially where Dalit women are concerned.

Part III: Caste Violence – Movements for Social Mobility

In Kilvenmani in Tamil Nadu (1968), caste violence broke out as the Dalit labourers were asking for higher wages. Sporadic violence on Dalits continued to occur reflecting the churning in the rural areas. No police or legal action was taken against the upper caste accused. In 1985, the upper castes in Karamchedu village in Andhra Pradesh brutally assaulted the untouchable Madiga community. However, the state was forced to take cognition of the violence and announced an aid package for the victims as the Naxalite movement delivered swift justice against the accused. The SC/STs were getting restive unwilling to take the injustices meted out against them meekly. Subsequently, the Atrocities Act was passed in 1989. The majority of the caste conflicts in the rural areas revolved around issues of land, labour, wages, and access to water and public spaces. There were even incidents of sexual violence against Dalit women. In more recent times, incidents in Jhajjar in Haryana, Una in Gujarat, and Hathras in Uttar Pradesh exemplify the ruthlessness of caste-based violence.

The caste conflicts continued to plague society, and the political leadership was ill-equipped to deal with them effectively. The late 1980s also witnessed fractured political governance, with the right wing slowly gaining centre stage. In order to consolidate his hold on power, V.P. Singh unleashed the Mandal Commission Report (reservations for Other Backward Castes) which revealed the fault lines inherent in the caste-based society. To undo the damage and unify the masses under the framework of religion, the BJP resorted to the Rath Yatra and the Babri Masjid demolition which led to widespread communal violence. The polarisation and violence due to caste and communal turmoil triggered human rights violations at the level of both state and civil society. Only the Dalit movement and the radical left ideology provided an alternative reading to the orgy of violence and focused on issues of justice and rights.

While the nation was battling both caste and communal conflicts, the economy was also in a crisis. In a desperate situation, the paradigm of

Liberalisation and Privatisation was accepted amidst the hope that once India joins the bandwagon of globalisation, the economy will develop quickly, and the benefits will trickle down to the masses. However, the marginalised people were further excluded from the market as the structures of class, caste, and gender made it an unequal playing field. They were further pushed into poverty and deprivation. The social conflicts continued – Tsunduru in 1991, Bathani Tola and Lakshmanpur-Bathe, Jehanabad, all signposts in the continuing trajectory of caste violence. In order to assuage the masses, the Bhopal Declaration of 2002 called for the implementation of the constitutional provisions for the welfare of the SC/STs. The Dalit and other movements of the oppressed people took the battle to an international audience in Durban in 2001 where caste was recognised as a human rights violation. This phase also witnessed mobilisation around sub-caste identities.

Despite the economic growth, employment generation for SCs/STs has remained a major concern. The gradual withdrawal of the state from the public sector, the prevalence of caste-based stigma in the job market, and the denial of reservations in the private sector have foregrounded the idea of "merit". The identity movements and the demand for a share in the nation's wealth raised questions about inclusive planning. The state responded with special component plans, and the 11th Five Year Plan discussed socially inclusive policies in all the sectors of the economy.

How have the subaltern people fought for social justice? A possible thematic map would be political movements, conversion movements, social movements, and human rights movements at the grassroots as a response to the violence against Dalits and the failure of the state to prevent it. The emergence of the Bahujan Samaj Party and other political leaders in various states also needs to be contextualised. The internal divisions amongst the Dalit communities as reflected in the Madiga Dandora Movement are a fresh challenge for Dalit mobilisation. The internal divisions amongst the Dalit communities as reflected in the Madiga Dandora Movement pose fresh challenges for Dalit mobilisation as noted by P. Muthaiah.

Continuing the discussion, K.S. Chalam focuses on post-Ambedkar political developments in united Andhra Pradesh which influenced Dalit politics, the caste atrocities, the flowering of literary and cultural expressions, and the emergence of Madiga Dandora Movement. Prakash Louis and Surinder Jodhka discuss the exceptional case of Punjab as compared to the rest of India, the influence of the Sikh Gurus, the entrepreneurial skills of Dalits which enabled them to attain a better standard of living vis-à-vis their brethren in other parts of the country. They present a case of conflict involving members of Dalit caste of *Ad-Dharmis* and the dominant landowning Jats over the participation in the management of a local shrine in a village called Talhan in Punjab which points to some interesting trends in the nature of caste conflict in the region.

This part further revolves around globalization and the various discourses on development and exclusion. It also acknowledges the failure to address the prevailing social inequality which has increased under the impact of globalisation and led to social exclusion of Dalits in education, employment, and development programmes. Anand Teltumbde analyses the larger question as to whether globalisation has really helped the marginal groups to prosper or worsened their situation with the formation of Special Economic Zones, the corporate takeover of land, etc. He argues for a broad-based social struggle by the oppressed communities in order to realise their rights.

For Dalits to have equitable access to resources, it is essential to strengthen democracy at the grassroots. Karunakar Singh raises the question as to whether the Panchayati Raj institutions are inclusive. For a community which is at the bottom of the socio-economic hierarchy, any slight mishap will push it to the edge. In such a scenario, social security attains significance. Access to education is a life-changing scenario. However, for Dalits this is similar to running a hurdle race. Even if they happen to reach elite educational institutions, their "merit" is always questioned. Paul D'souza and Teena Anil provide a perspective from below as to how caste in education has spread across in various states, leading to discrimination and exclusion of children, especially those from households engaged in "unclean" occupations. A case of caste-based discrimination at Delhi University provided by N. Sukumar and Shailaja Menon reflects the roadblocks that Dalit students experience in accessing higher education in a Brahmanical universe. Despite approaching various constitutional and administrative bodies, the issue could not be resolved and ultimately the student concerned was forced to leave the university and join another course.

Future India needs to be visualised for establishing an egalitarian ethos that was aspired by anti-caste ideas. In a democratic endeavour, caste and its allied institutional mechanisms need to be taken seriously and dealt with from a structural political perspective by adopting policy remedies rather than temporal mechanisms. At the societal level communities need to be sensitised and the relations need to be democratised. A strong rights-based approach becomes necessary to address the concerns of the marginal groups, and to achieve it the social and community consciousness needs to be strengthened by both the state and non-state agencies to make the constitutional vision in practice.

References

ACCCR (The Ambedkar Centenary Celebration Committee Report). (1991). "Untouchable Still", *Frontier*, Vol. 23, No. 47, July 6, pp. 4–6.
Chatterjee, Debi. (2004). *Up Against Caste: Comparative Study of Ambedkar and Periyar*, New Delhi: Rawat Publications.
Desai, I. P. (1976). *Untouchability in Rural Gujarat*, Mumbai: Popular Prakashan.
Dirks, Nicholas B. (2002). *Castes of Mind – Colonialism and the Making of Modern India*, New Delhi: Permanent Black.

Fraser, Nancy. (1996). "Social Justice in the Age of Identity Politics: Redistribution, Recognition, and Participation", https://tannerlectures.utah.edu/_resources/documents/a-to-z/f/Fraser98.pdf

Fraser, Nancy. (2005). "Reframing Justice in a Globalizing World", https://sicologias .files.wordpress.com/2015/01/13-fraser-n-reframing-justice.pdf

Gooptu, Nandini. (1996). "Urban Poverty and the Politics of Caste and Religion in Early 20th Century North India: Implications for Development Practice and Research", *Oxford Development Studies*, Vol. 24, No. 3, pp. 221–240.

Gupta, Dipankar. (ed.). (2004). *Caste in Question: Identity or Hierarchy? Contributions to Indian Sociology Occasional Studies 12*, New Delhi: Sage Publications.

Guru, Gopal. (2000). "Dalits: Reflections on the Search for Inclusion", in deSouza Peter Ronald (ed.), *Contemporary India – Transitions*, New Delhi: Sage Publications.

Habib, Irfan. (2000). "Caste in Indian History", in Irfan Habib (ed.), *Essays in Indian History, Towards a Marxist Perception*, New Delhi: Tulika.

Harihar, Bhattacharyya. (2021). "Partha Chatterjee's Concepts of Civil Society and 'Uncivil' Political Society: Is the Distinction Valid?", *Journal of Civil Society*, Vol. 17, No. 1, pp. 18–33, DOI: 10.1080/17448689.2021.1886759.

Human Rights Watch. (1999). *Broken People: Caste Violence against India's Untouchables*, New York: Human Rights Watch.

Kamble, Ramesh. (2002). "Untouchability in Urban Setting: Everyday Social Experience of Ex-Untouchables in Bombay", in Ghanshyan Shah (ed.), *Dalits and the State*, New Delhi: Concept Publishing Company.

Moffatt, Michael. (1979). *An Untouchable Community in South India: Structure and Consensus*, NJ: Princeton University Press.

Mohanty, B. B. (2002). "Development of Scheduled Castes: An Overview", *IASSI Quarterly*, Vol. 20, No. 3, pp. 108–117.

National Campaign on Dalit Human Rights (NCDHR). (2000). *Broken Promises and Dalits Betrayed: Black Paper on the Status of Dalit Human Rights*, Delhi: NCDHR Publication.

Partha, Chatterjee. (2006). "Beyond the Nation? Or With In?" in Carolyn Elliott (ed.), *Civil Society and Democracy: A Reader*, India: OUP.

Parvathamma, C. (1984). *Scheduled Castes and Tribes: A Socio-Economic Survey*, Delhi: Ashish Publications.

Pinto, Ambrose. (2000). Editorial, *Social Action: A Quarterly Review of Social Trends* (January–March 2000).

Shah, Ghanshyam. (2002). "Untouchability in Rural Gujarat: Revisited", in Shah Ghanshyam (ed.), *Dalits and the State*, New Delhi: Concept Publishing Company, pp. 129–146.

Srivastava, S. P. (1997). "Dynamics of Dalit Oppression: An Appraisal", *Eastern Anthropologists*, Vol. 50, No. 3–5, July–December.

Part I

The Trajectory of Caste in Post-Independent India

1 A Critique of Right-Based Policies on Justice[1]

Ambrose Pinto

What should be the approach to the question of justice? This is a difficult question. There are many approaches to justice. Justice can be obtained through claims, mobilisation, rationality, or reason and through laws as well. Rights are basically collective claims of the people. The state merely confers rights through an enactment of a law and legally grants them. The state grants them because of the pressure of the people. Universally people have fought for their rights. India's Independence was as a result of a long-drawn struggle against the British. The Blacks both in the USA and in South Africa obtained their rights for equality through struggle. In our country a number of small states were formed as a result of people's assertion. The tribals of India fought for their protection for the tribal self-rule law. What any state does is only to recognise such claims and give them a legal sanction. That is why it would be wrong to say that the state grants rights. States finally give in to people's demands when they cannot resist any longer. The source of most laws is somewhere else.

State and Rights

The state is unable to provide legal sanction to all claims. While the states grant certain rights due to people's pressure, there are claims states are unable to grant. This can be due to several reasons. Every claim made has consequences. Those in power weigh the consequences and accordingly respond to the claims made. There are times when the state is unable to resist the demands of the people. Take the example of the creation of small states. If the choice was left to the central government, it would have been impossible to have smaller states. The government was made to yield. To protect their identity and livelihoods, the discriminated communities fought for the creation of small states. Due to people's agitation, the central government had to yield and make it possible the creation of small states. However, the purpose for which these states had fought for their creation may not have been realised. Once the state comes into existence, powerful social forces take over, often negating the very rationale for the existence of the new state.

There is very little the central government can do once the state is created. While the right has been granted, the state is unable to protect the right.

DOI: 10.4324/9781003317173-3

There are a number of other rights guaranteed by the constitution which have not been implemented. The right against untouchability is one of them. The Constitution of India has abolished untouchability. But the practice continues. Across the country the Scheduled Castes are kept out of the mainstream due to untouchability. The social practice has been so powerful that the state has proved ineffective. Manual scavenging is done away with by law, but its practice is still widely prevalent. Similarly, there are rights against child labour, bonded labour, trafficking, and violence against women. Day after day, newspapers still report numerous cases of violation of all these rights. There are many more unreported cases than the many reported in the newspapers and the media. What does this mean? It means that the very fact of the state granting rights to citizens does not mean that individuals can enjoy their rights. That rights provide justice is not true. While the state confers rights, the states have been unable to protect the rights of the discriminated and marginalised. The prime reason is simple. Powerful caste forces in state and society resist any implantation of measures that affect their interests.

States Violate Rights

State confers rights and there are more and more cases where the state violates rights conferred by it. Take the land acquisition law. The state is not permitted to acquire tribal land or Dalit land. And yet the major projects of development have all come up in recent years on the land of these communities. POSCO is a Korean steel project in the tribal belt of Orissa. There are other mega projects coming up in the tribal belt in Orissa. The tribals have fought against their land being taken over in the name of development to further impoverish them. The Comptroller and Auditor General of India has found that the Naveen Patnaik government has "misused" the Land Acquisition Act for acquiring land for several big industrial projects, including the proposed mega steel plant by POSCO: "Emergency Provisions of Section 17 (4) were misused and applied arbitrarily even without indicating detailed justification for the same and without fulfillment of prescribed conditions", the CAG has stated. According to the CAG, under the Act, the government is empowered to acquire land in case of urgency, invoking provisions prescribed in Section 17 (4), without giving land losers the opportunity to contest the propriety of the acquisition and the opportunity to be heard as per Section 5A of the Act. Such acquisitions are to be made for a specific purpose, subject to fulfilment of prescribed conditions, and the acquisition process is to be completed within six months, the report says. There can never be a denial of citizens' rights under the garb of urgency or necessity.

The CAG report says:

> An examination of 85 land acquisition cases, in which provisions of Section 17 (4) of the Land Acquisition Act were invoked by the government, revealed that 4,967.08 acres of private land valued at

Rs. 165 crore (approximately the present market value is Rs. 901.305 crore) was acquired, between July 2002 and March 2011, for establishments by six promoters.

The six companies are POSCO (India) Limited in Jagatsinghpur, Vedanta Alumina Limited in Kalahandi, Dhamra Port Company Limited in Bhadrak and Aditya Aluminium Limited, Bhusan Power and Steel Limited, and Viraj Steel and Energy Limited in Sambalpur district. It was noticed that none of the conditions prescribed in executive instructions of September 1985 for invoking the emergency provisions was fulfilled in all these cases. Instead of giving a detailed justification for applying such provision, only general remarks like "the project is being executed on a priority basis" and "requirement of land was emergent in nature" were indicated in the applications by the requisitioning officers, it says. Also, the state government invoked emergency provisions for acquiring 437.86 acres for POSCO projects.[2] What happens to law when the state decides not to follow it to cater to the interests of the corporations? The state becomes unjust.

Even the Supreme Court has found states violating the land acquisition law in several states. Frowning at increasing incidents of government forcibly acquiring land for industrialisation and residential schemes, the Supreme Court cynically observed that the Land Acquisition Act ought to be scrapped as it is a "fraud" devised by some "sick people". Issues of farmers and the poor being uprooted are pouring in from all states. The court cautioned that if remedial measures are not initiated in five years musclemen would take over private land and utter chaos would prevail as the prices of land are shooting up everywhere. "The Act has become a fraud. It seems to have been devised by people with a sick mind who have scant regard for the welfare of the common man", Justice Singhvi heading the bench had observed. The Supreme Court made the scathing observations while dealing with a bunch of petitions filed by aggrieved farmers from Uttar Pradesh's Hapur district on the forcible acquisition of 82 acres of land by the state for developing a leather industry. "We are coming across several cases of land being acquired in the name of emergency and public purpose. The poor farmer is being uprooted from his place and deprived of his only source of livelihood". The Supreme Court told senior counsel Pallabh Sisodia appearing for one of the litigants that it was unfair on the part of the authorities to frequently invoke the emergency clause provided under Section 17 of the Act. "If you are uprooting people of their only sources of livelihood you (government) should make alternative arrangements for their livelihood and accommodation. It is time the Act is scrapped", the bench remarked while reserving its verdict.[3] Under such circumstances of violently taking over land from the owners and tillers, one may not be able to speak of the state providing justice and establish a relationship between rights and justice.

Ideology and Rights

While on the one hand the state that confers rights is unable to protect rights, on the other the state itself violates rights. Besides, the understanding of the people about the concept of rights is not uniform. There are some rights that one part of the world considers as central for a just world while another part of the world considers another set of rights as just. While the capitalist world speaks in terms of rights, it does not make sense to the socialist world to speak the language of rights at all. If one has to approach the question of justice from a position of rights, in different political and social systems rights and justice are understood very differently. What justice means in the capitalist world is not the same as in the Communist, Marxist, or socialist world. While food, clothing, and shelter along with education and employment are essential ingredients of a just socialist order, the liberal states do not have these rights as fundamental in their constitutions. For liberal states the notion of democracy has become so central that they think the right to vote, contest elections, and freedom of thought and expression are enough for a just state. Does it mean that these states do not believe in the right-based approach to justice? Any discussion on the issue of justice needs a theoretical foundation. The concept of justice in the socialist world is based on the social theories, and the liberal concept of justice is based on liberal theories.

Rights and Culture

The other aspect of justice is the impact of cultural norms and the laws of the state. We have a large number of cultural norms. "All humans are equal" is a universally accepted statement. We can examine this statement empirically and culturally. Experience suggests that every human person feels pain when he or she is hurt as a result of an accident. But different humans feel the pain differently and their response to that pain also varies. Does this mean all people are the same? The social system of the country practises the system of caste. In the caste order all people are not treated as humans and all people do not have the same value. While any attack on the upper and dominant castes is considered a grave violation of rights and the state's administrative and judicial machinery function, when there are atrocities or human rights violations of the tribals and the Dalits, the law simply does not work. If all human beings are equal, why aren't they treated equally? Blacks were not treated as equals. Even now, individual Africans not only in different European nations but in African states too, do not enjoy equal standing in international transactions due to their impoverishment and race. Such complexities do not make any easy to talk about the right-based approach to justice.

Human societies and the norms that they are expected to follow are too complex to reduce to a statement. People stress different aspects of this complexity depending on their cultural and political backgrounds. One of the questions that have been raised is what principles of justice should be reflected in such norms and laws. While people should treat each other in a just manner, social goods have to be distributed in a fair manner. What principles of justice should guide the distribution of economic goods in a society? I think that would be the key question. And yet even in the distribution of economic goods different political systems have different ways of conceptualising justice. While the liberals will hold that individuals could have as much access as possible to goods, the socialists provide a prominent place to the state to make a just state possible.

Recent Debates on Rights

In recent years, we have created a political utopia where there are wonderful rights – right to work, right to education, and very soon we will have the right for food. The state has enacted fundamental laws and conferred basic rights to protect the rights of people. The Supreme Court has upheld the Right to Education. Would this mean that every child would be given a meaningful education? Will the state be able to provide qualitative education for all? The judiciary has favoured the extension of fundamental rights, which is also the extension of the state's obligations and powers. There are basic questions that need to be raised with regard to these entitlements – right to work, right to education, and right to food.

> Are there enough jobs or is there social security of sorts to make the right to work meaningful? Can the state create jobs to meet the obligation of right to work? Can the state force the private sector to create jobs? Can they employ all those who need a job irrespective of whether they have the required qualifications? Do they – the state and the private sector – have the capacity to create a skilled workforce through educational institutions? Does the right to education mean that the individual gets an education that makes him employable? Is this the definition of the right to education? Or does it also include the individual's right to seek the education he or she wants?
>
> Would the right to food mean that an individual must have the necessary education and the required employment so that he or she can buy food? Or does it just mean the right to stand in the queue at a soup kitchen or langar, run by the state or by a private organization? The other set of basic questions with regard to these rights are: What is the meaning of right to education if there are not enough schools in the state and private sectors to accommodate every child? What is the meaning of right to work if there are not enough jobs on offer and economic expansion becomes a counter-productive and self-defeating initiative? What is the meaning of right to food if every hungry person is not provided with food? Is it not better to have a vibrant economy with enough food and jobs for all rather than a mere right to food which cannot be implemented? And if there are enough schools,

enough jobs, enough food, is there need for these empty assertions of fundamental rights to work, to education and to food? But such is our intellectual malnourishment that we do not have the stomach to face tough questions about creating a good society. We think it is enough to create the political rhetoric and the constitutional rights framework and that the reality will take care of itself. This is to indulge in self-delusion and hypocrisy. A good society needs hard work and open debate, enough doubts and dissent about goals and values, to create conditions that ensure dignity and freedom for the individual without making him or her a cog in the wheel, which would defeat the liberal ideal of being human. Until then, right to this and right to that will remain hollow gestures, loud talk and empty tokenism.[4]

Therefore, all said and done mere rights cannot provide what they promise.

Justice and Human Rights

The next important question is the meaning of justice. What do we understand by justice? Definitions vary. The liberals would say access to justice is the ability of people to seek and obtain a remedy through formal or informal institutions of justice, and in conformity with human rights standards. Justice intersects with human rights in a number of ways. First, it is a fundamental human right as set out in Article 8 of the Universal Declaration of Human Rights:

> Everyone has the right to an effective remedy by the competent national tribunals for acts violating the fundamental rights granted by the constitution or by law. Secondly, it is a means to protect and enjoy other rights. Thirdly, for the right to access to justice to be truly enjoyed, a number of other human rights must also be protected, such as the right to information, the right to physical safety, the right to confidentiality and the right to privacy. A fair and efficient system for providing justice is crucial to the proper functioning of society. Not only does it hold individuals, including state officials, accountable for their actions, but it also sets norms of behaviour for other citizens. This system must be available to the most disadvantaged. Ideally, the justice process underscores the dignity of the person, as well as being a step for individuals to move with their lives. Unfortunately, in reality the system is sometimes used to entrench power imbalances and reinforce stigma and gender discrimination.[5]

In the liberal discourse, therefore,

> justice includes the right to a fair trial; a public hearing before an independent impartial tribunal; be presumed innocent until proven guilty

when accused of a crime; not be tried or punished more than once for the same offence, sometimes known as double jeopardy; protection against prosecution for retrospective criminal offences, or behaviour that was not against the law at the time, but only criminalized afterwards; and individual and collective remedies for an injustice. These rights are protected under the International Covenant on Civil and Political Rights (ICCPR). For every right, there should exist a remedy if it is infringed. The right to justice therefore involves the right to both individual and collective remedies for an injustice. The individual right to justice under the criminal law includes the right of an accused person to a fair and public hearing before an independent and impartial tribunal. The criminal law is intended to provide justice by deterring and mitigating criminal acts, and punishing those who commit them, as well as rehabilitating offenders. The criminal law should also protect the rights of people accused of crimes.[6]

However, the problem with such notions of justice is that it is only restricted to the legal sense of the term. But justice is more than law.

The socialist discourse is different. Socialism is an economic, social, and political system in which all things are communally centred. In other words, socialism is characterised by social ownership and cooperative management. Socialism is fundamentally grounded by what is needed, not what is wanted. It veers from a privatised sector of society and business. Socialism calls for a government to have virtual control over taxes and capital within the market economy so that goods can be distributed among all the people in an equitable manner. One of the original proponents of socialism is Robert Owen. Although he was inspired by Marxism, and later Leninism, he sought out a system in which private businesses were regulated by the states and free market exchange and prices were duly implemented. Mirroring traditional Communism-Lenin-Marxism, socialism never directly addresses protection of human rights, options for the poor, or social equity. Those tenets neglected by Owen and socialism are actually basic institutions within social justice. Has the socialist system provided justice to the people? The review of literature that has been published on this state does not provide enough data to prove that these states have been totally just. In fact, the revolt against the society system was precisely because the state was found to be unjust. The question then is, how do we create a just state?

Change in the Notion of Justice

Amartya Sen opined that central to the idea of justice is a strong sense of injustice. Taking the example of American attack on Iraq in 2003, he views different arguments to arrive at whether the war was just or not. The war did not have a global agreement through the United Nations. The USA was not well informed on the presence or absence of nuclear weapons of mass destruction in Iraq, and yet the country went for war on the allegation that the nuclear weapons amassed by Iraq would pose a threat to the security of the world. Democracy is a government by discussion where might is not right. It is not right for a powerful state to go for a war on a weaker nation by adopting bullying tactics. And finally did the war bring peace and order to the invaded country? Iraq still is going through turmoil with violence and bloodshed. When one reflects on these, the war may have been a big mistake on the part of the USA. What becomes central to the whole debate on justice is the engagement of reason on the issue. Beyond reasoning there is a need for sensitivity and intolerance to injustice as well. However, the requirement of justice includes bringing reason into the play of justice and injustice.[7] Where then is the place of justice as right? What is right is often very subjective. What was right and just to the President of the USA was not found right by a large section of the international community on the American invasion of Iraq. Back home is another example of the nuclear establishment at Kudankulam in Tamil Nadu. While the Indian state has concluded that nuclear energy is key to India's energy needs, the people think differently. How do we conclude what is just? Every effort is made by the state to sell to the public that the project is safe, in the best interest of the local people and the country. People, on the other hand, are convinced that the project would harm their life, livelihoods, environment, and even their existence in case of any explosion at the site.

In both the cases, there is a possibility of listening to public reasoning away from the voices of the state or government. While the state of the USA is determined to exhibit its might as the international police and by consistently waging war on those who pose threat to their interest, in India the state has sold itself to corporations. When state power takes over the state, then there cannot be public reasoning with the states. Public reasoning is the reasoning of the people that takes place as a result of discussions, debates, and, at the end of it all, even referendums. People are trusted, and they feel that they are participating. When decisions are arrived at without reference to people, then the attack is on public reason.

Legal Frameworks Are Not Enough

Administration of justice is by lawyers. There are good lawyers and bad lawyers. Not all lawyers are guided by the norm of justice. There are other interests that work in the process of legal verdicts. That is why a mere legal framework cannot be the basis of obtaining justice. Justice can be obtained through long-drawn struggles, people's movements, and assertion for what is due to the people. Take the example of the struggle for freedom in South Africa. Civil society organisations played a vital role and shared a common analysis of what they were and are confronting: the apartheid state. In South Africa, there was a lull in political activism following the banning of opposition political organisations in 1961. This lull ended only with the resurgence of civil society organisations which reactivated openly anti-apartheid struggles. Civil society activism had started again in earnest by the early 1980s following an uprising by students in Soweto and with the emergence of other civil society interest groups across the country. These organisations pursued a range of social justice issues on different fronts. They included religious groups, women's groups, youth formations, labour unions and academic societies, business chambers of commerce, journalists who created local newspapers, and a range of other issue-based formations which sprung up from the grassroots and became engaged in local struggles for social justice. Organisations of lawyers, for example, such as the National Association of Democratic Lawyers (NADEL) and the Black Lawyers Association (BLA), played a key role in actively providing legal defence for activists inside the country who often found themselves in apartheid courts. Community-based legal advice centres also played a pivotal role in educating people about their rights; hence the emergence of the slogan "each one teach one" during the 1980s. Meanwhile, icons such as Bishop Tutu exposed the immorality of the apartheid regime through religious critique. Progressive white civil society joined some of these grassroots struggles and launched numerous campaigns of their own. These included the end-conscription campaign which resulted in wide-scale defiance of compulsory conscription laws that obliged young white men to join the apartheid army. In the absence of overt leadership from any political formation, it was the people themselves, as represented by civil society formations, who carried the torch of liberation and pushed for social justice in all spheres of life during the 1980s. This era in South Africa saw ordinary people take the struggle into their own hands. In the end, it was this democratisation of the struggle for social justice that made the continuation of apartheid policies unsustainable. This movement effectively made it impossible for the minority regime to govern over the oppressed majority. Furthermore, by linking the internal struggle to the activities of South African activists in exile, the growing coalition of civil society movements contributed immensely to the stimulation of international solidarity action, including the growth of the international anti-apartheid movement and the spread of the Boycott, Divestment and Sanctions (BDS) campaign. It was a combination of these factors that made the struggle for social justice in South Africa broad-based and democratic in character, accelerating the demise of apartheid. It is furthermore important to note that the benefits of a democratic and grassroots struggle in South Africa did not end with the demise of apartheid. Positive spin-offs are still felt today, with civil society in South Africa – though weakened somewhat after 1994 – continuing to be vigilant and take grassroots action to challenge and curb some undemocratic tendencies of incumbent ANC governments. From time to time the materialism of the new elite is challenged and the rising economic apartheid that excludes the majority of poor people from economic opportunities is also made visible by grassroots demands and initiatives. The struggles for freedom in South Africa did not end with the end of formal segregation. There continue to be efforts to stifle freedom of expression, including the "Protection of Information" bill introduced by the South African government. If passed, this bill would make it difficult for citizens to access information held by the state. The passage of this bill will prevent ordinary citizens from exposing abuses of power by politicians and public officials. However, through a well-organised civil society challenge, this bill is being opposed. Democratisation of pre-1994 struggles for social justice in South Africa also served as an investment in the country's future democratic dispensation. "South Africa's strong legacy of civil society involvement continues today to help safeguard gains made following the defeat of apartheid".[8]

Conclusion

One of the major concerns today is environmental justice which is defined in terms of the distribution of environmental goods. Activists and scholars have focused on issues of cultural recognition and political participation in providing environmental justice to the poor. The Forest Act is one of those acts in the direction. Environmental challenges raised by indigenous communities demonstrate a broad, complex conception of environmental justice focused on a range of capabilities and basic functionings, at both the individual and community levels. But such justice simply does not come. The corporates are keen to commercialise forests for gain. Without ongoing democratic movements, it is unlikely that justice will be made possible on the environmental front. This is equally true on other fronts. What the globe needs is an awakened community of people who are determined not to allow ruling regimes to undermine people's power. Justice then can be obtained through struggles, assertions, and civil society movements where citizens play an important role. Instead of looking towards laws or a legal framework we may have to go for a mobilisational approach to obtain justice from an oppressive state and society. Of course, such mobilisation has to have public reasoning as Amartya Sen has rightly said (Sen, 2009).

Notes

1 This chapter is a revised version first published in *Published in Social Action: A Quarterly Review of Social Trends* (January–March 2000).
2 Satyasundar Barik, *The Hindu*, March 31st, 2012.
3 *Indian Express*, Editorial, Aug 4, 2011, New Delhi.
4 Parsa Venkateshwar Rao J in *DNA*, Do we really need right to education? April 16, 2012.
5 http://www.gaatw.org/atj/index.php?option=com_content&view=article&id=105&Itemid=116.
6 http://www.ihrna.info/ihrna-justice-and-law/what-is-the-right-to-justice.
7 Sen Amartya, *The Idea of Justice*, Penguin Books, 2009, pages 2–6.
8 Bangani Ngeleza and Ghadija Vallie, Some Reflections on Social Justice Struggles in South Africa and Palestine, in *Development Issues*, Vol. 13, No. 1, 2011, International Institute of Social Studies of Erasmus University Rotterdam.

2 Dalits and Cultural Identity[1]

Ambedkar's Prevarications on the Question of Culture

Valerian Rodrigues

The issue of cultural identity is a central question in the Dalit movement from its very inception. It has led to seeking different kinds of recognition by segments of Dalits at different times. They have sought recognition as Hindus, first settlers, labouring masses, depressed classes, untouchables, Indians, Buddhists, and simply as human beings at different phases of the movement and in different parts of the country, although such claims need not necessarily be exclusive. Some of these identities were commendatory as they mapped out and laid claim to certain resources and orientations as constitutive of their identity. Others drew attention to disabilities and disadvantages and sought their removal to enable Dalits to become different or to bring about a desired state of affairs. Ambedkar's intervention in this movement was to prove decisive in shaping this search for belonging and recognition for significant sections of Dalits in large parts of the country.

We are confronted today with a widening base of a shared Dalit identity, but it is in deep contestation. What are the deprivations and resources common across Dalits all over India? Whom to include among Dalits? These and other related concerns are not settled issues in India awaiting merely a policy response. There are those belonging to the erstwhile untouchable castes who continue to recognise themselves primarily as members of their respective castes. This makes it difficult for any long-term and comprehensive interventions as their identities are so fractured. Hence, the Dalits are forced to either appeal to public conscience, act as a pressure group, or are reduced to limited influence in the electoral arena. There are those who identify themselves as Dalits or as members of specified castes but who at the same time claim themselves as belonging to certain encapsulating identities such as Hindus, Christians, Indians, and workers. Many of them may consider the latter as their primary identity.

Formulation and attribution of such identities have not brought about significant changes for the vast majority of Dalits as far as their specific disadvantages are concerned. Although Ambedkar contributed much more than anybody else to the making of a Dalit identity, today, this chapter argues that his stances in this regard shifted appreciably from time to time. These shifts and prevarications are as integral a component of the contested Dalit identity today as are affiliations to caste and religious identities. Ambedkar, however,

DOI: 10.4324/9781003317173-4

cannot be merely seen as oscillating; he also advanced a set of criteria and orientations to undertake the search for an identity.

India as a Homogeneous Cultural Domain

In several of his writings Ambedkar alludes to a shared culture prior to the emergence of caste in India. In his first published essay on "Castes in India: Their Origin, Mechanism and Development", he says,

> I venture to say that there is no country that can rival the Indian peninsula with respect to the unity of culture. It has not merely a geographic unity, but it has over and above all a deeper and much more fundamental unity, the indubitable cultural unity that covers the land from end to end.[2]

In fact, Ambedkar defined the caste system as arising from the closure of groups in an otherwise homogeneous culture. Given the cultural homogeneity that existed in India, the tendency to close on themselves into an endogamous embrace by a group beholden by the rest precipitates the diffusion of this tendency among others too. "When some people closed themselves, others followed suit".[3,4] He repeatedly drew attention to the shared cultural heritage of India in his other writings of the period. He talked of the civilisation of India as

> One of the oldest but like all of them has come to a dead stop, but it has lived to revive, and we may hope never to die again. The contact of the West has shaken the 'fixity' and restored her old dynamic power.[5]

Lest this be construed as the enthusiasm of a young Ambedkar; this position is repeated by him in several places in later writings. In the *Annihilation of Caste*, published in 1936, he says:

> The caste system cannot be said to have grown as a means of preventing the admixture of races or as a means of maintaining purity of blood. As a matter of fact, caste system came into being long after the different races of India had comingled in blood and culture.[6]

As per this understanding, if the caste system is annihilated in India a homogeneous culture, belief system, values, ideas, and corresponding practices, widely shared across all sections, would emerge to the forefront. It will give rise to fellow-feeling and intimate levels of communication for which the caste system would prove a hurdle.

Culture Suffused with Brahminism

In several of his other writings Ambedkar rejected the notion that one can retrieve a shared cultural identity by annihilating the caste system or its ideological anchor, Brahminism.[7] In fact, Brahminism impregnates cultural life as a whole. There is no cultural realm shorn off the caste system. Indian culture has no alternative expression except as represented by the caste system:

> The caste system prevents common activity and by preventing common activity it has prevented the Hindus from becoming a society with a unified life and consciousness of its being.[8]

No communal solidarity becomes possible as the caste system comes in the way. Even if castes occasionally come together such association does not result in their mutual blending and a sense of community. Ambedkar sometimes compares *them* to nations pursuing their interests without consideration for others:

> The anti-social spirit, this spirit of protecting its own interests is as much a marked feature of the different castes in their isolation from one another as it is of nations in their isolation.[9]

The mutual ranking, deference, and condescension in-built into the caste system make the pursuit of a common culture not possible. Ambedkar saw them as reasons why in the heart of so-called civilisation there are millions of aborigines who remained untouched by it:

> "Civilising the aborigines means adopting them as your own, living in their midst and cultivating fellow-feeling. In short loving them. How is it possible for a Hindu to do this? His whole life is an anxious effort to preserve his caste."[10] Caste system, therefore, comes in the way of fusing a common culture. It erects walls to prevent diffusion of beliefs, values and ways of life.

> "Caste is, therefore, the real explanation as to why the Hindu has let the savage remain a savage in the midst of his civilisation without blushing or without feeling any sense of repugnance."[11]

The Brahmanical principle of ranking affects everything and not merely social relations. Even the scriptures do not remain immune from it. The Shastras came to regard themselves as superior to the Vedas, Puranas to the Vedas, and Tantras to the Smritis, and each one of them against the other.[12] In the Annihilation of Caste Ambedkar argued that the Hindu scriptures constituted the principal agencies defending the caste system. He found that popular customs and traditions were deeply imbued with Brahminism. In fact, this ideological system acted as a bulwark against the pursuit of any serious reform. The code of Manu may no longer be regulating the legal system. But social institutions and ways of life are pervasive of its influence.

> It may well be asked how much of this dharma of Manu now remains?
> It must be admitted that as law in the sense of rules which a court of
> judicature is bound to observe in deciding disputes the dharma of
> Manu has ceased to have any operative force.... But if it has gone out
> as law, it remains as custom. Custom is no small thing as compared
> to law. It is true that law is enforced by the state through its power;
> custom, unless it is valid, it is not. But in practice this difference is of
> no consequence. Custom is enforced by people far more effectively
> than law is by the state. This is because the compelling force of an
> organised people is far greater than the compelling force of the state.[13]

Since the whole culture is impregnated with the spirit of the caste system, there is little hope of reforms from within Hinduism. What about alternative ways of interpreting texts and traditions? Ambedkar found that tradition has prescribed what were the legitimate ways of interpretation. It has to be undertaken from the perspective of the central concepts of tradition. A reform is acceptable to the extent to which it is in tune with the explanations and prescriptions of this tradition:

> There have been many who have worked in the cause of the aboli-
> tion of caste and untouchability. Of those who can be mentioned,
> Ramanuja, Kabir and others stand prominently. Can you appeal to
> the fact of these reformers and exhort the Hindus to follow them?
> It is true that Manu has included Sadachar as one of the sanctions
> along with Sruti and Smriti ... but what is the meaning of Sadachar.
> Sadachar does not mean good acts, or acts of good men. It means
> ancient customs good or bad.[14]

In relation to their perspectives castes and untouchability are matters of religion for Hindus, and Ambedkar argued that the efforts of Gandhi would not serve the purpose.[15] Eliminating them will be perceived by Hindus as an affront. On the other hand, if they perceived Gandhi as an authoritative religious spokesperson, then his utterances will be interpreted from the perspective of tradition. In either case Gandhi's novelty, if any, will be made to be in consonance with the imperatives of tradition.

The hierarchised culture of Hinduism does not provide a cultural access to a vast number of people. "Higher caste Hindus have deliberately prevented the lower castes who are within the pale of Hinduism from rising to the cultural level of the higher castes."[16] Since there is no space outside the caste system, there is no possibility of conversion in Hinduism. In fact, Ambedkar thought that initially Hinduism was a proselytising religion but once the caste system engulfed Hinduism, there was no possibility of conversion. "Where to place the convert, in what caste"[17] prevents the possibility of Hindus embracing others.

There is thus a persistent dilemma in Ambedkar about delimiting the relative roles of culture and the caste system in India. This dilemma persists in him long after, up to the time of monitoring of the Hindu Code Bill during 1948–1951. If cultural homogeneity makes possible the formulation of a common set of beliefs, values, and concepts to explain and regulate, castes act like nations, pursuing interests and beliefs distinctive to them, making themselves apart from others.

This dilemma between what to emphasise, the shared bond or cleavages divisive of such a bond, is visible in Ambedkar's reflections on Muslims and Christians as sharing a common Indian culture. Sometimes, he finds both these communities deeply embedded in caste considerations and discriminations. At other times, he distinguished between practices of caste and religious considerations drawn in favour of its defence. Muslims and Christians might be adhering to caste practices, but they have no religious defences behind them; while the absence of religious legitimacy behind caste made these religions more attractive than Hinduism, their continued adherences to caste practices made them repugnant and their appeal limited.

Buddhism as the Cultural Alternative

Following the position that Indians or Hindus are bound in a homogeneous culture and caste as both fragmenting this belonging and violating claims of equality and freedom, Ambedkar set up the agenda of abolishing caste and untouchability and founding a system of rights on the basis of a shared culture. But he found that such a task was increasingly unrealisable.

On the understanding that caste and untouchability have irretrievably marked the Hindu society, Ambedkar thought that only Buddhism succeeded in advancing an alternative to the Brahmanical culture as it suggested an alternative perspective and concepts and categories fundamentally different from Hinduism. Ambedkar also argued that the best of the pre-Buddhist culture is salvaged in Buddhism as the Buddha was in constant dialogue with the central facets of tradition.[18] Buddha approved and acknowledged certain strands of the pre-existing tradition but transformed their meaning and significance as he relocated them in terms of his perspective. As an illustration, we can consider the way Ambedkar reduced the notion of religion. Religion generally meant "Belief in God, belief in soul, worship of God, curing the living soul, propitiating God by prayers, ceremonies, sacrifices etc.". Buddha rejected such a notion of religion. He substituted Dhamma in its place. For him, Dhamma meant something different. "Dhamma is prajna and Karuna",[19] reason and consideration towards others. To the extent that these qualities and akin characteristics are found in Hinduism, Buddha considered them as valid.

Interpolations

Given the fact that the perspective of Buddhism was markedly different from Hinduism, Ambedkar thought that the cultural domain in India, till the stage of Brahmanical hegemony was a field of combat and contestation between two different and largely opposed tendencies.[20] He also thought in the process of relating and combating different interpretations were deployed with dramatic turns and shifts. He found that Brahmins adopted vegetarianism in their combat with Buddhism. They also interpreted significant tests of Buddhism and considered them as their own. While certain Buddhist concepts were given a substantially different meaning, several others were ignored. For instance, the concept of Karma Niyama collapsed into the Brahmanical theory of Karma. Certain concepts such as Nibbana that came to be ignored were resuscitated and were deployed for very different purposes. Ambedkar thought that the primary reason for the weakening of Buddhism is due to the weakening of the Sangha. Once such a defence was weakened, other hostile forces could easily play havoc. Its capacity to act was undercut in the process. Its link with the masses came to be snapped. Once its central concepts were poached upon and recast, Buddhists had to fight their battles with the intellectual tools supplied by others in a terrain which had already caved into others. The task of reconstitution and reform of the cultural domain is caught in the terrain of combat. Culture becomes the ground where the different positions are challenged, and alternatives are posed. But there are positions which are in tune with reason and morals. They are appealing to the masses. Cultural contestation, therefore, need not be anarchic.

State power can enable a cultural strand to become dominant or ensure a level playing field to diverse cultural strands. Ambedkar thought that in the cultural battle with Buddhism, Brahminism deployed political power as in the case of Pushyamitra's counter-revolution. It was due to the partisanship of state power that Buddhism came to be subdued.

Ambedkar felt that state power should not advance a specific conception of the good but certain general conditions conducive to reason and morals. The state should enable people to live a life befitting reason and morals.

Co-option of Elements of Buddhism by Hinduism

Ambedkar thought that Brahminism was able to establish its dominance not merely through interpolation but also by co-opting certain central elements of Buddhism. In "Krishna and His Gita"[21] he argued that the Vedic religion was not able to withstand the challenge posed by Buddhism. Therefore, Krishna deployed singular elements of Buddhism to defend the position of Jaimini's Karmakanda.

The key to the reading of the Gita is not a transcendental ethic that purportedly upholds the debate from within tradition. Buddhism had contested the positions of the Vedic religion on rituals and practices from the perspective of reason. Krishna defends the Vedic positions by taking recourse to and viewing issues from the perspectives of Buddhism on several counts.

There are therefore four notions of Indian culture that Ambedkar advanced: (1) Unity and homogeneity of Indian culture which is fragmented by the caste system. (2) Indian culture as impregnated through and through with Brahminism. There cannot be cultural elements that can be salvaged from it from within its framework. (3) The morally defensible culture of India was Buddhist. Buddhism however came to co-opt certain elements of Hinduism which were in consonance with it. (4) However, existing Buddhism is driven through and through with Brahmanical concepts and interpretations. Therefore, if Buddhism is to be nurtured in India it can be done only by salvaging it from Brahmanical intrusions through appropriate exegetical interventions. Hinduism came to establish its cultural sway over India by co-opting certain elements of Buddhism.

Constructing Dalit Identity

The kind of prevarications that mark Ambedkar's conception of culture in India is also found in his conception of Dalit identity in India. There are two ways that Ambedkar attempted to construct a Dalit identity: the first pronouncedly in the class direction, in terms of the shared situation of exploitation and exclusion of untouchables all over India; and the second in the ethnic direction, in terms of a common ethnic identity based on common descent. The first called for a radical restructuring of social relations through collective mobilisation and struggles against the structures of deprivation and contempt, while the second construed a common belonging not merely to Dalits but to larger non-Brahmanical masses.

i) *Untouchables as Sharing the Common Lot of Deprivation and Exploitation*

Ambedkar discussed forms of exploitation common for untouchables all across the country. Some of the most common forms that he highlighted are the following:
Prohibitions in terms of dress and appearance:

> They cannot wear gold-lace bordered pugrees; They cannot wear dress with coloured or fancy borders; Women should not wear fancy gowns or jackets; Prohibition to give presents that upper castes bestow on their dear and near ones; The bridegroom cannot wear the glitter crown that upper castes wear; Only the specified patterns of dress can be worn.[22]

Duties that untouchables are bound to carry out:

> Convey the news of the death of a touchable Hindu to his/her relatives. Attend the confinement of Hindu women. Render all traditional

services without demanding remuneration, that vary from place to
place and are sometimes sub-caste specific; Play nautch and tamasha
for touchable lords; Compulsory eating of the left-over; Undertake;
Begar or forced labour, perform hereditary menial work; Eat stale
food and meat of the dead cattle; Bend low and look down to the
ground while passing through the houses of the upper castes.

Prevented from the following:

Residing within the precincts of the village, playing music before marriage processions, sitting on cots and smoking, wearing the sacred thread
after going through the shuddi, polies and palkies in the marriage procession, wearing of footwear near the houses of the touchables, burning
of the dead, drawing water from village wells from which upper castes
draw water, using butter or ghee for weddings, engaging doctors and
lawyers, riding on a horseback in the village, travelling by public vehi-
cles, drinking from common glasses in a hotel, worshipping gods of the
great tradition, eating good food; halva, employing words for salutation,
address that the upper Castes employ such as namaskar, Ram Ram etc.

The Upper Castes express strong resentment on the following:

When untouchable children go to school; If untouchables purchase
agricultural land; If untouchables construct pucca houses; When
untouchables expand their circle of interaction.

Assault on Fair Name:

Typecasting: naming leaders such as Ambedkar as Harijan leaders while
other leaders can represent common masses without raising eyebrows.
Rumours; attributing aggression and low character. Control over sources
of information; Discrimination in service; attribution of inefficiency.

Distinctions to be observed:

Touchables and untouchables and their relative rankings gender and
age, space and time, The sacral and the profane. The residential space
is clearly marked. The untouchables are outside the village. Ambedkar
saw the touchables and untouchables as two hostile camps. While
the untouchables want to negotiate terms on contract the touchables
want to acknowledge status. Ambedkar also referred to some of the
most humiliating ways employed traditionally towards the untouchables. Tying a pot across their necks so that they do not spit and pollute
the surroundings; Tying a broom on their back so that they can clean

up the path they have trodden; hiding from the sight of the touchables and make themselves as un-seeable.

Ambedkar documents some of the most violent forms employed to suppress the untouchables in case they do not adhere to any of the injunctions, prohibitions, and attributions mentioned above:

> Refuse employment. Prevent the untouchables, particularly young girls and women, from going to the fields for ablutions. Fill wells with human excreta. Prevent cattle from grazing in the fields. Do not let untouchables pick up firewood. Close down water springs. Prohibit passing through the lanes located in the land of the landlords.

While most of these ways can be resorted to without violating law, the touchables in general and landlords in particular resort to other ways:

> Rape and assault, Physical attack, Filing false charges, Burning the houses, Collective punishments, Force parents to inflict punishments on their children.

Ambedkar felt that such a situation of the untouchables led to the development of certain attitudes and approaches. For instance,

> The inferiority complex of the untouchables is the result of their isolation, discrimination and unfriendliness of the social environment.[23]

Ambedkar felt that such deprivation has left the untouchables little space for alternatives and protest; he found that a lot of the untouchables were far worse compared to those of other parallel cases. Although the Roman law declared that the slave was not a person, Roman religion did not accept this legal view. Alternatives were available for the slave such as falling on the altar and thereby surrendering oneself to the arbitration of the gods or seeking another master. Slavery, by and large, preserved the sanctity of the person of the slave as a human being. There was no social or religious gulf that separated the slave from the rest of society. As a result, one finds so many bequests for the education of slaves in modern times but none from touchable castes, for the untouchables. Similarly, even though the Jews were very badly treated particularly in medieval Europe, their lot was far better than the untouchables.

Caste Hindus mete out such treatment to the untouchables, provoking no agony of their conscience:

> If the Hindu observes untouchability, it is because his religion enjoins him to do so. If he is ruthless and lawless in putting down the untouchables rising against the established order, it is because his religion not

only tells him that the established order is divine and therefore sac-rosanct but also imposes upon him a duty to see that the established order is maintained by all means possible. If he does not listen to the call of humanity, it is because his religion does not enjoin him to regard the untouchable as human being.[24]

Given such conditions of the untouchable, Ambedkar thought that Hinduism is not a civilisation but felony. He refuted the argument that just because Hindu civilisation has survived unlike several other civilisations there must be greater truth with it. Mere survival does not constitute a warranty of the worth of a social institution.

"The main point is not whether the civilisation is ancient and whether it has survived. The main point is what are the merits of civilisation? What is its worth, if it has survived, on what plane? In other words, the principal question is, is this Hindu civilisation, the social herit-age a burden, or a benefit? What does it offer by way of growth and expansion to classes and individuals".[25]

In this version of dalit identity, everything drives to undermine the given culture. There are no spaces, except those which can be salvaged from the ghetto, to be protected. It calls out for an absolute negation without an anchor for reconstruction. There are no points of evalu-ation. There are no solidarities, except those of the experience of the ghetto, that are trustworthy. The dalit can only long for a culture teared out from the unfathomable depths of the universal and from the bridgehead of the impersonal. The exploitation of the dalit is pri-marily moral. Dalits fight for a moral revolution.

(ii) The Untouchables as an Ethnic Constituency

Against the class conception of the untouchables Ambedkar sometimes attempted to present them as an ethnic group or saw them as a community sharing a system of values, beliefs, and practices. This led to the possibility of a dual construction: first, Dalits as autonomous constituency subject to exploitation and humiliation and given the refusal of Hindus to make repa-rations left with no option but belong to a potential community which can consider them as human beings. He considered Buddhism as such a potential community that Dalits can authentically belong to. But it is not any exist-ing Buddhism but a Buddhism that expresses universal human emancipa-tion. Apart from constructing them as such a potential community based on certain social relations, he attempted to construct an ethnic identity of the untouchables as a whole by making them as broken men living outside the village. They were Buddhists and ate beef. When Brahminism reasserted itself, these broken men, however, continued to pursue Buddhism and persisted on eating beef for which Brahminism declared them as untouchables.[26] Thereby, Ambedkar attempted to work out a common ancestry to all untouchables in India and as an ethnic identity made claims for the social capital that belonged to it. Such a construction asserted that culturally the untouchables have a residual presence in Buddhism. The untouchables thereby were counterpoised to Brahminism.

Ambedkar attempted to link up such an ethnic identity of the untouchables with the broader non-Brahmin masses. He equated Nagas=Dasa=Dravidians. He suggested with Oldman that Dravidians of South India were of the same stock as the Asuras or Nagas of the North. The Nagas, he felt, were ardent Buddhists and Nagpur was their major citadel. The conversion at Nagpur was a message not merely to untouchables but to all the non-Brahmin masses in India. In fact, one of the major works that Ambedkar planned was on the Nagas. Ambedkar did not pay much attention how to negotiate between an ethnic identity as Buddhists attributed to the untouchables as a whole and Buddhism as a proleptic community of universal human emancipation. If Brahminism had a deep impact on untouchables as on Indian culture in general, there were no anchoring points for the striving from within for a reconstituted universal. The appeal to grow out of Dalit cleavages into a community sharing thick bonds could be as elusive as the venture to retrieve an Indian culture shorn off the caste system.

This tension between rights and identity persists when Ambedkar considered other akin cases. However, this tension is of a very different kind compared to the claims of Dalits and their cultural identity.

Ambedkar rallies the minorities to fight for a common set of safeguards known as minority pact at the Round Table Conference and reasserted the same position in "States and Minorities" in 1947. But at the same time, he felt that Muslims could coalesce themselves into a nation if they come to perceive that their rights were violated. At the same time Hindus and Muslims have adequate cultural resources shared in common to live together.

> There is much in the Muslims, which if they wish, can roll them into a nation. But isn't there enough that is common to both Hindus and Musalmans which if developed, is capable of moulding them into one people? Nobody can deny that there are many modes, manners, rites and customs, which are common to both. Nothing can deny that there are rites, customs and usages based on religion which do not divide Hindus and Musalmans. The question is which of them should be employed.[27]

However, for Muslims nationalism was seen as a solution to secure their rights. But for untouchables, the scenario is different. The solution to the question of Dalit identity becomes possible only by reordering social relations into a universal moral community. Buddhism becomes in his imagining such a community of communities.

There is a third kind of identity that Ambedkar paid close attention, i.e., the linguistic identity. He handled it within the majority-minority and rights framework by encapsulating identities within a regime of right claims. He saw the danger of a linguistic majority dominating the minorities. His preferred solution became that the official language of the province should not be the language of the majority. It should be the national language, the terrain of rights equally available to all. Let the language of the majority prevail in civil arena, he suggested. He attempted to countervail the power of the majority by the countervailing power of the state.

This was not, however the solution that satisfied Ambedkar while handling other identities. The realm of the state equally available to all is not able to engage with the issues confronting Dalits as nationalities. He, however, does not tell us why cultural identities involving normative frameworks, in a stronger sense, such as being Muslims and Christians, need to be treated differently from identities of a linguistic kind.

Ambedkar's prevarications on cultural identity in general and Dalit identity in particular left behind a complex legacy. If India is a homogeneous cultural terrain sans the caste system, once the realm of rights are extended or potentially in sight Indians are expected to extend an unswerving loyalty in upholding a common cultural identity or will do so depending upon the way one perceives the role of culture. However, if Indian culture is suffused with Brahminism, the cultural domain becomes a terrain of struggle. Emphasis is not on salvaging but on construction of cultural identity. With respect to Dalits Ambedkar toys around three possible identities: Dalits as members of a redeemed human community regulating its relation on the basis of rights and defended by the organised strength of the community; Dalits as members of a Buddhist community where Buddhism is constituted as the expression of reason and morals and can therefore be a community of communities; and finally Dalits as an ethnic Buddhist community. Further, while he recognises other identities such as based on religions and linguistic affiliations, his solutions to discrimination in these respects are markedly different from those he advocated with respect to the issues of Dalits.

Notes

1 This chapter is a revised version, first published in *Published in Social Action: A Quarterly Review of Social Trends* (January–March 2000).
2 http://www.columbia.edu/itc/mealac/pritchett/00ambedkar/txt_ambedkar_castes .html.
3 The following two extracts from the poems of Namdeo Dhasal make it amply clear:

From Dr. Ambedkar
You are the one
Who dances from shrub to shrub like the butterfly

Namdev, Dhasal. 1975. *Golpitha*, trans. D. B. Karnik, Pune: NilkanthPrakashan [Reproduced in Eleanor Zelliot], 1992. *Untouchable to Dalit: Essays on the Ambedkar Movement*, New Delhi: Manohar.
   Ambedkar: 1980
4 Vasant, Moon (ed). 1979–1999. *Babasaheb Ambedkar Writings and Speeches* (BAWS) Vol. 1, Bombay: Government of Maharashtra, p. 6.
5 BAWS, Vol. 12, p. 4.
6 BAWS, Vol. 1, p. 48.
7 Ambedkar identified the following elements as characteristic of Brahminism "1. It established the right of the Brahmin to rule and commit regicide 2. It made the Brahmins a class of privileged persons 3. It converted varna into caste; 4. It brought about a conflict and anti-social felling between different castes 5. It degraded the Shudras and women 6. It forged the system of graded inequality 7. It made legal and rigid the social system which was conventional and flexible" (B.R. Ambedkar, 'Revolution and Counterrevolution in Ancient India', *BAWS*, Vol. 3, p. 275).
8 BAWS, Vol. 1, p. 51.
9 Ibid., p. 52.
10 Ibid., p. 53.
11 Ibid.
12 See B. R. Ambedkar, *Riddles of Hinduism,* BAWS, Vol. 4.
13 BAWS, Vol. 5, p. 283. In fact, this theme has found a forceful expression in Dalit poetry. See Eleanor Zelliot, op.cit., p. 283.
14 BAWS, Vol. 1, 74.
15 See *Reply to the Mahatma,* Vol. 1: See also *What Congress and Gandhi Have Done to the Untouchables.*
16 "Annihilation of Caste", BAWS, Vol. 1, p. 9.
17 Ibid., p. 54.
18 See, *The Buddha and His Dhamma.*
19 Ibid.
20 For a lucid explanation see Brian, Fay. 1996. *Contemporary Philosophy of Social Science*, Oxford: Blackwell, p. 57.
21 "Krishna and His Gita", BAWS, Vol. 3, pp. 360–371.
22 *Dr. Babasaheb Ambedkar Writings and Speeches Vol. 5*, Govt of Maharashtra, 1989, pp. 305–308, https://www.mea.gov.in/Images/attach/amb/Volume_05.pdf.
23 BAWS, Vol. 5, p. 418.
24 BAWS, Vols. 5, p. 90.
25 Ibid., p. 136.
26 B.R. Ambedkar, *Writings and Speeches, Vol. 7*, Govt of Maharashtra, 1989, pp. 277–281 https://www.mea.gov.in/Images/attach/amb/Volume_07.pdf.
27 Vol. 8, p. 53.

3 Ambedkar's Quest for Social and Economic Democracy

Pradyumna Bag

Despite being the most popular form of government, democracy has its own drawbacks. Success of democracy, Ambedkar believed, to a considerable extent depends on institutional arrangement, mental and moral disposition of the citizens, and the attitude and the philosophy of life.

Caste culture has evolved with modern concepts of democracy and has infiltrated into state as well as non-state transactions. Competitive politics has reinforced caste codes and religious morality instead of democratic values and constitutional morality. Democracy failed to cultivate scientific temper; progressive values and sensible attitude have succumbed to traditional morality and hierarchy. Politics has done little to include the excluded and work together to advance the cause of democracy. Ambedkar warned that in the absence of social and economic democracy, political democracy will be only a top dressing in Indian society.

Ambedkar was a visionary, and despite all drawbacks in society and democracy, his leadership offered a new direction and hope for the millions of depressed classes. He wanted democracy to address the disabilities suffered by women, Dalits, tribals, and other minority groups. The dominant discourse often reduced him to his Dalit identity overlooking the herculean efforts he put in to uplift the status of the millions of underprivileged in the country. The objective was to establish a society based on universal values of liberty, equality, and fraternity.

Ambedkar on Democracy

With formal checks and balances, where the executive is subordinated to the legislature and judiciary keeping both within their prescribed bounds, parliamentary democracy has all the appeals of a popular government, often defined as a government of the people, by the people, and for the people. But are these people homogeneous and possess identical rights and privileges? Do these people have common objectives which bind them together or are their group interests larger than the collective interests of society or nation? Ambedkar was deeply apprehensive about the functioning of democracy in a highly graded and unequal caste-based society. These inequalities are not purely economic in nature but with considerable social sanctions made it

DOI: 10.4324/9781003317173-5

excruciating to the lower castes. Ambedkar believed that "democracy is more than a political machine. It is even more than a social system. It is an attitude of mind or a philosophy of life" (Ambedkar's Writings and Speeches Vol. 4 p.283).

It is no secret that caste views are diametrically opposed to democratic principles, such as liberty, equality, and fraternity. Are the upper castes willing to change their attitude towards lower castes? Are they willing to subscribe to a universal value system instead of being governed by caste codes? How receptive are the higher castes to accept constitutional morality instead of religious morality? Democracy could be the most popular form of government, but its success depends on the mental and moral disposition of the people. The history of democracy is a witness to the fact that it is doomed to fail if the society for which they were set up were not democratic. He believed that the democratisation of social and economic institutions enables political democracy to take root and succeed.

Caste divides society and allocates unequal rights and privileges to different caste groups. This inequality has been institutionalised and retained through socio-economic sanctions. Caste principles are diametrically opposed to the democratic principles of liberty, equality, and fraternity. In a society deeply divided on every aspect of life, how will the government discharge its task of governing with justice and fair play? Castes are conflicting social groups with belligerent attitude towards each other, and they jealously guard their caste culture which makes it irreconcilable. Caste has eclipsed the larger vision of society as each caste group wants to further its own interests. What could be expected from the individual from different caste groups who runs the state administration? Will these planners, policymakers, and administrators give up their caste code and caste visions once they are recruited to be agents of the state? Society built on hatred and contempt could hardly find common interests. Even legitimate issues get disrupted as each caste wants to outdo the other, in terms of claiming credit and being a beneficiary of a policy. In such a hostile situation, democracy is just a mere formality where the government may in form be a government of the people and by the people, but can it be a government for the people? Barring Bahujan Samaj Party (BSP) all major political parties are dominated by upper castes, and the same goes with the executive, judiciary, and the intelligentsia, what Ashok Rudra aptly called "intelligentsia, ruling class" (2006). They did not allow others to access the knowledge and have been an obstacle to the growth of an organic intellectual. It all points to the fact that caste rule remained unimpeded and continues to influence the entire socio-economic and political arrangement of the country. Ambedkar had forewarned the country against the class rule, but it paid no heed to that. Caste continues to play a significant role in the socio-economic and political landscape of the country (Thorat & Newman, 2012; Mencher, 1974).

Ambedkar argued that countries have made a mistake by reducing democracy to a political machine which has resulted in its failure. The primary function of democracy according to this assumption is to conduct elections, form a government, and subsequently formulate and implement legislations. Why has democracy failed in many countries? Are we aware of such failure? And what have we done to avoid such mishaps and the subsequent consequences? (see also Ambedkar op. cit. Vol. 4). Ambedkar stressed that the foundation and success of democracy lies in the mental and moral disposition of the people, mode of association, and organisation in the society. It is fallacious to assume that only the form of government will be democratic and the rest of all the institutions in society remain undemocratic ridden on caste and nepotism. Law of the state alone wouldn't be sufficient to protect and preserve these fledgling ideas – liberty, equality, and fraternity. These are new to Indian soil which needs to take root and grow. The underpinning idea of democracy must stand on fraternity or what the Buddha called Maitree, which Ambedkar called the root of democracy.

Caste is anti-social and undemocratic and a great hindrance to social harmony. Even enlightened Hindu intellectuals did not feel the necessity for agitating for the abolition of castes. They confined their activities to abolishing enforced widowhood, child marriage, etc. According to him, social and religious reforms were led by saints, but the issue of political independence during the freedom movement sidelined all social reforms. Even the socialists did not fight against the monster of caste. For them caste is inconsequential without economic power. Unfortunately, cutting across political ideologies, upper-caste Hindus were reluctant to work towards a new social vision based on the ideals of liberty, equality, and fraternity.

Maitree the Root of Democracy

One of the widely quoted definitions of representative democracy is "of the people, by the people and for the people", a quote by Abraham Lincoln. Since people are at the core of democracy, one would like to understand who are these people who occupy the centre of democracy? Are they homogeneous groups having identical rights, privileges, and dignity in society? Have they got equal representation and enabling political environment to voice their concerns in society as well as in governance? But we will return to the question later after looking at the underpinning ideas of democracy: liberty, equality, and fraternity. An ideal society, Ambedkar believed, must be organised on these principles.

Equality is one of the three basic principles on which constitutional democracy underpins, the other two being liberty and fraternity. But is it enough to have political equality, in the sense, giving voting rights to the adult? Can this formal equality bring substantive equality? Democracy eludes equality with sugar-coated waffles. In the matter of equality, it does not go beyond giving political equality, i.e., voting rights, despite knowing the fact that society is highly unequal in economic and sociocultural standings. In the absence of substantive equality, "liberty swallowed equality" and has made democracy a farce. Reluctance to realise the significance of equality or to say substantive equality has made inequalities an integral part of democracy. This has resulted in the reproduction of inequality and "the rulers are always drawn from ruling class and the class that is ruled never become the ruling class" (Ambedkar cited in Rodrigues, p.62). In this power struggle between the ruler and ruled, if at all any, the former maintains its supremacy over the latter, as the resources and the state power are at their disposal. After generations of social reproduction of governing and servile classes, the latter internalised the inferiority complex and "regard the member of the governing class as their natural leaders" (ibid., p.62) and willingly elect them to political positions. As a result, there is dynastic succession under democratic politics. This defies the essential character of democracy, as Ambedkar predicted; it can never be a government for the people:

> This happens because generally people do not care to see that they govern themselves. They are content to establish a government and leave it to govern them. This explains why parliamentary democracy has never been, a government of the people or by the people and why it has been in reality a government of a hereditary ruling class. It is this vicious organization of political life which has made parliamentary democracy such a dismal failure. It is because of this that parliamentary democracy has not fulfilled the hope it held out to the common man of ensuring to him liberty, property and pursuit of happiness.
>
> (ibid., p.63)

Imitation of democracy resulted in cultural lag, where only the framework has been replicated without the essential democratic culture and values. Every institution in India is infected with the virus of caste which stands on inequality. Apart from being undemocratic, caste also is a closed social system. Believers in caste are in perpetual fear and trepidation for any change. Even progressive individuals among the upper castes are subdued by the caste code which prevents any change regardless of the desirability in the system. While inequality is at the core of the caste system, equality is a prerequisite for a democratic government. In the absence of equality, democracy becomes a class rule.

> A government for the people can exist only where the attitude of each individual is democratic, which means that each individual is prepared to treat every other individual as his equal and is prepared to give him the same liberty which he claims for himself. This democratic attitude of mind is the result of socialization of the individual in a democratic society. Democratic society is therefore a prerequisite of a democratic government
>
> (Ambedkar, op. cit. Vol. 4, p.283)

Ambedkar's vision of democracy was based on substantive equality rather than mere formal equality. "Equality and liberty are no doubt the deepest concern of democracy. But the more important question is what sustains equality and liberty?" he questioned. The off-the-rack answer to the question is, of course, "the law of the state" which is expected to protect and sustain equality and liberty. But knowing the attitude of the upper castes, he expressed doubt about the answer. Technically, statutory provisions would provide equality, but it is far from clear that law alone will not be adequate to sustain equality, as the caste code directly confronts the principle of equality. For equality to sustain in this inimical social setting, Ambedkar qualified,

> what sustains equality and liberty is fellow-feeling or fraternity or more accurately what the Buddha called, Maitree. Without fraternity, liberty would destroy equality and equality would destroy liberty. If in democracy, liberty does not destroy equality and equality does not destroy liberty, it is because at the basis of both there is fraternity. Fraternity is therefore the root of democracy.
>
> (ibid., p.283)

Ambedkar attributed special significance to fraternity which "gives unity and solidarity to social life". Without that "liberty and equality could not become a natural course of things". He was inspired by John Dewey's idea of "social endosmosis" – that individuals are not "isolated non-social atoms" but essentially social beings. He believed democracy is a mode of "associated living" and for a society to become democratic, it should facilitate free exchange of ideas and practices across different social groups.[1] Caste hierarchy and the strict rules of endogamy, commensality, and restrictions on communication constrained reciprocal relations between social groups. Ambedkar stated, "It is the isolation of the groups that is the chief evil. Where the groups allow for endosmosis, they cease to be evil, for endosmosis among the groups makes possible a resocialisation of once socialised attitudes". This "sense of common brotherhood of all Indians" was something he felt India desperately lacked. India was not "yet a nation in the social and psychological sense", especially because of the presence of castes which "bring about separation in social life" (Ambedkar, op. cit. Vol. I). In one of his renowned works, *The Annihilation of Caste*, he stated

> There should be varied and free points of contact with other modes of association. In other words, there must be social endosmosis. This is fraternity, which is only another name for democracy. Democracy is not merely a form of government. It is primarily a mode of associated living, of conjoint communicated experience. It is essentially an attitude of respect and reverence towards fellowmen.
>
> (Ambedkar, op. cit. Vol. 1 p.57)

After considering the widespread patronising attitude of upper castes he cautioned that "democratic governments have toppled down largely due to the fact that the society for which they were set up was not democratic" (Ambedkar, op. cit. Vol. 4 p.283).

Social Democracy

Democracy may be the best available form of government as politicians claim, but democratic institutions of society are vital prerequisites for a democratic government. While social processes such as competition and conflict are essential for democracy, rigid social barriers and anti-social feelings between groups could upset democracy. "It may not be necessary for a democratic society to be marked by unity, by community of purpose, by loyalty to public ends and by mutuality of sympathy" (Ambedkar, op. cit. Vol. I, p.222). But it does involve two things – first the attitude of respect and equality towards fellow members of society; and second, an open society without barriers to social mobility and reciprocity. Unless there is a fellow-feeling among those who constitute the society and subsequently the state, democracy is incompatible and inconsistent with isolation and exclusiveness, resulting in the distinction between the privileged and the unprivileged. For him, democracy "was not a form of government: it was essentially a form of society" which the politicians failed to realise. Of all, Ambedkar praised Ranade for his visionary leadership and progressive ideas which the Indian leaders were never able to realise.

The Indian social structure is highly unequal and undemocratic, and the Karmic philosophy justifies such inequalities. Under this world view, everything is unequal and to uphold the divine provisions it must remain so. When the basic institutions of the society are governed by religious codes which are highly undemocratic, it is erroneous to assume that democracy, a borrowed idea, could succeed in a hostile environment. Social democracy is an essential prerequisite for political democracy. "There cannot be a democratic government unless the society for which it functions is democratic in its form and structure" (Ambedkar, op. cit. Vol. 4, p. 282). The success of democracy lies in the organisation of basic institutions of society. "A democratic form of government presupposes a democratic form of society. The formal framework of democracy is of no value and would indeed be a misfit if there was no social democracy" (Ambedkar, op. cit. Vol. I, p.222).

Government, a distinct and separate body solely elected to govern, is ill-defined. In fact, the government is no less an institution than any other institution in society. The office-bearers were not foreign but members, who were born, brought up, and socialised in the society. Society plays a leading role in preparing those leaders, administrators, and bureaucrats. "Government is one of the many institutions which society rears and to which it assigns the function of carrying out some of the duties which are necessary for collective social life" (Ambedkar, op. cit. Vol. 4, p.282). How democracy would play out in society hinges on the mental and moral disposition of those office-bearers. They are expected to conform to constitutional morality and impartially execute their jobs but must actively engage in dismantling caste codes which are undemocratic. Democracy demands restructuring of the existing social structures where not only the graded inequality needs to be dismantled but rights and privileges assigned on the basis of birth need to be redistributed democratically. The fledgling institution of democracy could take root only when the societies, especially the office-bearers, shun caste codes by following constitutional morality. The conflicting caste groups could work together to advance the cause of democracy.

> A government is to reflect the ultimate purposes, aims, objects and wishes of society and this can happen only where the society in which the government is rooted is democratic. If society is not democratic, government can never be democratic. Where society is divided into two classes, governing and the governed, the government is bound to be the government of the governing class.
>
> (ibid., p.282)

To maintain democracy not merely in form, but also in fact, he wanted society to hold fast to constitutional methods of achieving social and economic objectives. Democracy demands universal values and the principle of equality. For that reason, he was in favour of the principle of one man, one vote, one value.

Ambedkar was attentive, in fact, prophetic, that the Indian social structure was no friend of democracy as there are hostile social groups attempting to impair and conquer others. Discrimination, nepotism, and suppression have resulted due to group hostility, as one group want to outwit the other. It has perverted the course of justice and equality and has obstructed peace and progress.

> In a heterogeneous population divided into groups which are hostile and anti-social towards one another the working of democracy is bound to give rise to cases of discrimination, neglect, partiality, suppression of the interests of one group at the hands of another group which happens to capture political power.
>
> (Ambedkar, op. cit. Vol. I, p.103)

Under such hostile conditions, democracy falls victim to crooked dominant groups. Power, instead of being used impartially and for the benefit of all, will be used for political vendetta against the opposition. Instead of enlarging the progress and prosperity of the larger society, power often has been used to the detriment of the opposition and the weak. The present scenario has witnessed the gradual decline of constitutional institutions and is being used to get political mileage.

Whether the democratic form of government will result in good will depend upon the disposition of the individuals composing society. If the mental disposition of the individuals is democratic then the democratic form of government can be expected to result in good government. If not, democratic form of government may easily become a dangerous form of government.

(Ambedkar, op. cit. Vol. 4, p.282)

It is a widely held misperception that for democracy to function it is enough to have a democratic form of government. Regular election, formulation of good legislations, and proper administration of the laws suffice as the requirements of democracy. In popular belief, this is the essence of democracy and good government. But there is an important element on which the success of all these rests and that is representation. Democracy loses its essence in the absence of representation as lack of representation produces class rule, where there will be governing class and the class that have been governed. In this circumstance, instead of working for the larger good of society, especially the disadvantaged masses, the governing class furthers their own interests through the state power. "Now there cannot be a good government in this sense if those who are invested with ruling power seek the advantage of their own class instead of the advantage of the whole people or of those who are downtrodden" (ibid., p.282).

Under the rigid caste division caste groups are isolated from one another and every individual member of a caste exhibits loyalty to his/her caste above everything else. Castes are charged with anti-social feelings and the spirit of assertiveness and belligerence. The government functionaries are hardly sincere about the discharge of the duty of the state. Their allegiance to caste prevents them from executing their constitutional duties. In such a political climate, it is futile to expect the governing class to be just and impartial. Despite being an administrator or state actor, he continues to adhere to his caste code and caste interests. This loyalty comes in the way of executing his/her duty with impartiality and fairness. This leads to a miscarriage of justice. Living in caste compartments he is

> bound to place the interests of his class above the interests of others, use his authority to pervert law and justice to promote the interests of his class and for this purpose practices systematically discrimination against persons who do not belong to his caste in every sphere of life, what can a democratic government do.

(ibid., p.283)

Ambedkar made abundantly clear that strict caste and religious upbringing inhibit questioning the caste order.

> whether the government would be good or bad, democratic, or undemocratic, depends to a large extent upon the instrumentalities,

particularly the Civil Service, on which everywhere government has to depend for administering the law. It all depends upon the social milieu in which civil servants are nurtured. If the social milieu is undemocratic the government is bound to be undemocratic.

(ibid., p.282)

Instead of formal democracy, Ambedkar was a firm believer in substantial democracy, and the Constitution clearly demonstrates his commitment. He firmly held that political democracy must stand on the base of social democracy, in other words on the principles of liberty, equality, and fraternity.

Economic Democracy

There has been a selective application of the foundational ideals of democracy – liberty, equality, and fraternity. A few of them object to liberty in the sense of a right to property, right to life, and right to keep the body in a good state of health. "Why not allow liberty to benefit by an effective and competent use of a person's powers?" (Ambedkar, op. cit. Vol. I, p.57). But the caste enthusiasts "would not readily consent to liberty in this sense, inasmuch as it involves liberty to choose one's profession. But to object to this kind of liberty is to perpetuate slavery" (ibid.). Under the caste-based division of labour, liberty to choose one's own occupation has been proscribed. Traditionally the upper castes have monopolised the so-called pure and lucrative occupations and made these occupations only inheritable. Elaborate socio-economic sanctions have been institutionalised, and religion has legitimised the forced division of labour and condemned Dalits to carry out the so-called polluting and low-paying jobs. Religion has barred Dalits from any dignified source of living.

> For slavery does not merely mean a legalized form of subjection. It means a state of society in which some men are forced to accept from the other the purposes which control their conduct. This condition exists even where there is no slavery in the legal sense. It is found where, as in the caste system, some persons are compelled to carry on certain prescribed callings which are not of their choice.
>
> (ibid., p.57)

Ambedkar believed that a person's competency depended upon his socio-economic inheritance which is otherwise known as social and cultural capital and his/her inclinations and efforts. For centuries caste has made India a closed society and inequality is inbuilt in the generality of the socio-economic system. Social mobility had been outlawed. Should the government treat them as unequal because they are unequal? Equality may be a fiction, but nonetheless one must accept it as the governing principle. To sustain a just and fair society, it is imperative to adopt the policy of equity and give required incentives for actualisation of self. In the absence of social justice, the existing social inequality continues to reproduce and widen the gap between the rich and the poor. Ambedkar asked,

> But what would happen if men were treated unequally as they are, in the first two respects? It is obvious that those individuals also in whose favour there is birth, education, family name, business connections and inherited wealth would be selected in the race. But selection under such circumstances would not be a selection of the able. It would be the selection of the privileged.
>
> (ibid., p.58)

Government is duty-bound to upset the traditional hierarchy and differential treatment against different caste groups. Ambedkar believed that government must treat all men "as equally as possible" and provide enabling conditions to the less equal to realise their fullest potential. It works in the interest of the society as well as of the individual. The traditional hereditary system has degenerated the competitive environment of society, as it allocates roles on the basis of ascribed criterion. It rules out the competition by making everything inheritable which has made the society incompetent and promoted nepotism and favouritism.

Ambedkar categorically rejected the hereditary system of occupation which he believes is averse to democracy and social progress. Taking a cue from the hereditary priesthood, he questions the measures applied to recruit a priest. Why not every person who professes to be a Hindu be eligible for being a priest? What criteria are used for assessing a priest's ability? How one of the revered and honoured occupations among the Hindus could be handed to someone on the basis of birth? Moreover, they claimed themselves to be the conscience keepers of the society which expect them to be stringent followers of the principles. Considering the significance of priests in the Hindu society, it is important to bring them under the state and the priest should be subject to ordinary laws of the land. This could be a small step to democratise the institution.

Since every profession in India is subjected to law and controlled by the state, why are a few exempted? Apart from displaying proficiency in their respective occupations, Ambedkar argued that they must also obey the special moral code prescribed by their respective professions. "Why not the same principle be applied to the priests in fact, they should be subject to stricter discipline but why is it otherwise? The priestly class among Hindus is subject neither to law nor to morality. The priesthood is the only profession where proficiency is not required. The profession of a Hindu priest is the only profession which is not subject to any code. All this becomes possible among the Hindus because for a priest it is enough to be born in a priestly caste" (ibid., p.77). By throwing it open to everyone, it retains not only the sanctity of priesthood but also democratises the institution.

Hereditary occupations have wider socio-economic implications, and one such outcome is the issue of distributive justice. Since the role, status and wealth have become inheritable, the lower castes do not get any opportunity, let alone equal opportunity, to advance their socio-economic status. For society to progress, it needs to advance beyond prejudice and superstitions and recruit people on the basis of their skill, virtue, talent, and inclination and not on the basis of birth.

Does Self-Government Mean Good Government?

"Swaraj", or "self-government", was a rallying cry and a widely celebrated slogan all through, the freedom movement. The slogan gained substantial credence as it was grounded on the assumption that there cannot be a better government than self-government. Indeed, it is true that self-government is the best government, but what it fails to recognise is the hierarchy of "self" and the location of Dalit "self" in Indian society. Is this "self" a homogeneous category independent of any hierarchy? Have these selves all got equal representation and are governed by identical principles? Is the Dalit social self equally recognised and entitled under the caste system? Do they have equal representation in decision-making and resource-sharing?

Since time immemorial Dalits had been placed at the bottom of the socio-economic and political hierarchy. This exclusion and subjugation have been fully justified on religious grounds. The upper caste continues to deny a dignified existence to the Dalit self, and the exclusion continues with different forms and intensity. In the absence of equality and universal moral principle, "self-government" is an empty slogan, an eyewash aimed at baffling the masses. Therefore, Ambedkar believed that the slogan "self-government is good government" is founded on a series of fallacies.

Decentralisation is an important political reform to institutionalise local self-government. Powers and responsibilities are delegated to panchayats to make decisions on multiple local issues like land, water, forest, and sanitation. The objective of this ambitious plan was to include the excluded in the political processes. It has special provisions for weaker sections such as Dalits, tribals, and women. But the local self-government idea encountered stiff opposition from the upper castes since the statutory panchayat challenged the traditional caste panchayat which was dominated by the upper castes. Today any individual from any caste, community, or gender could be the sarpanch, which has circumscribed the power and the caste-based privileges of the upper castes. The appearance of Dalits in electoral politics, no matter how insignificant the post they might hold, has wounded the upper castes, as it goes against the principle of caste.

Instances of atrocities against Dalit elected representatives are not uncommon. They were routinely subjected to cruel and degrading treatment. Though a few extreme individual instances capture headlines, the everyday experiences often go unnoticed and unreported. NortiBai of

Rajasthan (The Hindu, February 08, 2012) or Badami Devi of Madhya Pradesh (Hindustan Times, July 23, 2014), or Indira Kushwaha all suffered the same fate – they are all being punished for getting elected into political positions. A 25-year-old Jaysukh Madhad, a Dalit sarpanch in a village in Amreli district of Gujarat, was hacked to death by upper castes, as he dared to contest the election and became a sarpanch in upper caste–dominated Varsada village (The Hindu, March 01, 2017). They suffered such fate at the hands of their upper-caste adversaries who did not want them to occupy those political positions. Despite having been elected to those positions, their lives and the lives of their family members and on occasions even the life of their community became ever more desperate. In addition, the upper castes put insurmountable obstacles for Dalits in the local self-government.

There is a great disinclination among the upper castes to accept Dalits in public life and treat them equally. They are reluctant to change their attitude towards the Dalits – the untouchable, useable, and unapproachable self of Dalits. The upper castes do not extend common courtesies to Dalits while enjoying their own freedom. They want Dalits to remain enchained under the yoke of their own unjust practices. As Ambedkar said, there is nothing new for the upper-caste hypocrites (Ambedkar, op. cit. Vol. I).

Conclusion

Even today Dalits continue to live in isolated areas with little or no provision of basic facilities. Even their limited success has failed to provide them the facilities otherwise available to their upper-caste counterparts. It is imperative to address gross socio-economic inequality and the indignity suffered by the Dalits to institute political democracy. Throughout his life, Ambedkar was a staunch advocate of social and economic democracy. He knew the consequences of political democracy in the absence of social and economic democracy.

India has witnessed the falling and rising of political parties of different ideological affiliations, but all have failed to bring any substantial change in socio-economic institutions. In fact, caste has penetrated both state and market institutions (Thorat & Newman, 2012, Shah et al. 2006). Where have we gone wrong? The answer is simple because most social institutions are undemocratic and regressive.

> For the answer to this question is to be found in the wrong social system, which is too undemocratic, too over-weighed in favour of the upper classes and against the masses, too class conscious and too communally minded. Political democracy would become a complete travesty if it were built upon its foundations. That is why nobody except the high caste Hindus will agree to make it the case of a political democracy without serious adjustments.
>
> (Ranade, cited in Ambedkar, op. cit. Vol. I, p. 224)

Note

1 Mathew Idiculla, Ambedkar's Vision of Democracy, https://www.newindianex-press.com/opinions/2017/apr/22/ambedkars-vision-of-democracy-1596282.html, 22nd April, 2017.

References

Babasaheb Ambedkar: Writings and Speeches Vol. I, II, III, IV (Govt. of Maharashtra 1979) re-printed by Dr. Ambedkar Foundation, 2014.

Mencher, J. P. (1974). "The Caste System Upside Down, or The Not-So-Mysterious", *Current Anthropology*, Vol. 15, No. 4, pp. 469–493.

Rodrigues, V. (2015). *The Essential Writings of B. R. Ambedkar*, New Delhi: Oxford University Press.

Rudra, A. (2006). *Intelligentsia as a Ruling Class*, New Delhi: Critical Quest.

Shah, G. (ed.). (2006). *Untouchability in Rural India*, New Delhi; Thousand Oaks, CA: Sage Publications.

Thorat, S. & Neuman, K. S. (2012). *Blocked by Caste: Economic Discrimination in Modern India*, New Delhi: Oxford University Press.

The Hindu, March 1, 2017 & February 8, 2012.

The Hindustan Times, July 23, 2014.

Part II
Dalit Culture and Identity

4   Dalit Culture

A Perspective from Below

Raj Kumar

Introduction

India is considered to be the most stratified of all known societies in human history with its peculiar form of caste. The caste system is "peculiar" in the sense that it is one of the greatest separating forces that have been used to divide human beings, mainly into two categories: higher castes and lower castes. This simple division is hacked by certain religious sanctions, which yield to what sociologists' term 'purity' and 'pollution' concepts. These religious sanctions make possible a renewal of legitimacy to the Indian caste system even after it is challenged throughout the course of history. Thus, the caste system with its myriad variations of super-ordination and subordination, with confusions and contradictions, rites and rituals, vices and virtues, dogmas and doubts, professions, and protests, still exists in all the regions of India with different degrees of rigidity.

It is due to this irrepressible caste system that the untouchables of India, who number more than 220 million and are known today as Dalits, have been systematically neglected and ostracised in Indian society for ages. Variously known as ati-Sudras, chandalas, panchamas, antyajas, mlecchas, depressed classes, harijans, and the Scheduled Castes in different periods in Indian history, the Dalits still suffer the stigma of untouchability even after it has been declared an offence under the law. They are socially frail, economically needy, and politically powerless. They continue to be so despite protective discrimination policies being given effect by the government under various constitutional provisions. Even though a small section of them has become well-to-do under government patronage and has moved up economically and professionally, socially they remain downgraded and unaccepted. When the Dalits endeavour to rise up in the social scale, they are too often brutally crushed by the upper castes and sometimes by the state machinery.

Their oppressors resort to mob-raids, murder, arson, and rape. Thus, the Dalits have been subjected to deliberate insults and calculated humiliations of an inhuman kind over millennia.

An attempt has been made in this chapter to interpret Dalit culture from below. Given the fact that Dalit communities are extremely heterogeneous groups having divided into hundreds of castes, sub-castes and sub-sub-castes

DOI: 10.4324/9781003317173-7

and spread out all over India, a question may immediately arise: is there a common Dalit culture in India? It is too early to draw a conclusion. However, one can argue that despite the differences in languages, religious practices, life-styles, etc., Dalit communities all over the country share one thing in common. They all suffer from oppression based on caste inequalities, some way or other, though the magnitude of their sufferings may vary according to time and situation. The present chapter attempts to locate the historical causes that gave birth to the caste divisions, the net result of which is a Dalit culture. Before analysing different aspects of Dalit culture, however, it is perhaps, necessary to make ourselves clearer about what we understand by the term "culture".

Defining Culture

Culture, according to social scientists, includes beliefs, values, behaviours, and material objects that define a people's way of life. It includes "what we think, how we act, what we own. But culture is also a bridge linking the past, the present and the future. In short, culture is nothing less than an ongoing social heritage" (Macionis, 1995). Thus, the term "culture", like the terms "communication" and "development", is multidiscursive. It can be used in the context of a number of discourses-revivalism, religion, anthropology, arts, nationalism, consumerism, etc., and its meaning in each instance will be relationally derived. For example, as early as 1871 the famous British anthro-pologist Edward Brunnett Tylor defined culture as "that complex whole which includes knowledge, belief, art, morals, customs and other capabilities and habits acquired by man as a member of society" (Tylor, 1891). Mathew Arnold, a literary critic, at about the same time defined culture as the "dis-interested pursuit of perfection … simply trying to see things as they are, in order to seize on the best and make it prevail" (Arnold, 1932). Thus, there are intimations of growth and deliberate cultivation embedded in the term, but such historical residual elements coexist today with the notions of the oppositional – punk culture, rock culture, black culture, subaltern culture, Dalit culture, etc. It is in this sense that the term "culture" is no longer used in Arnoldian ("it is a study of perfections"), Elitesque ("the way of life of a particular people living together in one place"), or Brahmanic sense to refer to perfection in the arts and to the cultivation of the aesthete. It has been decolonised and cultural studies have been involved in democratising the meaning of culture, explaining the links between the social production and reproduction of sense, meaning, consciousness, and community, particularly in the context of oppositional discourses such as race, gender, class (and, of course, caste), and mapping the terrain of cultural struggle at global and local levels (Thomas, 1997). It is in this note we examine the Dalit culture.

Dalit Culture

Known for their hardworking body, intelligent mind, and sagacious heart, it is believed that the Dalits had a rich cultural tradition. Historians agree that they were among the original inhabitants of the Indian subcontinent and founders of the Indus Valley civilisation which was rich and sophisticated. Later they came to be economically and politically subjugated not by one but by many successive invaders. The history we know from Aryans onward is one of domination and subjugation, division and dictation, devaluation and deregulation – all carried out subtly but tactically in the name of God, religion, and Karma theory. Brahmanical culture, which became the hegemonic force in the subcontinent, refused to integrate the Dalits religiously and culturally. It assimilated and subordinated the gods, priests, myths, and cult practices of the Dalit groups into its religion characterised by the central values of purity and pollution. Various disabilities were imposed in worship and in mode of life, occupation, skills, dress, ornaments, food, etc., on Dalits.

The overall outcome of this historical process was that the culture of Dalits remained structurally dependent and submerged beneath the socio-religious tradition of the caste Hindus, which acted as a stranglehold rendering the Dalits culturally a powerless people. The main themes of Brahmanical culture such as purity and pollution, devaluations of manual work, conceptions of swadharma, karma, and ancestor worship built a low image in Dalits of their culture. In other words, Dalit culture is dominated by a culture that is not of their own making and does not serve their interests but is the making of another people, serving another's interest. As a result, while there are many diverse cultural practices among different Dalit groups, this common oppression has unified them.

The Role of the Aryans

Although debatable, the theory that the Aryans are believed to have come and settled down in the region of Punjab from their original home in Middle Asia has gained a measure of acceptance. As mentioned earlier, they were basically nomadic, chariot-driving tribal groups, and reared cattle. They were at a relatively primitive, non-urban stage of culture compared to the Indus Valley civilisation and also did not possess the art of writing. However, they were essentially a race of warriors who were bold, hardy, unscrupulous, superstitious, and even cruel adventurers who steadily extended their migrations, overcoming and sometimes mercilessly extirpating the aborigines who opposed their march, until they were able to establish powerful kingdoms in the Gangetic valley. Swami Dharma Theertha, in his book *History of Hindu Imperialism* (1992), describes the ways and means of the Aryans who could defeat the Dravidians, the inhabitants of the land. Swami writes,

> Dominated by the military and predatory spirit, they (Aryans) lived the life or activity, adventure and enjoying of all the good things of the world. They invoked their gods … constantly to destroy the aboriginal tribes whom they contemptuously called "dark-skinned dasyus" and "rakshasas" (demons). Many hymns of the Rig Veda are fervent appeals

to the gods to annihilate Dasyus. "We are surrounded on all sides by the Dasyus. They do not perform sacrifices. They are unbelievers. Their practices are all … different. They are men! O! destroyer of foes! Kill them, destroy the Dasa race" (Rig Veda, 1, 100-8) … Health, wealth, prosperity and power in this world were the chief and almost sole concern of the Aryans, and to them religion was a means of acquiring these.

(Theertha, 1992)

These views of the Aryans are supported by the famous historian D. D. Kosambi who sees the *Rig Veda* as the source of the story of Aryan invasion, destruction, and conquest. He substantiates this view by saying that the decline of the Indus Valley civilisation by archaeological evidence occurred about 1250 B.C. and the *Rig Veda* actions were put around the same time. The rest of the Vedas were composed much later, probably about 1000–900 B.C. It is during these Vedic times that a kind of social division – but not necessarily caste division as we know it today – was created which was the forerunner of our social structure today.

The Consolidation of Caste Society and Untouchability

With the chaturvarnic order Indian caste society gradually came to be established during 500 B.C.–500 A.D. period. It is during this time that many caste laws and restrictions were made for the Sudras to keep them permanently away from the so-called dwija society and degrade them to the position of virtual slaves without rights of citizenship. The caste rules were mostly made by the Brahmans with the active support of the orthodox Kshatriya kings. The dominant characteristic of all the caste rules was to suppress the masses of the Sudras by prohibiting them from all knowledge and status, the process which continued for quite a long time. Thus, the caste scheme proved to be a very effective instrument of domination and exploitation, for keeping the masses of people ignorant in order to make them submissive, and for keeping them weak by increasing divisions and disunion among them.

It is believed that during Pushyamitra Sunga's rule (187 B.C. onwards) we begin to hear of untouchability. Pushyamitra was a Brahman and the commander-in-chief of the last Mauryan king Bruhadatra, who was Sudra by caste. Pushyamitra is understood to have killed Bruhadatra and established Brahman rule which continued till 800 A.D. Fearing that the Sudras would organise and revolt against his action, Pushyamitra asked Manu, a Brahman pandit of his time, to do him favour. In order to suppress the potential revolution, Manu codified all inhuman and unethical laws against the Sudras in the name of religion. His work is later known as the *Manushastra or Manusmriti*. This was the beginning of Brahminism. During this time, Brahmans were given the highest status in society and caste divisions were enforced by the kings. The role of the king was seen to be in protecting "dharma" and dharma was now interpreted as "varnashrama dharma" or the law of the castes (and ashrama or stages of life). To keep the upper caste interest intact, varnashramadharma was often supported, propagated, and reinterpreted through numerous Brahmans, the Sutras, the Smritis, and the Puranas, which are known in combination as the Dharma Shastra today.

Thus, through the centuries, the ancient Dharma Shastra of the Hindus imposed a series of social, political, economic, and religious restrictions on the lower castes, nuking the untouchables completely dependent on those above them. As a result, the Panchamas lived a life of physical degradation, insults, and personal and social humiliation for quite a long time. They were relegated to menial occupations only. They lived outside the village and fed on the leftovers of the high-caste people. Physical contact with the untouchables was said to be "polluting" and worse still, even their shadows were considered defiling. Even as late as the early part of this century the untouchables had no access to public facilities such as wells, rivers, roads, schools, and markets (Galanter, 1984). The most perverted practice of untouchability was that which, at one time, compelled the untouchables to tie an earthen pot around their neck so that their sputum should not fall to the earth and pollute others. Another such practice was the compulsion to tie a broom behind them so that their footprints would be erased before others set their eyes on them (Dangle, 1992). All these forced conditions made the untouchables destitute, deprived, and the most depressed section of human beings, as a result of which they remained socially degenerated; economically impoverished; politically servants of the upper classes.

In ancient times, apart from monopolising the state power and property, the upper castes also made sure that learning and using Sanskrit language was exclusively their privilege. The untouchables, the Sudras, and women were barred from access to this language. Thus, the Sanskrit language, which was the repository of knowledge and wisdom, became a closely guarded terrain, where no outsiders were permitted. Knowledge and power are closely linked, Foucault has stressed. For him, knowledge of all sorts is thoroughly enmeshed in the complex activity of domination:

> What makes power hold good, what makes it accepted, is simply the fact that it does not only weigh on us as a that says no, but that it traverses and produces things. It induces pleasure, forms knowledge, produces discourse. It needs to be considered as a productive network, which runs force through the whole social body, much more than as a negative instance whose function is repression.
>
> (Foucault, 1984)

This is precisely what happened in the history of Hindu society. The hegemony of the high caste became pervasive because all knowledge was generated and processed by them. People who enjoyed the fruits of knowledge and power did not let it go out of their hands. Some of the immediate effects of this policy were the non-proliferation of the Sanskrit language and the creation of an outer group, the Sudras and the untouchables, whose sole purpose of existence was to serve the interest of the upper-caste people. As a result, for centuries a community remained permanently at the periphery of society, even though they very much participated in the production process. Thus, the people at the lowest strata were considered untouchable, but not the goods they produced.

It is mostly the theory of Karma, with the aid of religion, which dissuaded the untouchables and other exploited classes from undertaking any revolt against their oppressors. What was worse, the untouchables believed that if they performed the prescribed duties in this life, which were ordained by Providence, uncomplainingly, willingly, and obediently, they would probably be born in a higher group in their next birth. Thus, the Indian caste system made the untouchables to be meek, passive, and so much docile that an organised revolt was hardly expected from them.

Challenges to Caste: Lokayat

At different points of time in history the institution of caste has been questioned by various philosophers and reformers whose philosophy created the background for either new religions or new philosophies. The first challenge to the caste system came from a band of rationalists known as Lokayat which literally means "restricted to the world of common experience or Charvakas" which came to be established in the 6th century B.C. (Brolov, 1984). Headed by the famous materialist philosopher Charvaka, the movement revolted against the slave system, caste exploitation, and the existence of God. The Lokayata propagated materialistic philosophy as opposed to the idealism of the Upanishads and the Vedas. They preached the abolition of slavery, rational behaviour, and development of moral man rejecting all forms of sacrifices, rituals, and ceremonies. Thus, the Lokayata emerged as a progressive and optimistic philosophy supporting the cause of the oppressed people.

Buddhism

During the 6th century B.C. both Jainism and Buddhism set for themselves the task of questioning the Brahmanic orthodoxy. The religious scriptures were scrutinised to interrogate the truth. Although compared to Buddhism Jainism did not do much for the oppressed class of the people – for the simple reason that it spread mainly among the traders and businessmen – nevertheless it made a dent against Brahminism. In this sense Buddha was the first social revolutionary who challenged Vedanta philosophy, rejected the authority of the Vedas, and revolted against the caste system. His simple way of preaching the righteousness of conduct over social aspects such as social tyranny, slavery, and inequality made his philosophy understandable to the common people. Buddha did not prevent any caste from becoming his followers. Untouchables could find a respectable place in society for the first time by embracing Buddhism.

It is unfortunate that in spite of its radical philosophies, Buddhism lost its battle with Brahminism. As a result, the teachings of Buddha influenced the Hindu religion and he was given a high place in the Hindu pantheon as an avatar of Vishnu. Once Buddhism started declining Hinduism laid emphasis on caste distinctions. And it was Brahminism, the militant part of Hinduism, which took charge of devising different sinister designs. Puranas, especially the *Gita*, were written incorporating parts of Buddhist philosophy.

Bhakti Movements

In the medieval period the Bhakti movement (roughly from the 8th to 18th centuries A.D.), which threw up radical thinkers and mystic reformers, was yet another force that challenged the varna system and stratification of human society on the basis of caste. The movement cut across barriers of caste, creed, language, and religion. Most of the poets, singers, and saints *in* the Bhakti cults were from lower castes: Namdev (1270–1350 A.D.) belonged to Shimphi (tailor) caste.

Chokamela (13th–14th centuries) was a Mahar (untouchable); Kabir (1398–1518 A.D.) was a weaver; Raidas (a contemporary of Kabir) was a cobbler; Sena (another contemporary of Raidas) a barber; Tukaram (born in 1608 A.D.) was a farmer's son. The languages these saint-poets used for their songs, dohas, and abhangas were the local languages spoken by the common people, and very often they used metaphors connected with their daily work. Though there is no evidence to suggest that Chokamela ever protested against the traditional limits of Mahar village work, the internal evidence of his abhangs suggests some protest about the concept of untouchability. Kabir's strong note of dissent and protest against the existing reality, the glaring disparity between the rich and poor, the discrimination by Brahmans and high caste Hindus towards the low castes, especially the untouchables, and his emphasis on a direct relationship with God without the mediation of Brahmans and the Mullahs, i.e., the clerics whom he ridicules as greedy and ignorant, had a profound impact. Surdas (1483–1563 A.D.) graphically described the hard life of the peasants and the oppressions of the local officials, landholders, and even high officials such as wazir.

Of late, the Bhakti movement has been examined critically in terms of its social contributions. The objection here is that it was never a mass movement because the saint-poets of this tradition sought only personal salvation. Whatever it may be, ultimately, the Bhakti movement, which had started as a radical movement of dissent and protest, gradually became appropriated by the dominant discourse of Hindu society. In the course of time, the Bhakti ethos became a supplement to Brahminism.

The Caste and the Role of Islam

It is quite surprising to note that even during Muslim rule in India (roughly 800–1600 A.D.) Brahminism made its presence felt by enforcing its caste rules. The Muslim rulers called and treated all non-Muslims as "Hindus". This helped the higher castes to claim leadership of all Hindus against the Muslims who, in fact, retained some authority and power during the Muslim rule. This provided an opportunity to enforce caste laws and restrictions in different walks of life. Even the matrimonial alliances that many Hindus made as they cooperated with the Muslim rulers made it possible for the caste system to continue as it weakened by remaining Muslim opposition to caste.

Thus, the conditions of the untouchables and other lower-caste people in the Hindu community remained the same in the Muslim period as earlier. Probably as a protest against this continuing discrimination, a big chunk of Hindus, mostly from the untouchables and backward castes, became Muslims through conversion. Particularly the Moplas of Malabar and the Chitagonians of East Pakistan are examples of en masse conversions to Islam. The process of proselytisation was, however, never on an organised scale. Only some of the so-called lower ranks, mainly comprising the artisans and wage earners, the real producers of wealth, willingly embraced Islam, attracted by its democratic structure and fraternal approach. It was true that compared to Hinduism Islam granted relative equality to everyone irrespective of caste or class status. More than anything else, it provided every follower of the prophet opportunities to rise to any position according to one's own capacity. More recently, the conversion of more than some 200 untouchable families at Meenakshipuram, Tamil Nadu, in 1981 to Islam speaks about the renewal of the faith of untouchables in Islam.

Colonial Experience of Dalits

After suffering under the dominance of Brahmanic culture for so many centuries, it was only during British rule that certain remarkable changes in the lives and culture of the Dalits could be seen. All through the 19th century the building of roads and railways and introduction of post and telegraph, printing press, and many industries by the British made provisions for a new legal system, a new system of property relations, and new modes of mobility. It was during this time that old powers and prerogatives were abolished; occupations and learning were rendered obsolete or marginal; new opportunities for gain and advancement were introduced; power and access to it were distributed (Galanter, 1984). It was on this background that India went through a reformation movement. But the kind of Hindu renaissance brought by upper-caste reformers like Raja Rammohan Roy, Dayananda Saraswati, Vivekananda, Mohandas Karamchand Gandhi, and others left untouched the sociocultural and religious lives of Dalits. In fact, the Hindu renaissance strengthened and politicised the caste Hindu culture and their national dominance vis-à-vis the Dalits.

Contrasting to the elite renaissance were the efforts of Phule, Periyar, Narayana Guru, and Ambedkar, some of the prominent figures of the "Enlightenment" who fought against the caste system and untouchability. All of them talked about creating a new society with a new culture and new religion based on the universal ideas of "liberty, equality and fraternity", a call given birth after the French Revolution of 1789. In order to realise these, they struggled relentlessly against all the oppressive casteist forces. This, in Indian history, is known as non-Brahman movement.

Jotiba Phule

The origin of the non-Brahman movement, otherwise known as the "anti-caste movement", started with Jotiba Phule (1827–1890) in Maharashtra. Phule, who hailed from Mali (gardener), a Shudra community, attacked the domination of the Brahmanas and the caste system. He attempted demythification of the Hindu concepts. The Hindu god Brahma, for him, was not a creator of the world but, he is a stereotypical Brahman, an avaricious, cunning, and secretive clerk. Phule also condemned that the Vedic texts were full of fables, which were written down by the shrewd Brahmans to guard their vested interests.

Phule considered that the main instrument for awareness and anti-caste consciousness among the people of the lower caste was education, and for this it was necessary to fight against the upper-caste monopoly. To start his movement Phule in 1858 opened a school for the children of untouchables – the first of its kind – thus striking at the root of caste hegemony. In 1853, he established the Society for the Teaching of Knowledge to Mahars, Mangs, and other lower-caste groups. In 1873 Phule established the Satya Shodak Samaj (Society for Truth Seekers), an organisation which proclaimed the need to save the lower caste from the "hypocritical Brahmans and their opportunistic scriptures".[1]

To summarise briefly, Phule's movement was rural; it attacked the caste system, called for the usage of Marathi vernacular rather than English in schools, and claimed to speak for the Bahujan Samaj (Majority) against the Shetji-Bhatji (Moneylenders and Brahmans). Phule rejected the Hindu religion and other religions based on holy books and the prophets, utterances, and advocated an ethic-based monotheistic religion.

Narayana Guru

Narayana Guru is yet another contributor to the non-Brahman movement, who championed the cause of all the downtrodden, including the untouchables. He was the founder of Sri Narayana Dharma Paripalan Yogan, popularly known as S.N.D.P. movement, which originated among the Ezhavas (toddy-tappers) of Kerala in the late 19th century. Once Ezhavas were considered untouchables in the traditional caste hierarchy. As a result, they suffered from many disabilities and were not allowed to worship in the temples of caste Hindus. Toddy tapping was considered to be a defiling occupation. Ezhava women could not cover their breasts, and they could neither wear any footwear nor build pukka houses till the third and the fourth decades of this century.

Narayana Guru did not like the idea of people having different castes, several religions, and gods. That is why he preached a philosophy: "For man there is only one religion; only one caste; and only one God". In order to realise this philosophy, he undertook some concrete and active social actions. He built many temples; installed deities of Shiva, Narayana, and Sharada; and trained an order of monks, priests, and household-disciples. The temples he and his followers built were thus thrown open to the untouchables. He preached that worship of God should not be denied to any individual or caste group. An offence in this regard was an offence against God, he declared. Narayana Guru also got untouchables appointed as cooks or bearers and tried to give them equal opportunities in all the organisations he had set up. As part of his reformation, he pulled down the temples of Ezhavas, which were devoted to the worship of lesser deities and spirits and asked his followers to abstain from eating meat and drinking liquor. He also evolved simple wedding rites and abandoned many expensive and meaningless rituals. All these were meant to have an ideological protest against the Brahmanical hierarchy and pollution. Thus, Narayana Guru was fully responsible for a thorough transformation of the style of life of the untouchables involving new religious beliefs, rituals, and outlook.

Periyar

The non-Brahmana movement in Tamil Nadu came vigorously with the aggressive leadership of E.V. Ramasamy (1879–1973), who is popularly known as Periyar. Periyar began his Self-Respect movement in 1925, and the primary objective of this movement was to discard the priestly service of the Brahmans and their value-system and to resist Hinduism at large. Seeking a basic change in the traditional social system, Periyar wanted to establish an entirely new pattern of values in which all people, irrespective of their caste, creed, or sex, could enjoy equal self-respect. That is why the followers of his movement protested against the accident of birth as the only criterion to judge a person's individual worth. Citing the racial dispute theory that the migrant Aryans conquered the subjugated indigenous Dravidians, Periyar emphasised that the Dravidian culture was otherwise far superior to the Brahmanical Aryan culture. It is on this argument that Periyar could mobilise mass support, with the untouchables, women, rural youth, and uneducated masses joining in his movement.

As part of his non-Brahman movement Periyar carried out his propaganda for the separate non-Brahman or Dravidian country. In 1944 the Dravida

Kazhagam came into being, demanding a separate non-Brahman Dravidian nation, later to become a political party. Unfortunately, the Self-Respect movement which arose as a protest against Aryan culture was later to be broken into so many pieces.

Ambedkar

It was B.R. Ambedkar, the prime architect of the Indian Constitution, who made significant contributions to the anti-caste movement. An untouchable himself, Ambedkar championed the cause of the "broken men" as he terms the Indian untouchables, and fought relentlessly throughout his life to ensure equality, social justice, self-respect, and freedom for them. Ambedkar stood for the social liberation, economic emancipation, and political advancement of the downtrodden millions – a task never undertaken by any high-caste Hindu leader with so much vigour and force. That's why, perhaps, Gandhi described him as "fierce and fearless" and Nehru acclaimed him as a "symbol of revolt against all the oppressive features of Hindu society".

A radical reconstruction of Indian society, as Ambedkar imagined, cannot come without the intensification of the caste/class struggle. Since Hinduism is founded on scriptures, which sanctioned the caste-based social order, a just solution can only be possible through a new edifice, that is, the annihilation of the Indian caste system. For this, Ambedkar launched several protest movements. As early as 1926 he started a Marathi fortnightly *Bahiskrit Bharat* to give a voice to millions of voiceless people. Apart from these, Ambedkar also established several educational institutes, political parties, and published periodicals and journals as part of his movement.

As stated earlier, the sole motive of Ambedkar's movement was to establish equal status in religious, social, economic, and political matters to all classes, thus offering untouchables an opportunity to rise in the scale of life and creating conducive conditions for their advancements. For the total upliftment of the downgraded untouchables, Ambedkar came to realise that unless this socially suppressed section of the Indian society secured political power it was not possible to completely wipe out all social, legal, and cultural disabilities from which they suffered. That is why his slogan was: "Be a ruling race". But the political power which Ambedkar wanted for the untouchables during British rule could not be obtained due to the stiff resistance of the Congress with its caste Hindu character. For this Ambedkar characterised Congress as a "full-blooded and blue-blooded Hindu body" (Prasadi, 1993).

As the chief architect of the Indian Constitution, Ambedkar worked hard for a new constitutional order based on equality and social justice. Ironically, however, his dream has not materialised even after more than four decades of the working of the Constitution. The various kinds of torture perpetrated today on the Dalits are testimonials. As K. R. Narayanan very appropriately explains: "In a caste-ridden society all you can get is a caste-ridden democracy or caste-ridden socialism or caste-ridden communalism" (Baisantry, 1991).

Being dismayed and frustrated with the negative attitude of the caste Hindu people, Ambedkar towards the end of his life rejected Hinduism and embraced Buddhism. As we have seen earlier, Buddhism advocates a casteless and classless society against the Hindu society, which is based on graded inequality. Buddha's opposition to human exploitation is, perhaps, the main reason which Ambedkar finds Buddhism attractive as an alternative.

The Post-Independence Condition of Dalits

Despite the legal abolition of untouchability in independent India (the Untouchability Offences Act passed in 1955 followed by the Protection of Civil Rights (PCR) Act in 1976) and promises of official jobs in Legislatures, Parliament, etc., even to this day the effects of the caste discrimination continue. With the upper-caste people having all the powers in their hands, the lower-caste communities are continuing to be subordinated. The untouchables constituting the lowest strata are naturally in the most disadvantageous situation.

While in rural India the untouchables are still struggling to assert their degraded status in the orthodox rural caste structure, their urban counterparts who are a little better off, being educated, mobile, and organised are unitedly agitating against the various caste discriminations practised against them. But, whenever there are such attempts made by the untouchables, they have been easily suppressed and various kinds of atrocities are inflicted against them to curb their power. What is more amazing is that, in the recent past, the untouchables are also the victims of state-sponsored terrorism which is carried out subtly but systematically on the guise of various developmental programmes.

The New Dalit Movement

The anti-development social forces which were operating against the untouchables for ages now have become a subject of scrutiny with the new social movement which came forcefully at the beginning of the 1970s. It is no surprise that the movement incidentally started in Maharashtra, the homeland of B. R. Ambedkar who fought for the rights, liberties, and equalities of the downtrodden throughout his life. Thus, the awakened Dalit youths of Maharashtra who tasted the fruit of modern education organised themselves in 1972 under the banner of the Dalit Panthers movement. The main objective of this movement is to create an atmosphere of a counterculture and to bring a separate identity for the Dalits in society. The call given by the Panther for a social reconstruction was further activised by the Dalit writers, poets, and activists through their writings and speeches in various forms. Thus,

"Dalit literature" emerged in the early 1970s, which subsequently spread to the neighbouring states of Gujarat, Karnataka, Andhra Pradesh, and others.

Dalit Literature

Since the late 1960s and 1970s, an increasing number of poets and writers of the Dalit communities in various Indian states have been producing literary works, such as poems, short stories, novels, dramas, and autobiographies representing the themes of caste oppression, untouchability, poverty, repression, and revolution. Their writings also contain powerful denunciations of and tierce attacks on the caste system and on Brahmanical Hinduism. It has been pointed out that Dalit literature is considered to be a unique genre of modem Indian literature. The ex-untouchables themselves using the traditionally denied weapon of literacy are exposing the conditions under which they have lived, as well as directly rebelling against the Hindu institutions which have brought to them their perpetual subordination to the varna order.

Broadly speaking, Dalit literature has arisen from cultural conflict. Since the "downtroddens" have no place or hardly any place in the established canonical literature of India, Dalit writers call it "Hindu literature" and challenge its hegemony. In the words of Baburao Bagul,

> the established literature of India is Hindu literature. But it is Dalit literature, which has the revolutionary power to accept new science and technology and bring about a total transformation. "Dalit" is the name of total revolution; it is revolution incarnate.
>
> (Dangle, 1992)

Thus, Dalit literature aims at creating a counterculture and a separate identity for the Dalits in the society. Generally, Dalit writers are not against any groups (individuals, caste, or communal groups) but against the establishment, the government, and the social system, which, in their view, keeps them depressed and deprived. In other words, the search of identity is a basic dynamism of Dalit culture. That is why issues related to poverty, powerlessness, untouchability, hypocrisy, and several other corrupt social practices have generated a variety of responses among Dalit writers. These responses are basically forms of protest aimed at bringing social change through a revolution. It is unfortunate that this has been vehemently opposed by the establishment in our country.

In the Age of Globalisation

While the new phase of globalisation began in the 1980s, with the 1991 liberalisation policy declared by the Government of India, it has had a wider scope. But there are two trends of opinion about the impact of globalisation on Dalits. One group of scholars argue that in the Indian democratic polity, globalisation will not liberate people from the oppression and exploitation of the dominant power structure; rather, the forces of subjugation will continue more vigorously, often in invisible and remote ways. They fear that economic deprivation of the poor, especially the subaltern groups, will aggravate their political alienation at a time when such groups are trying to establish themselves in the power structure with state patronage. The Dalits who are mostly labourers and landless peasants will suffer under globalisation due to "jobless economic growth", they argue. They continue with an observation that there may be a clear-cut divide between the leaders and the masses among subaltern groups. The leader may cope with the system but may not patronise the cause of the subaltern masses.

Another view is that globalisation will lead to bigger development which will result in the growth of the service sector, generating employment opportunities for the lower rungs of society who are mostly jobless. Globalisation will also succeed, it is argued, in generating the income to provide greater social security measures like employment, poverty alleviation, and protection and promotion of the interests of the Dalits and other deprived sections of the population.

These are mostly economic arguments. Regarding the cultural effects of globalisation, the attitude of Dalits is clear. They need globalisation. Because they want to be part of the "mainstream" of the world, they want to claim the heritage of the ages, and they view resistance to this as largely a product of the Indian Brahmanic elite, descendants of the Aryans who wanted to keep the country closed off and considered all outsiders as "mlecchas" or dirty barbarians. Dalits want openness. There is a rich cultural heritage that has been submerged; the hope is that they come out of the enforced "culture of silence" and speak to the world. There should be a scope to show their creativity and talents in the arts to the whole world. Dalit literature and its English translation is one step forward.

Broadly speaking, the Dalits are not against globalisation or multinational companies (MNCs); what they are opposed to is the fact that MNCs cater more to the increasingly paranoid consumer needs of the upper castes and classes than to the minimum needs of the poor Dalits. The Dalits have already started realising that the dangers of globalisation are that the upper castes are getting globalised faster. This is partly because the Non-Resident Indian (NRI) network is dominated by the upper castes, in spite of small groups of Dalits who have mobilised here and there.

Conclusion

This is an age of likes and choices. Given the chance, the Dalits are ready to pick and choose whatever they like from the market (for example, whether they will watch Doordarshan, which is Brahmanic, or BBC, which is a western upper middle class). It is high time that we should revalue our symbols and practices. The revaluation of symbols and practices in the realm of culture and society is a recognition that pluri-cultural societies must evolve a political structure that is both decentralised in its operations and sensitive to the primacy and centrality of other cultures as the foundation of development policy. In spite of the various contributions to the making of an alternative "ethic" in India, no systematic attempt has been made so far either to map out this emerging terrain of cultural and social change or to define alternative cultural politics. There is, as Frederic Jameson (1991) has suggested, a need for a new "cognitive map" to help individuals understand the changes that are taking place in society. This concern, however, needs to be grounded in an understanding that situates cultures and decentres culture at the heart of social change (Thomas, 1997).

Note

1 For details refer to https://thesatyashodhak.com/jotirao-phule-on-why-he-started-a-school-for-dalits/, accessed 20/11/2022.

References

Arnold, M. (1932). *On the Study of Celtic Literature and Other Essays*, London: J.M. Dent.

Baisantry, D. K. (1991). *Ambedkar: The Total Revolution*, New Delhi: Segment Book Distributors.

Brolov, V. (1984). *Indian Philosophy in Modern Times*, Moscow: Progressive Publishers.

Dangle, A. (1992). *Poisoned Bread*, Bombay: Orient Longman.

Foucault, M. (1984). *Power/Knowledge* (ed.), Paul R. Robinson, New York: Peregrine Book.

Galanter, M. (1984). *Competing Equalities*, London: Oxford University Press.

Jameson, F. (1991). *Postmodernity or the Cultural Logic of Late Capitalism*, United Kingdoms: Verso.

Macionis, J. (1995). *Sociology*, New Jersey: Prentice Hall.

Prasad, R. C. (1993). *Ambedkarism*, Delhi: Motilal Banarasidass.

Theertha, S. D. (1992). *History of Hindu Imperialism*, Madras: Dalit Educational Literature Centre.

Thomas, P. N. (1997). "Communication, Culture and Social Change", *Religion and Society*, Vol. 44, No. 2, 53–65.

Tylor, E. B. (1891). *Anthropology: An Introduction to the Study of Man and Civilisation*, London: Watts.

5   Human Rights and the Subordinated People[1]

A Cross-Cultural Study of Dalit and Black Life World

Selvaraj Arulnathan

Human rights discourse and the life world of the subordinated people stand in opposition to one another. This poses a serious philosophical problem as much as it becomes a sociological issue to be tackled. To understand and locate the identities and life world that is experienced by the subordinated communities around the world, the author conducted an empirical survey between the Dalits (former untouchables) of India and the African Americans/Blacks (former slaves of African descent in North America) of the United States as a cross-cultural empirical survey for a fresh understanding of the subordinated discourse. This study is indicative in nature and inspirational in approach as one subordinated community was compared to another as cross-cultural and imitative process. This attempt becomes very significant when human rights discourse has been very much in the limelight in sociological, political, and philosophical disciplines and also very much in the activist world of grassroots organisations. It is very significant that human rights discourse stipulates the paradigm model for sociopolitical and economic emancipation of marginalised communities across the globe.

The preamble of the Universal Declaration of Human Rights sets the tone hitherto to all types of rights discourse that addresses the issues and life of the marginalised communities as their rights have been grossly vitiated and their livelihood resources have been ruthlessly and snobbishly taken away from them as it states, The recognition of the inherent dignity and of the equal and inalienable rights of all members of the human family is the foundation of freedom, justice and peace in the world. In the same preamble, it is stated,

> The disregard and contempt for human rights have resulted in barbarous acts which have outraged the conscience of mankind, and an advent of the world in which human rights shall enjoy freedom of speech and belief and freedom from fear and want has been proclaimed as the highest aspiration of the common people.

This already presents the possibility of the denial and violation of human rights and the subordinate people's yearning for justice as the a priori inquiry and necessity. The life world of the Dalits and Blacks will strengthen the philosophical search as they present the realities of life in day-to-day experience.

DOI: 10.4324/9781003317173-8

Who Are the Subordinated People?

A subordinated people are a sociological group that does not constitute a politically dominant voting majority of the total population of a given society. It may include any group that is subnormal with respect to a dominant group in terms of social status, education, employment, wealth and political power. From the sociopolitical and economic and cultural conditions, one can easily conclude that Dalits in India and Blacks in the United States are the most subjugated and subordinated in the name of caste and colour respectively. The word "minority" was used during the time of Ambedkar especially in the western context to denote the subordinated community of various categories like social minorities, linguistic minorities, ethnic minorities, and religious minorities. Ambedkar remarked, "minorities are an explosive force, which, if they erupt, can blow up the whole fabric of the state ... it is for the majority to realize its duty not to discriminate against the minorities" (C. A. Debates, Vol. VII, 39). His idea of minority people is what we call today the subordinated people.

Dalit Life World Is Marked by Oppression and Discrimination

Jeya Subramaniam, a social activist and educator from Madurai, Tamilnadu, experienced more social exclusion both in her neighbourhood as a child and in educational institutions, schools, and colleges. She experienced such exclusion in her neighbourhood in daily chores, in the school, and in college as an SC student. She would cringe at the revelation of her identity as her peers would look at her as if she was a *dirty thing thrown in their midst* (interview, 2009).[2] *Jakkian* experienced the worst form of exclusion/identity crisis when he was forced to introduce himself in the college as a cobbler. He locates his Dalit existence in its social ambience which denies his/her psychical, physical, socioeconomic, intellectual, and even moral space; the dominant world view ghettoises his being (Dalitness) within the walls of human wretchedness. The personal narrative of Jakkian is the case in point which foregrounds the whole gamut of the Dalit life world. According to him,

> for a Dalit the surrounding of our living, the historicity of our life world from childhood, the social and spatial setting of our living quarters everything imposes certain pressure upon us. Take my case; I come from a large but very humble and poor family; my father is a folk musician, plays Nagaswaram (a pipe instrument) for living. My mother is a daily wager (coolie) and my grandfather a cobbler and my uncles are all scavengers. This is my family background which is wrought in poverty and humiliation.
>
> (interview, 2009)

He contrasts the life of dominant castes through the occupation of their parents as

> when others introduce themselves in the school or college, "I am so and so; my father is a doctor, my father is an engineer, my father works in the bank, in the railway, etc." but when we introduce ourselves, we have to say, "my father is a drummer or my father sweeps the streets or cleans the toilet," is humiliating.… In short, our identity is inscribed on the tag of humiliation. So, this is the social background we have come from; on the whole the society looks at us as filth and dirt.
>
> (ibid.)

Yesumarian, a Jesuit lawyer and social activist from Tamilnadu, identifies three major areas where Dalits have been discriminated against. One is *denial of land*. Land has been the benchmark of a person's identity in the Indian context. Dalit lands have unjustly been appropriated by the dominant forces for centuries including the *Panchami* land accorded by the British regime. The same point is asserted by *Uma Shankar IAS*, an Indian Administrative Officer from the Dalit community. In his keynote address at the Mission Assembly held in Loyola College, Chennai, in December 2009, he said that land owning is self-esteem. Since Dalits in general are landless labourers, discrimination against them is very high. Number two is *denial of education*. Education has been a rarity for Dalits from the beginning of the Indian education system. Dalits have been grossly denied their share in education, especially, when education is considered the vehicle for mobility and social change. And the third is *denial of housing*. Dalits don't have proper housing as poverty and landlessness have been born with them and would never part with them. How it is possible even after so many centuries and millennia that Dalits have been kept under such a condition is the pertinent question one is inclined to ask (Yesumarian, interview: 2009).

T.K. John traces the root of the problem in the Hindu social order and traces the locus of Dalit self thus:

> I think in Indian society mud, cow dung, wood, rock all these are more appreciated than Dalits. Mud, you want for brick, you touch it no problem; rock also a Brahmin has touched, and anybody can touch it no problem; sleep over it, use it for a building and any of these materials is rated higher than Dalits in the Hindu consciousness.
>
> (interview, 2009)

This is the core value attached to Dalits by the Hindu social order which follows them like their shadows wherever they go, whichever religion they embrace, and whatever they do and achieve.

This clearly explains and expresses how Dalits have been denied their human dignity and respect for so long and so cruelly that today their struggle is not even to establish their human rights which is still a farfetched dream; it is very much a fight for their right to be human. This demolishes all logic, morals, and even human sensibilities that there is a community which has been grossly violated against all norms of human rights that are enshrined in every sensible human mind.

Black as Despised and Denigrated Colour

The problem of the 20th century is the problem of the colour line is the famous words of Du Bois, the world-renowned first African American soci-ologist. It is very relevant even today when racial discrimination is rampant in the United States. One will be shocked to notice the similar experience that the Blacks of America go through as the Dalits in India. The first and inevitable challenge that American society poses to any serious and system-atic inquiry of knowledge about African Americans is that American social, religious, and cultural norms and values are foregrounded in its "white social frame". Anything other than this is treated as the "unwanted other", "alien", and 'radical' and even "anti-American". Hence the core of Black experience in the United States lies in either accepting the "white frame" and surren-dering their uniqueness as people of different ethnic and cultural entities or contesting it to assert their legitimate social space to establish their specific life world to the effect of multicultural and pluralistic social milieu. This also implies that African American life world is viewed as the anti-thesis to the established white norms and allied practices. The black-white relationship has been marked from the very beginning by vertical relationship, not hori-zontal. A closer look at the life of the African Americans in narrative form to the researchers during his field survey will prove that it stands antithetical and critical to the white world view and framework. In this light, it is very insightful to view American society from the white and Black perspectives.

Eileen, an African American woman pursuing her doctoral studies in Chicago, USA, speaks about how she perceives America. She quips,

> *m*ost of my experience personally has been in mostly African American settings. The neighbourhood that I grew up in Detroit was black, African American. The schools that I went to were mostly black schools, the grade school, junior high and high school with another minority may be another Asian or two. But I think most of the students are African Americans and most of the teachers are African Americans. So, I really didn't have an experience of an exposure to a lot of white students until I got to college. So, my world is pretty black in that sense.
>
> (interview, 2009)

This is how America presents itself, two different and opposite worlds forced to co-exist: one world (the subordinated world) exists as the subservient society for the other (the dominant world). It is very interesting to note what Dr. Christopher Manning, an African American professor of History at Loyola University, Chicago, feels about American society. According to him, "there are two different worlds, the wretched one and the blessed one; the former is despised and deplored as the necessary evil while the latter as intrinsically good and noble" (interview: 2009). This is the social definition that the dominant world has constructed for itself by which the subordinated people are forced to live. In other words, the subordinated world exists for the sake of the dominant world. The former is made to believe that it does not have meaning, purpose, and goal independent of the latter. It implies that the dominant world has unlimited power, aspirations, and mode of existence, while the subordinated world has a borrowed and limited existence, an existence of concession by the dominant. This creates a serious sociological issue as the subordinated people don't have independent existence vis-à-vis the dominant people. This has been very much contested and confronted by the subordinated people and their allies in the wake of human rights discourse and sensibilities.

There is a split, a divide between these two social networks and their world views, perceptions, and perspectives. This is the basic structure based on the colour line upon which all other institutions and structures are constructed. One cannot understand America without understanding the divergent colour consciousness of different ethnic groups. But it is the white society which introduced colour consciousness in the society. When *Jonathan Swain* spoke about America and the place of African Americans in it, he makes a remarkable observation and says,

> I think it is not one or two problems that the African Americans go through but the very system. In America this circle of things that operate and it is connected to generations of generation. What we tried to do as Americans is to cut the circle, stretch it out and where we cut and fix and that is our real problem in my view. I think it is very much like a wheel. The American kids sit on the wheel and push it all around. It is kind of take that wheel and break it that is the real challenge'. The black-white relationship is not in a linear setting but in a circular fashion.
>
> (interview, 2008)

According to *Gregory Meyers*,

> there is more racism now than it was earlier when I was here in the 70s and 80s, because it is now more indirect, it was not as affront as it is now. Racist elements expressed when you highly move up in an organization you really do not get the respect what should have. When you walk in to such a position, where you are a supervisor or a manager

you have to fight your way to earn respect, because most of the time you supervise not only blacks, so you have to earn their respect, show them what you are doing when they are not doing their job.

(interview, 2008)

Mark Soderquist realises what happens behind the back of every Black in the white world.

> Still as you travel as an African American, you do notice that you draw undue attention in public places; when you examine a situation behind you what is going on, you find a lot still to know and be placed. And because we are building more relationship and friendship with Anglos, they begin to tell us things that are happening away from our presence. So, we know we are still a long way to match putting on our table of real brotherhood.
>
> (interview: 2008)

He further clarifies how whites sit in their ivory castle and believe that racism is over. But when you shed off all the layers of masks and get down to brass-tacks of the African American life world, one is exposed to the real world. He acknowledges that when he says,

> What I didn't see the systemic racism; racism and injustice that permeate our system; whether it is justice system, whether it is economic system, I didn't see that till I came down here; till I started working with Derrick (Derrick is an African American who works very closely with Mark in the black neighbourhood for its development). And it was like blinders in my eyes.
>
> (ibid.)

Cheryl Newson, an African American woman who observes very closely what is happening in the United States says,

> Life is very difficult for us. We just appear on the surface to have everything that everybody else has. … African Americans are the last considered to have all that others have. We don't have the finance to buy whatever we want to.
>
> (interview: 2007).

*Frantz Fa*non sounds exactly the same when he says,

> the native town is a hungry town, starved of bread, of meat, of shoes, of coal, of light. The native town is a crouching village, a town on its knees, a town wallowing in the mire. It is a town of Niggers and dirty Arabs.
>
> (Fanon, 1963)

Erick Styles describes it in a very philosophical language as *culture of depri-vation* as the basic identity of African Americans when he adduces,

> African Americans as Americans are apple pie especially when we talk about what is American. As the cultural landscape, we have been from the very beginning only preceded by the Native Americans. And yet the social vocation is always weak at best and challenging certainly collectively. But the situation of the African Americans continues to be one in need of work
>
> (interview: 2007).

While Newson and Styles tried to locate the African American experience in the modern economic, consumerist world as how they are systematically impoverished, *Dwight Burrow*, another African American from Houston, Texas, goes to the heart of the issue. He speaks about how they have been treated from the time they were brought into this new land and why.

> Our people were brought into this country from the countries of Africa. The people who brought them here did not consider them as human beings. They were considered properties, chattel. Some people like them to a work horse, or a work mule. In many cases they were not even considered to be human. So, they were not brought here to be citizens. They were not even brought here as people. That says a lot about how they were treated.
>
> (interview: 2007)

Thus, the African American experience in the United States is denial of their humanity. Denial of humanity is the a priori status which accounts for all other discrimination and oppression. This is in a way a primordial experience of every African American which produced the institution of modern slavery based on race. This became a permanent blot on the mental map of African Americans.

Racism expresses itself in various ways. One of the most prominent ways it exhibits is in the education system. This is what Angela Swain experienced in the college. "I have had many experiences, especially in the college where I was discriminated against, because I was black" (interview: 2008). Educational institutions, instead of acting as temples of learning and character formation, building up human community of brothers and sisters, in fact serve as the breeding ground for division and discrimination, and animosity. We can quote a number of events and incidents wherein schools and colleges have played a detrimental role in race relations.

Denial of Human Dignity and Humanness

From the foregoing case narratives, it is very clear that the subordinated people have to fight for their rights continuously and consistently until they join the mainstream. Today, more than any other time in history, the subordinated consciousness is widely prevalent and forges into the social agenda of Dalits and Blacks in a very special and specific way. Today it has become even dangerous as people like Gandhi propagated only political emancipation as the national agenda pushing both social and economic emancipation to the background. This has been the most miserable turn of events that instead of bringing about integral freedom, the dominant section of the society used its economic and social high-handedness to unjustly wield and usurp political power with its cutting edge by coercion, vandalism, and intimidation.

Resolution 32/130 of the Universal Declaration of Human Rights affirms that all human rights and fundamental freedoms are indivisible and interdependent and that the realisation of civil and political rights is, therefore, impossible without the enjoyment of economic, social, and cultural rights. In addition, all human rights are seen as inalienable, and their promotion globally is understood to involve different emphases in different parts of the world. Finally, realisation of the new international economic order is identified as essential for the effective protection of human rights (Mazairac, 1993). Hence the task before us is very huge to ensure social and economic democracy to the subordinated masses more than political democracy.

The Conception of Humans as Beings of Praxis

Mihailo Markovic speaks about human rights as seriously concerned about human beings. The ultimate foundation of human rights is constituted by those essential needs of each individual, the fulfilment of which is, under given historical conditions, a necessary condition of social survival and development. Law is just, humane, and universally valid only if statutes and legal acts express such universal needs; if they do not, then law is only the expression of naked force. If law is reduced to positive law, to what is written in the laws of a state, it is nothing but a justification of the particular interests of the ruling elite. In such a case law would be, as Thrasymachus in Plato's Republic put it, "what benefits the most powerful" (Markovic, 1981).

In this context, one has to ask if human history as a whole is a meaningful process or not. Before answering such a difficult and complex question, one could ask a simpler, more general one: What constitutes the meaning of any life process? Jacques Monod's answer was teleonomy: a unique, primary project of preservation and multiplication of the species. One could ask here: What makes this basic project "valuable"? Why is the preservation of species better than disappearance? Why is it better to multiply than to simply restore the already achieved quantitative level?

The only answer to such a question is the following: What is here described as "better" or "worse" is not merely a matter of subjective preference; it refers to a tendency which is a necessary part of the very definition of life. Surely not all individuals and species survive and multiply. But while they do, they are alive. In a similar way one should add that life involves a tendency to maintain and increase order and structural complexity; a process of change in the opposite direction toward lesser order and complexity is "bad" for a living organism since it leads to the destruction of life. It is therefore being described in negative terms: as a process of degradation.

In the same vein, we can seek answers to questions like what made human history possible and indeed unique – in view of the explosive development of the last few thousand years – was a specifically human activity: praxis. Praxis is purposeful (preceded by a conscious objective), self-determining (choosing autonomously among alternative possibilities), rational (consistently following certain general values), creative (transcending given forms and introducing novelties into established patterns of behaviour), *cumulative* (storing in symbolic forms ever greater amounts of information and conveying it to coming generations so that they can continue to build on the ground already conquered), and self-creative (in the sense that young human individuals, after being exposed to an increasing wealth of information and new environmental challenges, develop new faculties and new needs). Praxis is a new, higher-level form of the human species. Many human activities are clearly not instances of praxis, nor are they characteristic of human history. The repetitive work of a slave, serf, or modern worker resembles more a beaver's dam building than creative work.

Reconstruction of Social Democracy as the Historical Necessity

This reconstruction demands a new social culture, which sends the old caste and race culture based on discrimination and inequality on holiday. It implies that social emancipation is not possible from the available models as the very pillars of democracy and development stand on the foundation of the Hindu religious system whose soul is *Varnashramadharma* and racial superiority-inferiority duality. We need to first and foremost carve out a new action plan (praxis) and based on this demolish the old one. In other words, social democracy is the pre-condition to political democracy. Social democracy lies in the defiance of the so-called political democracy, the dominant discourse romantically propagated as the gateway to economic and social freedom.

Social Praxis as the New Paradigm

Social praxis of the subordinated people starts with their life experience. This life experience is basically and predominantly oppressive and discriminatory as we have seen above. Hence an action programme should be carved out to remove this oppression. The dominant discourse will never initiate social democracy as it would stand squarely against its own interest. It has always been from below. Just imagine, the Jesuits in India promulgate a policy not to employ anyone from Dalit or tribal community to service jobs like scavenging and cleaning and start rehabilitating in some other jobs all those who are already is such jobs. They can liberate not less than 50,000 Dalits and tribals from the social stigma of polluted identity within a year. If the different churches in India which claim to be working for the uplift of Dalits and Adivasis do the same, we can see hundreds of thousands of Dalits and Adivasis liberated within a year after which they can boldly speak of social justice. Till then it will be another political quarters which mouths words without any meaning.

While political democracy in the world nations was initiated by the elites, social democracy has always been initiated by the social underclass. Both in the United States and in India it was the social elites who spearheaded the political freedom struggle while the Blacks in the United States and the Dalits and Adivasis in India started the social protest movements. As it was Martin Luther King Jr and Malcolm X who spearheaded the emancipation of African Americans through the Civil Rights Movement, it was Ambedkar who spoke about social democracy as the precondition to political democracy. In the First Round Table Conference Ambedkar submitted a memorandum, in which he laid down eight conditions on behalf of the Untouchables. They were equal citizenship, equal rights, protection against discrimination, adequate representation in legislature and administration, right to demand adjudication in case of their neglect, and some special privileges and places in ministry. Ambedkar at the same time criticises the agenda of political democracy of Gandhi which did not have any programme for the emancipation of the Untouchables. A.K. Vakil opines that "Ambedkar criticized that Gandhi was determined to repudiate the rights of the untouchables" (ibid.).

Casteism and racism are basically social construction. Hence it can be deconstructed and also reconstructed through social democratic principles. We need to construct a different social order which destroys both caste and race. Difference is there, but there are differences in so many things and in so many ways. In his address to the General Assembly of the United Nations in December 1964, Che maintained, prophetically, that

> the time will come when this assembly will acquire greater maturity and demand of the United States Government guarantees for the life of the Blacks and Latin Americans who live in this country, most of them U.S. citizens by origin or adoption. This is possible only through social democracy, not political democracy.

Forms of Social Democratic Processes

Paulo Freire proposes *dialogue* as the way of learning and teaching as against the banking system in the education of Latin America. Paulo Freire was very critical about how the education system in Latin America was deeply oppressive and divisive of the elite from oppressed communities. He lays out a programme which holds participatory negotiation as the overarching principle as the praxis. All other elements of praxis for liberation includes in this (Friere, 1972). Sambiah Gundimeda contends that "rejection of any community's culture is a way of injuring the human agency of that community, and such injury can be healed only by a dialogical process, namely, the assertion of positivity and pride in their own culture by the injured and positive recognition of such assertion by the injurer. Secondly, democratization of the public sphere can be effectively actualized not only by according to the representation of the marginalized cultures, but such representation needs to be accompanied with respect to the other".

Ambedkar, the pioneer of and the ardent propagandist about social democracy as early as the 1920s while all other Congress politicians were busy with a transfer of political power without any real change, proposes a fourfold programme to Harijan Sevak Sangh which boasted of liberating the Dalits from their caste shackles as given under:

1. To try to get civil rights for the Untouchables: in order to achieve this objective, it was necessary to throw open schools, wells, *chavadis* (village Panchayat office), and means of transportation for the Untouchables.
2. To try to provide an equal opportunity to the Untouchables – the Untouchables were not allowed to sell milk, fruits, and vegetables. In the industrial sector low payment was given to the Untouchable workers. The Harijan Sevak Sangh should try to form a public opinion against such inequality.
3. To spread communication between the Untouchables and the *savarna* Hindus: Ambedkar opined that there should be constant communication between the *savarna* Hindus and Untouchables. He remarked that the *savarna* Hindus would not like it. Ambedkar appealed that as North America waged a civil war against South America, the progressive Hindus should wage a war against the orthodox Hindus.
4. To operate the organisation speedily – Ambedkar pointed out that organisations could not be run by mercenaries but by devoted social workers (Vakil, ibid: 34–35).

Equally important is *Advocacy and Networking*. It plays a very crucial role in social democracy. While the dominant discourse will not open its mouth either about its dominant approach to social and political policies as it would jeopardise its own interest, it will not even think of opening the subject of its subordinated people as the dominant discourse is the root of the issue. You won't see any dominant caste person, organisation, or state talk about casteism on international platforms or a white person, organisation, and white government advocating against the crisis of African Americans. Hence the affected parties, the Dalits and the African Americans, should take their cases to the international forum, human rights organisations, and nations to expose their crude realities and demand social and political justice by way of pressure upon the wronged nations, communities, and organisations.

Also, through networking the subordinated peoples of different cultures and nations should connect themselves and discuss a common praxis and pedagogy for all the subordinated people.

Conclusion

The Universal Declaration is remarkable in two fundamental aspects. In 1948, the then 58 Member States of the United Nations represented a range of ideologies, political systems, and religious and cultural backgrounds, as well as different stages of economic development. The authors of the declaration, themselves from different regions of the world, sought to ensure that the draft text would reflect these different cultural traditions and incorporate common values inherent in the world's principal legal systems and religious and philosophical traditions. Most important, the Universal Declaration was to be a common statement of mutual aspirations – a shared vision of a more equitable and just world.

Unfortunately, the celebrated ideals of human rights discourse were not translated into life and aspirations of the marginalised communities for whom it is more pertinent than to any other community. It has been mostly in the hands of the affluent majority whose interests and motives were taken care of by this philosophy. The present struggle for the practical realisation of civil and human rights is a new dimension of contemporary, emancipatory aspirations. To the extent that it stops being a mere phase of confrontation between governments and ideological camps, and achieves the character of a mass movement, it will contribute essentially to the abolition of present-day barriers to human freedom and social justice.

Human rights discourse has not so far appealed to the Dalits and Blacks in its full measure and dimension since it is still in the dominant hands of these countries as they set the standards and the interpretative tools by which they easily escape the international scanner. Hence the time calls for international human rights watch to monitor what happens with these communities and how they are still marginalised.

The next and very important movement of human rights discourse will be a movement from general and individual rights to specific, locational, social, and economic rights. One may argue that it is already enshrined in the Preamble and other periodic declarations. But it is also very necessary that geographic and other generic and specific dimensions like caste should be the benchmarks of human rights campaigns as the spirit of it is not just to stipulate the guidelines in terms of rights but also very much in terms of its stakeholders. This only can help different communities to take the cue directly from human rights recommendations in their own sociopolitical, economic, and cultural contexts. Finally, human rights discourse is the international law school that should find directions for all the social minorities who are still out of focus in the national and international development paradigm and programmes.

Notes

1 This chapter is a revised version of the article published in *Social Action: A Quarterly Review of Social Trends* (January–March 2011).
2 The author conducted an empirical survey between the Dalits (former untouchables) of India and the African Americans/Blacks (former slaves of African descent in North America) of the United States of America as a cross-cultural empirical survey for fresh understanding of the subordinated discourse. The interviews conducted at different time periods as part of the survey are indicated as interview, 2007; Interview, 2008; interview, 2009.

References

Fanon, F. (1963). *The Wretched of the Earth*, New York: Grower Press.
Freire, P. (1972). *Pedagogy of the Oppressed*, Portugal: Penguin Books.
Mazairac, L. P. J. (Director-General). (1993). *Human Rights Instruments*, The Netherlands: Ministry of the Foreign Affairs.
Mihailo, M. (1981). "Philosophical Foundations of Human Rights", *Praxis International.*, 4. Portugal

6 The Right to Selfhood[1]

The Paradox of Being a Dalit Woman

Subhadra Mitra Channa

Introduction

In this chapter we examine whether the concept of human rights can be applied to the situation of the Dalits in India with a special focus on the life of Dalit women. We must accept the premise that Dalit rights are human rights and the Dalit women have been at the receiving end of oppression in more senses than one. The Dalit issue should be examined in the light of the broader framework of sociological theory that has dealt with oppression in many social situations. The concept of cultural hegemony introduced by Gramsci was used by scholars to show that culture contains within itself a set of values and beliefs that rationalise and make domination and discrimination possible without the exercise of any external force or economic basis. Within the ambit of cultural beliefs, domination becomes natural and a way of life, taken as a matter of course and rarely contested.

These beliefs and values are taken for granted and reproduced through a set of practices embodied in the day-to-day existence of a people, which, taken together, reproduce the very conditions of existence, which produce it in the first place, like gift giving and marriage negotiations. This theory of practice, introduced and developed largely by Bourdieu (1977), is a useful tool of social analysis which not only describes the existence of domination but explains its continuation.

Continued relationships of domination have been or can be explained through the internalisation of the value system to an extent that there is an unquestioning acceptance of the hierarchy of relationships, what Bordieu has called "doxa". The strength or validity of such practices is that they are rooted not in "beliefs" that are conscious, but in the unconscious from where they cannot be removed until brought to the level of active discourse. This is the reason that systems of discrimination continue for long historical periods relatively uncontested except for occasional eruptions of dissent. The caste system, for example, was contested in several historical periods by Buddhism, by the Bhakti Movement, and by Sufism. But power hierarchies were able to redefine the situation in terms of existing belief systems to continue their hegemonic rule. In fact, the construction of people's self-hood has

DOI: 10.4324/9781003317173-9

been so entrenched within the idiom of caste that those at the receiving end are also reluctant to discard it altogether.

Those who are dominated live by the practices of a "contra culture" that negates and dilutes the oppressiveness of ideological domination. These are usually revealed only by a detailed ethnographic study and rarely form the subject of any verbal discourse. The dominated keep them as their "secret weapons" as it were, and even they may not be fully aware of them at a conscious level.

This is not to say that at the conscious level, cultural ideologies are unquestioningly accepted. Those who are subordinated would contest their position.

> As a matter of fact, in both the Southern United States and in India, the pariah groups can be shown to have a high incidence of active and intense resentment of their status, and a definition of themselves very different from that adopted by the dominant society.
>
> (Berreman, 1966)

But contested and conscious beliefs are subjected to hegemonic impositions, where the voices of the dominated are suffocated. What makes survival possible are the practices which are adaptive to the situation of oppression. The world view at the local level, obliquely placed to the dominant ideology, helps create a feeling of self-worth and a self-evaluation counter to the one superimposed from the top.

It is in the contradiction between self-evaluation and evaluation by others and the counteracting notions of personhood – one conferred, the other self-assessed – that the interface between domination and human rights can best be evaluated. Messer (1993: 221) suggests that the anthropological contribution to the subject of human rights lies principally in two aspects, by providing cross-cultural research on the questions of rights and who is eligible to be counted as a full person.

Thus, the dominating groups such as high castes dominating low castes and men dominating women frequently broadcast a stereotype of the "dominated" that gives them characters that make domination appear in a paternalistic light and "justified".

> Frequently they are defined as "non-persons" a social definition that undoubtedly serves a number of social functions – By defining them as not fully human, behaviour towards them can be excused that would be inexcusable if exercises towards a real human being.
>
> (Berreman, 1966)

Thus, the denial of full personhood is the basis of the denial of rights which can be physical, symbolic, and psychological. In the relationship between the dominant castes and the Dalits, all forms of violence may be executed, in one form or the other.

In this chapter we shall be concerned with one category of rights only, those related to a cognitive perception of self, which in turn are reproduced through practice in day-to-day life, a product of history and the environment. Further, in evaluating the relationship between domination and subjection, and relating it to gender we shall be touching upon another theoretical point, that neither the dominating group nor the dominated are homogeneous categories. Internal divisions, based on natural and conferred categories such as age, sex, economic status, and personal qualities, create multiple identities within a category. And, as Knauft (1996: 164) has pointed out, "In situations of fragmented and displaced identity, the fight against some in equalities is bound to reinforce others". Taking gender as one mode of fragmentation of identity in both the dominant caste and Dalits, we shall see that in terms of personhood and rights, women of both groups are placed very differently vis-à-vis both their own group and the other. And these identities neither match nor reinforce each other; neither are they homologous with the male identities.

The Symbolic Violence of Constructed Genderhood

Among all the various categories of rights to which human beings can stake a claim by the very fact of being human is the right to a cognitive perception of self and self-worth, which each individual forms of her-self and is collectively formed by a community. Whether or not a community can get its point of view accepted, including its own self-perception, by others is a matter of the power relations that exist in a society. Thus, the marginal and the dominated people are usually projected according to the stereotypes which others, the dominant groups, form about them. Although these projections may be quite contrary to a people's cognition about themselves, they are helpless in their position of powerlessness and cannot but accept what is heaped upon them from the "outside". The indignity of such a situation is symbolic violence which can be more painful than physical violence.

Most works on Dalit women have concentrated on the physical violence such as rape and sexual molestation to which they have been subjected by high-caste men. But few have shed any light on how society has systematically eroded their image and their dignity by a hegemonical imposition of a constructed image specifically designed to violate their inner being.

Superordinate–subordinate relationships between groups are usually centred on the creation of stereotypes, usually derogatory, about each other. Although both parties in a hierarchical power relationship, more so an exploitative one, have unfavourable views of each other, the dominated group suffers more because it is helpless in the projection of its point of view being deprived of a voice; the very consequence of its powerlessness. The Dalit women are such a muted segment of society whose voices are stilled by the male power holders who exploit them and simultaneously decry them. As Unnithan-Kumar (1997) has shown, the manner in which gender identities are constructed is a means of expressing differences between communities as well as inequalities. "The projection of an uncontrolled sexuality onto women of a community other than one's own is often connected with the desire to maintain a distinction and hierarchy between the two communities" (Kumar, 1997).

The ideals of womanhood in high-caste Hindu communities are the soft-spoken, demure woman who is physically restricted in her movements, delicate and dependent, non-assertive, and the epitome of motherhood. Needless to say, such an ideal type is perfectly suited to the needs of a male-dominated patriarchal regime, based upon the lineal transmission of property to male heirs. Resource-holding and powerful males ensure that the women give them male heirs and do not demand any share in the power. The women of their own groups are both sheltered and protected as symbols of their own manhood. Their roles, irrespective of the occupation of their husbands, confined to domestic duties. The more affluent and powerful a man, the less the productive contribution of his wife; the more she is relegated to an ornamental role and her personhood merged with that of her husband. The extreme expression of such a merging was the practice of immolation of the widows of high-status men. It was instilled into the value system of the women that their lives were meaningless without that of their husbands and that they were conditioned to follow their husbands willingly believing their existence to be totally merged with his. Such a woman then acquired the status of a goddess, but again this doubtful privilege was reserved only for the consorts of powerful men such as rulers and high castes. A Dalit woman was never given the right to attain this status. In fact, women of these castes were never accorded the status of pure widows and were most often required to remarry, if they were widowed at a young age. The stereotypical image of the lower-caste woman sees her as deprived of all virtues of ideal womanhood. She speaks in loud and harsh tones and is seen as aggressive and bold therefore shameless, devoid of feminine qualities of delicacy and charm. She moves about freely unprotected by her men and therefore viewed as easy prey. The concept of violating her modesty never arises because she is never viewed as having any. Thus, the high-caste men who sexually exploited a low-caste woman can do so without any qualms of conscience, viewing her as without the essence of womanhood which demands respect.

> High caste women, upon whom the precarious purity of the castes rests in both societies, are put on a pedestal of purity, honor and incorruptibility. Low caste women, the purity of whose offspring is not jeopardized by the possibility of high caste paternity, are assumed (by high castes) to be not virtuous and readily accessible to men of high caste.
>
> (Berreman, 1967)

Paradoxically enough the very fact that the low-caste woman was seen as a person in her own right and as not merged with her husband went against her image as not being a "Sati- Savitri", the epitome of pure womanhood. Her personhood, though separate, was viewed as inferior, like the person of an animal. She could be violated as she was not merged in identity with a powerful and pure man. Thus, rape and physical violence shadowed her existence, and often the aggressiveness and harshness of a Dalit woman was an outcome of the practical necessities of coping with this ever-present threat to her person. It is this manifestation of her personality that further led to the symbolic violence of denigration heaped upon her.

Thus the violence is not simply physical but also in the cognitive dimension of constructing an ideal of womanhood which violates the real existence of the high-caste women and the symbolic existence of the low-caste women. In the latter's case it goes against her own self-image as individuals struggle to define themselves and their place in society, from the inside out, contesting the way they are socially constructed trying to recreate culture to make meaning for themselves (Parish, 1997). When we look at the way a Dalit woman is constructed within her own community the significance of this statement becomes very clear. She is neither seen by others of her own group nor sees herself in the degraded image which the high-caste men construct of her. It is also relevant to mention that the high-caste women do not generally subscribe to the view held by their own men. A dhobi woman and her high-caste mistress may share a relationship that is informed by their common sisterhood of oppression. Secluded and immobile women of the high castes often had in the dhoban a confidante and a supplier of neighbourhood gossip, who, in the course of her daily work, went from house to house, collecting and distributing clothes.

The construction of gender within the subculture of each group is informed by the conditions of existence of that group and its material and non-material resources, and it must be understood in that context. The gendered lens needs to be more nuanced as Dalit women do not fit the stereotypes of traditional Hindu women. The former often appear to be more non-conformist in their behaviour. But the image that is interpreted through the categories of construction of the high castes does not comply with the meaning system of the Dalit groups themselves.

The Construction of Gender: Inner View

The Dalit women such as the dhobi women, whom I have encountered from time to time, show a construction of self-hood and self-perception that is an integral part of their historical existence. Such perception is linked both to their material conditions of social reproduction and to the cognitive dimensions of dignity and self-worth. Taking the example of the dhobi women, I will show the construction of the feminine in the dhobi's own mode of discourse and how it is adaptive to, as well as a product of, their way of life and an essential aspect of their adaptation to their own social environment.

The dhobis described in this chapter belong to an urban community of Old Delhi, known locally as the Sheheri Dhobis, studied by me in the 1970s

(Channa, 1985). The dhobis' hereditary occupation is washing clothes. The division of labour divides this work in such a manner that the men do the heavy work of beating the clothes and scrubbing (especially the heavy ones) and the women help in drying and in the collection and distribution of soiled and cleaned clothes from the individual households. The major contribution of women is to the ironing of clothes which is more or less regarded as a woman's job. The women are also entrusted with all the household duties such as washing utensils, cleaning, cooking, and looking after children. Since the urban dhobis have no agricultural work, the food grains and provisions are bought from the market, usually by the young girls, who take a male sibling along to carry the load. Besides the sex-wise division of labour, there is an age-wise division of labour. Most of the outdoor work, like collecting clothes, redistributing them, ironing, and helping the men on the banks of the river, in drying and squeezing of clothes, is done by older women. Ideally the young adult girls, both unmarried and married, are entrusted with household duties, which include taking care of the domestic finances and also taking day-to-day household decisions. As a woman grows older and is less burdened with childbearing and child rearing, she takes to ironing and older women gain prestige by their skill in this task. If there is no young woman in the house, the conduct of day-to-day household duties becomes difficult and sometimes impossible. Girls become economically productive from a very early age. Girls as young as seven or eight start taking care of their infant siblings, if any, or otherwise help in household chores like washing utensils or sweeping floors. By the time they are nine or ten years old, they also take up ironing clothes, starting with small and light fabrics and graduating to heavier ones. It is the daughter who, by the time she is fourteen or fifteen years of age, has the run of the house. She orders about her male siblings, keeps the household money, and takes all the decisions as to buying provisions and cooking. She is referred to as "gharkimalkin" (the mistress of the house). By the time she gets married, another sister may take over, or a young daughter-in-law. The latter does not take over as long as there are unmarried girls of mature age, to run the house. Thus, when a girl gets married, she usually undergoes a transformation in status from an independent and decision-making person to a subservient and rather quiet member of the household. However, this is only a passing phase, and the daughter-in-law takes over sooner or later, depending upon the status of the husband's female siblings. The significant difference from upper-caste households is in the powerful role played by young women in the domestic sphere and their indispensable contribution to the household economy.

This early control over household economic matters gives a girl self-confidence, rarely found in upper-caste girls. They are regarded as responsible members of society from an early age and are also usually regarded as more sensible than males. Since much of their work takes them onto the streets, knowing their own vulnerability as low-caste women, they learn to defend themselves, albeit by aggressive behaviour.

As women, their value lies more in their productive than reproductive role. The ideal dhobi woman is one who works hard and takes care of herself and her family, including the male members. She is adept at ironing clothes and helps her man get through the hard grind of life. Motherhood is seen as a natural aspect of womanhood but nothing to eulogise. The dhobis and other lower castes take the woman's role as mother as natural, biological aspect of life rather than giving it the sacred status as among higher castes. Too much time spent on looking after children is seen as a waste; children grow up any way. This is rational in their own setup as the woman's time, productively employed, brings bread and butter to the household.

The Status of the Girl Child

Children of both sexes are seen as equally important. The value of a child is in terms of its labour input into the household economy and not as heir to a line of descent. The male child is important less for himself than for the wife he will bring in to replenish the household labour pool and the subsequent children she will bear. Filial relationships and bilateral kinship take precedence over notional patriliny. The contribution of the male child is much less in terms of labour input than the girl child. The male child becomes important only when he grows up, but a girl child is productive from an age as early as six years. Parents desperately want to have female children. At the time I was doing field work, a couple with two sons was preparing to go to Vaishno Devi to ask for a daughter.

Since all marriages take place within the strictly endogamous "biradari" which is a localised kin group, the girl's displacement after marriage is minimal. Married girls can, and do, drop in to help out parents whenever required. Thus, a girl child is not lost to the parents even after marriage, in terms of her emotional and work support. In Northern India, upper-caste parents do not even drink water in their daughter's affinal household. The dhobis jokingly say that "If they cannot drink water, they can take liquor". In other words, eating and drinking takes place between all members of the "biradari", which includes all affines. Thus, the social and ritual distance between the bride giver and the bride taker does not exist for the dhobis; the parents of a girl are not accorded any lower status than the parents of the boy. The girl child is not a "parayadhan" (someone else's wealth) as she is referred to, among high castes in Northern India. She remains loyal to her parents and brothers, throughout her life.

Just like descent has little meaning for the dhobis who do not even have a family name to pass on to their sons, the other reason for the importance of a son for the Hindus, namely the performance of death rituals, has little meaning for the dhobis. In their preoccupation with the harshness of their daily grind, they have little time to think of the other world. The marriage and death rituals of the dhobis are substantially different from caste Hindus (Channa, 1991). Thus, the value of a child is per se related to their labour power and emotional value to their parents. It has nothing to do with descent or patriarchal notions of the other world.

A third criterion which evaluates the relative status of male and female children is in terms of the marriage prestations, which again hold little significance for the dhobis. Traditionally, there was no concept of dowry, as the girl was welcomed into her husband's home, for her own value. If at all, under particular situations, the boy's side was pressurised into giving money to get their bride. This was when they were badly in need of a productive, young woman to run the house.

Male vs. Female

The relationship between the dhobi male and female is one of equality. The Dalit husband has little power to dominate his wife. She is more than his equal partner in productive work. She also does not suffer the extreme inequality suffered by women within strong patriarchal regimes. Patriarchy, which draws strength from a broad resource base, is existing in a very diluted form in these people with neither political nor material resources to draw upon. The high-caste males have the advantage of ritual, material, and political superiority, which is denied to their own wives, placing them in an extremely unequal power gradient with respect to women of their own group. The relationship between exploitative external relations and the exploitation by men of the women of their own group has also been pointed out by Leacock (1980) where she equates the exploitative colonial relations of the western societies with the exploitation of their own women. From historical times till today, low-caste women have been spared male domination at least within their own groups. The high castes had reserved the notions of purity and sacredness only for their own women, thereby subjugating them totally. Low-caste men, by virtue of their lack of power, are situated in a relation of far greater equality to their own women. The woman here is evaluated in terms of her own personal qualities, especially her labour, but there also exists an emotional bond between husband and wife who regard each other as comrades. I have seen dhobi women address their husbands as friends, in a familiar tone, using the familiar "tu". The husbands are not averse to helping their wives with household chores, including cooking. If, for example, a wife is sick, then the husband may have to do everything around the house if no one else is available. Such relaxation of the division of labour has been reported by other works among the Dalit groups, for example among the sweepers (bhangi) by Searle-Chtterjee (1981) who found the husbands willingly sharing in the work of their wives. Also, Rao (1998), in talking about the pastoral Bakkarwals, says that what men do depends more upon their status than upon gender as poor men who cannot afford servants do many more tasks assigned only to women and servants among the rich.

There is no separation in the consumption level among the dhobis, on the basis of gender, only by age and productivity. Women eat and drink like men, consuming non-vegetarian food and liquor. Older women also smoke, though young women rarely do. A woman is given a nutritious, though cheap, diet of boiled meat bones during pregnancy. After delivery also she is put on a special diet of sweet meats, made with nutritionally high-valued nuts, semolina, and pure ghee. The dhobis realise the labour value of their women and take care to preserve it. Women are not subjected to any taboos during menstruation or after childbirth. A woman sometimes resumes work, a few hours after delivering a child. A woman's labour cannot be sacrificed for the sake of ritual purity, a concept anyway alien to the dhobis. The important point to note is that women are not discriminated against for consumption purposes as among high castes, where they are quite often prevented from taking non-vegetarian foods and certainly tabooed from alcoholic beverages. The high castes, at the same time, denigrate the low-caste women for specifically these consumption habits.

Thus, being an equal partner to her husband in terms of production and consumption, a dhobi woman's constitution of her own self-hood in no way puts her in a subordinate position to any man, husband or brother. Sisters may reprimand and order their brothers around, since most often they are in charge of the household. The same is true of wives. Women may openly abuse their husbands and the latter often meekly comply. Any fight or argument is always on a one-to-one basis.

The Inner vs. Outer: Paradoxes Constructed and of Perceived Self-Hood

The very qualities which contribute towards the positive womanhood of Dalit women place them in a negative light in the eyes of the patriarchal high-caste society. The high-caste men are both attracted and repelled by these women, who attract them sexually with their freedom of movement and their uninhibited body language, which is translated as sexual in the idiom of upper castes, but which is merely an outcome of their active participation in the process of production. Their voices are branded as coarse and loud, their postures vulgar, and their character loose. This links up with the double standards of a patriarchal society that it cannot respect women in their sexual role. The men are sexually attracted to women whom they cannot respect and respect only those women to whom they do not assign sexual roles. This is the root cause of the age-old exploitation and simultaneous social denigration of Dalit women.

Herein lies the contradiction of the Dalit woman's position. The Dalit man who is powerless to protect his woman is therefore also powerless to dominate her. The very conditions which give the Dalit woman her advantage to develop a positive self-image in relation to her own men give her a disadvantage in relation to the outside world. The high-caste women are both dominated and protected by their men; the low-caste women are neither dominated nor protected.

Upward mobility in the Dalit man's position only translates into a disadvantage for his wife. Educated men who do jobs want their wives to give up traditional work and become housewives. The wife consequently loses her independence and self-respect and becomes dependent. She is then expected to conform to high caste standards of modesty and so-called decency by her husband, for the very fact that he can support her materially.

Human rights are often translated into advantages of education and improved material standards. However complex models of human interaction intervene in such simplistic causal relationships. The advantages of leading a more carefree life, free from hard toil, have the disadvantage of the loss of personal freedom. Self-worth and human dignity suffer with material prosperity. Educated boys among the dhobis expect a dowry. They also look for superficial qualities such as beauty and fair skin in their prospective brides. In the traditional setup a woman was valued only for herself. Even dark-skinned and ugly women faced no disadvantage. In fact, concepts of physical beauty were practically absent. The introduction of these ideas brought about symbolic violence on womanhood itself. Women started to evaluate themselves and are evaluated by others, by external standards of beauty and the dowry that they may bring, which have nothing to do with her intrinsic worth as a person.

I remember an elderly man saying,

> What is this idea of bringing in a beautician to decorate the bride? Does she not have two hands and two feet, two eyes, and a nose? What else does a woman require? Is the beautician going to give her an extra limb?

It is these simple, earthy attitudes that are being eroded by the so-called modern values. Earlier a woman was a person, valued, because she could work and produce children.

The upper castes turn up their noses and say that the lower classes have no concept of aesthetics: they have no concept of beauty. They overlook the fact that they had the concepts of human worth and dignity. A person had value by being just a human being; it did not matter if she was dark or cross eyed. Just by being born a woman could expect to lead a life of fulfilment, as a wife and as a mother, most importantly as a socially respected being. Infiltration of high class and caste values stifles the "inner being" of the woman, though it may give her more leisure. If girls become a burden to their parents for reasons of dowry and loss of productive value, similar discrimination against them as that exists among the upper strata of society will come up. Educated boys among the dhobis started demanding educated girls as brides. To meet their demands the parents of girls have to withdraw their girls from productive work and put them in schools. Most parents compromised by educating their girls up to the primary level and then taking them out of school.

There is a severe contradiction in that the very weapon which is seen as the means to women's empowerment serves to worsen their condition. An elementary level of education only leaves the girl totally dependent, as she is not fit to pursue any occupation, either traditional or modern. Highly educated girls have to sacrifice their family life, as they find it impossible to get married. They do not find grooms from within their own groups and no one from a higher group is usually willing to marry them. Neither do the girls themselves willing to exert such an option as it means an alienation from their own families. Most of the highly educated women from the Dalit communities have had to compromise on their family options.

Thus, as Knauft has already pointed out, in a postmodern situation of multiple identities, oppression of one form may be alleviated only to reinforce or introduce it in another form. The struggle of the Dalit men to improve their position in relation to high-caste men through education and occupational diversification leads to a reversal in the position of their women with respect to their own self-image and in-group status. But, on the other hand, their seclusion leads to an enhancement, even if superficial, in the eyes of high-caste society. To a practical extent this may only be their relative inaccessibility as housewives and as the wives of men of greater social status. Symbolically they are still denigrated both in speech and in action, like a low-caste doctor is looked down upon as having secured his medical seat through reservation and not merit. But his wife may be accorded an ambiguous status as being practically inaccessible but nevertheless not quite up to the merits of a high-caste woman. She may be labelled as not having the housewifely skills or the motherly qualities of a high-caste woman. People may turn up their nose and say, "her house is dirty, her children are unruly" and add, "what else do you expect from a woman of her caste? These imagined barriers prevent most men from even contemplating marriage with a woman of a lower caste. Even men of the Dalit castes, who have risen in the social ladder, prefer to get themselves wives of higher castes to reinforce their newly found social status.

Thus, a human being's right to live a life of fulfilment is usually denied to Dalit women: who find a proper place neither in the traditional system nor in the modern system. To give them this right, modern society must look at them with the eyes with which they look at their own selves. They should be able to retain the independence and confidence that they had inculcated in their traditional enculturation and be acceptable to society retaining these positive qualities. For this the high-caste society has to re-socialise itself to reconstruct its gender model, to accept with respect the unabashed and unfettered femininity, that is, the Dalit woman.

Note

1 This chapter is a revised version of the article published in *Social Action: A Quarterly Review of Social Trends* (October–December 2001).

References

Berreman, Gerald D. (1966). "Caste in Cross-Cultural Perspective: Organizational Components", in G. DeVos and H. Wagatsuma (eds.), *Japan's Invisible Race; Caste in Culture and Personality*, Berkeley: University of California Press.

———. (1967). "Stratification, Pluralism and Interaction: A Comparative Analysis of Caste", in A. V. S. de Reuk and Julia Knight (eds.), *Ciba Foundation, Symposium on Caste and Race: Comparative Approach*, London: J & A Churchill Ltd.

Bourdieu, P. (1977). *Outline of a Theory of Practice*, Cambridge: Cambridge University Press.

Channa, S. (1985). *Tradition and Rationality in Economic Behaviour*, New Delhi: Cosmo.

———. (1991). "Caste, Jati and Ethnicity-Some Reflections Based on a Case Study of the Dhobis", *Indian Anthropologist*, Vol. 21, No. 2, Pp 39–55.

Eleanor, Leacock & Etienne, Mona. (ed.). (1980). *Women and Colonization: Anthropological Perspectives, Praeger, Praeger Special Studies: Praeger Scientific*, New York: J.F. Bergin Publishers Book.

Knauft, Bruce M. (1996). *Genealogies For the Present*, New York: Routledge.

Messer, E. (1993). "Anthropology and Human Rights", *Annual Review of Anthropology*, Vol. 22, Pp 221–249, published by Annual review Incorporation.

Parish, S. M. (1997). *Hierarchy and Its Discontents: Culture and Politics of Consciousness in Caste Society*, Delhi: Oxford University Press.

Rao, A. (1998). *Autonomy: Life Cycle, Gender and Status among Himalayan Pastoralists*, New York: Berghahn Books.

Searle-Chatterjee, M. (1981). *Reversible Sex Roles: The Special Case of Benaras Sweepers*, Oxford: Pergamon Press.

Unnithan-Kumar, M. (1997). *Identity, Gender and Poverty: New Perspectives on Caste and Tribe in Rajasthan*, Oxford: Berghahn Books.

Part III

Caste Violence: Movements for Social Mobility

7   Dandora[1]

The Madiga Movement for Equal Identity and Social Justice in Andhra Pradesh

P. Muthaiah

All over India, Dalits have been organising themselves to fight against caste-based inequalities and for respectable identity for the last eight decades. Liberation movements of various Dalit sections began to take form in the 1920s in the context of strong social reform anti-caste movements.[2] Adi-Dharm movement of Punjab, Mahar Movement of Maharashtra, Adi-Andhra movement of Andhra, Adi-Dravida Movement of Tamil Nadu, and Adi-Karnataka movement of Karnataka created a struggle history of their own during this period against the caste system.

The Madigas, one of 59 sub-castes of Dalits of Andhra Pradesh (AP), have been struggling for a respectable identity as early as the 1920s but entered a unique phase with the struggle phase of Madiga Reservation Porata Samithi (MRPS) which is popularly known as Dandora. The Madiga consciousness reached a militant phase after passing through eight decades of search for respectable identity. The MRPS has been fighting for the last nine years for categorisation of 59 Scheduled Castes into ABCD groups for equal distribution of reservation benefits among all sub-castes under the leadership of Mandhakrishna.[3] To counter the MRPS the Malas, one of the Dalit sub-castes, which has been cornering reservation benefits disproportionate to its population, has been opposing categorisation under the auspices of "Mala Mahanadu", stating that categorisation divides the Dalits in AP.[4] The Malas have been advancing all the arguments of anti-reservationists in order to enjoy lion's share of reservation benefits in the guise of Dalit unity.[5] In response to the demand of MRPS the government of AP, under the leadership of N. Chandrababu Naidu, issued orders categorising Scheduled Castes into ABCD groups. The Malas challenged categorisation in court on grounds that it is unconstitutional and is intended to divide the Dalits. Now, the Madigas are fighting for justice in the Honourable Supreme Court of India. The Dandora organised various programmes to exhibit its popular strength and high-level consciousness in fighting for their rights. It also triggered similar sub-caste movements among the tribals in the name of Tudumdebba of the Koya Tribes, Banjara Bheri of Lambda tribes, and Doludebba of Yadavas, in Andhra Pradesh.

DOI: 10.4324/9781003317173-11

Identity Formation and Struggle for Respectable Identity

From the beginning the Madigas have been struggling for respectable identity while the Brahmanic class has been designating them as low or polluting. Arundathiya Mahasabha was the first pioneering association that began
a search for respectable identity and awakening of Madigas. The first-generation educated Madigas have gone through the oral and mythological
tradition of literature to locate their respectable identity and their genesis.
The Madigas realised that the love story of the pious woman Arundhathi
and Vashistha reveals the genesis of Madigas that they were the first born
on the planet earth. Based on the love story of Arundhathi, the Madigas
believe that they are the grandchildren of the aborigine king Jambavantha
and Arundhathi, the daughter of Karthamaprajpathi. The Madigas identify their genesis with Arundhathi–Jambavantha and believe they were the
first rulers of Indian land. A Telugu Madiga, L.C. Guru Swamy, established
"Arundathiya Mahasabha" in 1920 in the Madras Presidency to initiate
the struggle for respectable identity. Guru Swamy propagated the story of
Arundhathi and Vashistha and tried to project a high self-image of Madigas
indicating Brahmanic matrimonial relations with Madigas.[6] The story of
Arundhathi and Jambavantha gives a proud account of Madigas. Today,
the mythological woman, Arundhathi, is an ideal and pious woman for all
Hindus in India.

The genealogy of Madigas also tells us how Madigas in the past were
cheated and projected as unseen, un-approached, and untouchables. The
story narrates that Karthama Prajapathi, the father of Arundhathi, allowed
Agasthya Maharishi to stay in Dakshinapatha for some time for his ritual
activities. But Agasthya did not leave the Dakshinapatha, instead claimed
ownership of the Dakshinapatha. Karthama Prajapathi claimed that he was
the original owner of Dakshinapatha as he has been moving and living on
earth from the very beginning. Agasthya Maharishi created a story to drive
Karthama away from the land, according to which says Karthama was born
to a Brahmin woman and a Mangali (Barber) man, so he is an untouchable
and unseen.[7] Then Karthama Prajapathi left the Dakshinapatha in humiliation losing the ownership of the land. The Madigas of AP believe that the
Jambavantha is their grandfather and Karthama is their great-grandfather.
The Madigas narrate this story to prove that they have a respectable identity
and that they have been there on the earth from the very beginning. They
believe they are born much before the earth takes its birth.

The MRPS which entered a struggle phase used three identities – Arundhathi
Jambavantha, the Madiga, and Dandora – to mobilise people for struggle
and to capture for themselves a respectable position in the society. The triple
identities of Madigas worked as the ideology of their movement, and these
symbols did miracles in mobilising Madigas in lakhs, in exhibiting its popular strength, and in achieving their demand for ABCD and equal rights. In
all public meetings the Madiga leaders narrated the story of Jambavantha as

their grandfather, the known warrior and aborigine king of ancient India. They also educated that they should feel proud of their mythological and pious woman, Arundhathi as then Adapaduchu (female child of the family) as an ideal woman for all Hindus who witness the Arundhathi star on the occasions of their marriages.

The leaders of Dandora took a pledge to make the abused term Madiga as respectable. For this purpose the activist propagated the etymological meaning of Madigas. The Madiga means Maha (very) + Adi (from the beginning + ga (moving)). That means the original inhabitants of India moving and living on the earth from the very beginning.[8] The MRPS resolved to use Madiga as a suffix to the names of its activists like Sharma, Reddy, and Rao and fight to make the society accept Madigas as equals in the society. They declared that there is nothing wrong and nothing to be ashamed of using their caste as the suffix. The movement gave a sense of pride to Madiga community to introduce themselves as the Madigas and raise their voice against injustice done to them. The MRPS has been successful in its struggle to gain self-respect and honour by popularising Madigas as the aborigine kings of India. It is also successful in projecting the Madiga identity as of equals as against an inferior image.

The drum-beating of Madigas is popularly known as "DANDORA" which means broadcasting. MRPS made their traditional musical instrument "the drum" as a symbol to cry for Justice. The Madigas have been the traditional messengers who communicate messages of village administration crying in the streets beating drums. The traditional occupation of drum beating has been made a subjugated service in the village jajmani system. Now they are beating the drum to cry for Justice and the emancipation of Madigas from suffering. Today, the Dandora has become a synonym for social movements, protests, rallies, and struggles in Andhra Pradesh. The President of MRPS, Mr. Krishna Madiga declared that their "weapon is not a gun but drum. We will beat so loudly that the ruling class will have to heed, or their ear drums will burst".[9]

Arundhatheeya Mahasabha was the first association established in Hyderabad state for the welfare of Madigas based on respectable identity in the year 1931. It originated out of the sub-caste cleavages between the Malas and Madigas of Hyderabad. There was a galaxy of Dalit organisations in Hyderabad State. Bhagya Reddy Varma, B.S. Venkat Rao, and Ariga Rama Swamy were considered to be Trinity of Dalit leadership. Bhagya Reddy Varma was the president of Adi-Hindu Social Services League in the 1920s which was the pioneering organisation of Dalits in Hyderabad State. Ariga Rama Swamy and B.S. Venkat Rao were President and General Secretary of Adi-Hindu Mahasabha respectively. These two organisations worked for the rights of Dalits. Bhagya Reddy Varma was a pioneering Leader of Dalits in AP, but his Mala partisan attitude was responsible for the emergence of Arundathiya Mahasabha in 1931.[10] Bhagya Reddy Varma opposed marriage between a Madiga boy and a Mala girl rescued from

Devdasi. Ariga Rama Swamy, the then Dalit leader, performed this marriage under his personal supervision. Adi-Hindu Social Services League under the leadership of Bhagya Reddy Varma ex-communicated all these leaders who attended the marriage, stating that Mala Tradition does not accept a marriage between Malas and Madigas as the Madigas are inferior to Malas in social hierarchy.[11] It was also said that Bhagya Reddy Varma refused to encourage Madigas education in all 32 schools established by the League. Adi Hindu Bhavan was also a bone of contention between Madigas and Malas. It was reported that Varma claimed the ownership of the Adi-Hindu Bhavan only to Malas because Madigas did not contribute a single paisa to the construction of the Bhavan. In fact the Bhavan was constructed by collecting contributions from different philanthropists of the Hyderabad state for the common educational purpose of the Dalits in the 1920s. To counter this partisan attitude of Bhagya Reddy Varma, the ex-communicated leaders established Arundathiya Mahasabha in 1931 for Madigas. Seshagiri Rao and S. Babaiah were prominent Madiga leaders of Arundhatiya Mahasabha. By the 1950s, the Sabha had become a defunct organisation as most of its members joined the Hyderabad State Dalit Jeteeya Sangh, patronaged by Jagjeevan Ram.

Arundhatiya Bandhuseva Mandali was established in 1981 by first-generation Madiga employees under the presidentship of Dr. Kishan Lal which inaugurated the era of prayers and petitions. There was a proposal to name the association Madiga Sevemandali. That was discussed and rejected by a majority of members, as the name of Madigavaru is a perverted form of Madiguvarar, which means people below us. Madhava Rao, former President of Bandhu Seva Mandali, organises DASARAMILAP every year in the Twin Cities a cultural function of Madigas. Various cultural programmes were conducted on these occasions. Through this association the organisers strengthened the kin feeling among the Madigas in the Twin Cities.[12] In 1982, the Mandali published a booklet with the title "Status of Arundhathiyas" with detailed statistics showing the inequalities between Mala and Madiga sub-caste in various fields. Through this document, the Mandali demanded categorisation of SCs into ABCD groups for the distribution of reservation benefits in proportion to the population of each sub-caste.[13] This document marks the turning point in Madigas' movement. The Mandal had chosen prayer and petitions as a method to ventilate their demands. The Mandali made representations to the successive chief ministers of AP demanding proportional representation in all the fields. The political response to the demand of Madigas in the form of promise came from Telugu Desam Party in the 1982 Assembly election.

Struggle Phase of Madiga Movement

The Andhra Pradesh Madiga Sangam was the first Dalit Association based on the sub-caste category in 1982.[14] It began the militant struggle phase of the Madiga movement. This sangam gave a number of representations to the governments in the 1980s for an equal share in the fields of education, employment, and politics by providing separate quotas for Madigas. The activists of Madiga Sangam entered the State Assembly in 1982 while the session was going on and threw pamphlets, titled "separate reservation for Madiga", from visitors' gallery, demanding separate reservations for Madigas. Consequently 12 activists of Madiga sangam were convicted by State Assembly for throwing pamphlets violating the rules of Assembly proceedings.[15] The activists also demanded the appointment of an enquiry commission for redressal of Madigas' grievances. After some time the Madiga Sangam gave up its struggle for categorisation as its activists felt categorisation will have to be done only by the Parliament of India.

Dakshina Bharatha Adijambhava/Arundathiya Samakhya was established in 1990 to organise the Madigas of South India to fight for their rights, with Bangalore as their headquarters.[16] Sri D. Manjunath was elected as President and Chikka Venkata Swamy and Dr. M. Jagannath of AP were elected as General Secretaries of the South Indian Samakhya. Dr N. Venkkata Swamy and Dr M. Jagannath were also elected as President and General Secretaries, respectively, of the AP State wing of the Samakya. Mythological identity of Arundhathi and Jambhavantha was chosen by the organisers as a common name acceptable to all sub-castes who were traditionally leather workers in South India. The AP wing of Samakhya organised three successful public meetings.

The then Chief Minister of AP N. Janardhan Reddy promised to do justice to Madigas. The first notable meeting was held on 12 June 1992 at Gandhi Bhavan in Hyderabad.[17] They also organised a public meeting in Nellore District of AP in 1994 with one lakh Madigas and demanded categorisation of SCs into ABCD groups.

A very significant meeting organised by Samakhya was held on 2 May 1994 in Nizam College grounds of Hyderabad at the instance of the Congress Government headed by Vijaya Bhaskar Reddy. During those days, the Congress party organised a series of sub-caste meetings of SCs/BCs/STs in AP to consolidate its vote bank after witnessing the success of the B.S.P.-S.P. combine in U.P. In this particular meeting, Congress C.M. Vijaya Bhaskar Reddy criticised B.S.P. leader Kanshi Ram and requested the Madigas not to listen to such North Indian leaders who criticised Gandhiji. Then the audience shouted saying, "We listen, we listen" indicating the readiness of Madigas to follow the North Indian Madiga leader Kanshi Ram and his Bahujan movement.[18] Few days after this public meeting was over, Koneru Ranga Rao, a Madiga leader, was made Dy. Chief Minister of AP by the Congress party with the sole purpose of retaining the Madigas with the Congress party and stopping the growth of B.S.P. in the state. It bears clear testimony to the fact that Madiga leaders of the Mandali and Samakhya worked as organic intellectuals and entered into bargaining politics and were successful in capturing some political space at various levels.

Assertion of Madiga Identity

The Dandora movement emerged in changing the socio-economic and political conditions of the state. The conditions prior to the launching of the Dandora movement clearly indicate the factors that shaped the Dandora movement of Madigas. By the 1980s Madigas were released from leather goods work which they inherited in the form of traditional occupation as the landlords stopped buying handmade leather chappals and leather goods of Madigas and started buying from urban chappal shops made of synthetics and rubber. As a result, Madigas who depended on leather work became unemployed. The Madigas feel that their due share from reservation benefits concerned Malas. Anti- and pro-Mandal movement in the State of AP has given rise to new terms of political discourse. Mandalisation of politics questioned the continuance of upper-caste leadership in Marxist and non-Marxist parties in the state. Naxalites like K.G. Sathya Murthy and Gaddar who were prominent leaders in the People's War Group of CPI (ML) left the party over questions of caste politics. The Mandal discourse reduced the caste blindness of Madiga youth working in Marxist and non-Marxist parties, and it sharpened their caste consciousness.[19] During the early 1990s, BSP's slogan "Vote Hamara Raj Tumhara Nahi Chelega, Nahi Chelega" had gone to every Madiga street and enlightened them on the importance of their votes as a source of political power in India. The whole process sharpened Madiga consciousness, particularly of the youth, in favour of the struggle for their rights.

The Madiga movement entered its struggle phase with Dandora. This phase was led by unemployed full-time activists with different outlooks on disabilities suffered by the Madigas in the traditional socio-economic and political structure. Most of its leaders were former Marxists who left the party as a result of Mandalisation and Bahujanisation of state politics.

Madiga Reservation Porata Samithi emerged as a fighting organisation in these conditions with special qualities of its own in the history of social movements. This organisation was established by 20 youths at a small kutcha house in a small village by name "Eedumudi" in the Prakasam District of Andhra Pradesh under the leadership of Mandhakrishna on 7 July 1994.[20] The participants of the meeting worked out a strategy to develop MRPS step by step from village to Mandal, Mandal to District, and from District to State level. They resolved to adopt the philosophy of Dr B.R. Ambedkar and Babu Jagjeevan Ram as the guiding spirit for Madigas Rights.

Struggle for Equal Identity Social Justice

Madigas' struggle for equal opportunities is the struggle for equal identity and social justice from the very beginning. Due to their relative backwardness the Madigas are not able to avail reservation benefits equally compared to their co-sufferers, the Malas. It is a fact that the special treatment benefits have often been appropriated by the more educated, articulate and organised among the S.C. communities.[21] As per the census of India the Madigas and the Malas constitute 37,37,609 (46.94%) and 32,63,675 (40.99%), respectively, of the SC population. But the Malas have been cornering reservation benefits disproportionate to their population. This new inequality triggered the Dandora movement in Andhra Pradesh. Table 7.1 gives a clear picture of the disparity between Madigas and Malas in the field of education, employment, and politics.

Out of 1,07,579 matriculates, 53.15% belong to the Mala caste, 28.02% to Madigas, 15.58% to Adi-Andhra, 1.33% to Adi-Dravida, 1.90% to other, and a negligible (0.002%) to the Dakkal community. Out of 14,415 graduates, 56.28% belong to Mala and 25.07% belong to Madiga sub-castes. From the rest of the graduates 16.21%, 1.46%, 0.96%, and 0.006% belong to Adi-Andhra, others, Adi-Dravida, and Dakkal communities, respectively. It is evident from data that there is glaring inequality within major sub-caste groups, with Mala at the top and Dakkal at the bottom of the educational ladder of Scheduled Castes.[22]

The Scheduled Castes have been granted reserved seats in State Assembly proportionate to their population, 39 out of 294 Assembly seats. Out of this 70.50% and 29.50% of seats were represented by Malas and Madigas respectively. It shows that from the days of Independence Malas have been appropriating political positions disproportionate to their population and maintaining their dominance throughout over Madigas.

Representative bureaucracy is one of the features of pluralism. It is a necessary condition that every social and economic group has to be represented in the bureaucracy in a plural society. But the data pertaining to Scheduled Caste shows the representation of Malas is more than 75% (75.90%) in public sector undertakings while Madigas represent less than 25% (24.10%). Inequality between Madigas and Malas in the appropriation of reservation benefits in the reserved field of education, employment and politics in the 198s negated equal identity and social justice for Madigas. This reflects the injustice that happened to Madigas.

The Dandora movement organized a number of programmes in the past 9 years to oppose the inequalities and demand for equal distribution of reservation benefits. "Chalo Nizam College" on 2 March 1996, "Chalo Assembly" on 2 September 1997, and Mahapadayathra in June 1997 are remarkable programmes in the history of the Dalit movement in AP. In the first place, in order to realize the social justice, in a public meeting of at least 5 lakh Madigas, at the Nizam's College Grounds in Hyderabad, the Dandora sought opinion on the ABCD categorization. In the second programme, Chalo Assembly, Dandora was successful in forcing the Government to appoint the Justice P. Ramchander Raju Commission of Inquiry to go into the differential benefits of reservation by Mala and Madiga sub-castes and to recommend the need for categorisation of SCs into groups for equal distribution of reservation benefits. The third programme, Mahapadayathra (Long March), was a novel method adopted by Dandora to shape public opinion in support of

Table 7.1 New inequalities within SCs

Sl. no.	Caste	Matriculation/ secondary	Graduates (other than tech.)	Public sectors undertaking	IAS	1957	1962	1967	1972	1978	1983	1985	Total
01	Adi Andhra	16,763 (15.58%)	2,338 (16.21%)	–	–	–	–	–	–	–	–	–	–
02	Adi Dravida	1,429 (01.33%)	13 (00.96%)	–	–	–	–	–	–	–	–	–	–
03	Mala & Allied	51,194 (53.17%)	8,113 (56.28%)	3,080 (75.90%)	26 (72.27%)	34 (77.27%)	33 (78.37%)	27	27 (67.50%)	29 (72.50%)	26 (66.66%)	27 (69.23%)	203 (71.15%)
04.	Madiga & Allied	30,148 (28.02%)	3614 (25.07%)	978 (24.10%)	10 (27.28%)	10 (92.75%)	9 (21.43%)	13	13 (32.50%)	11 (27.30%)	13 (33.80%)	12 (30.77%)	81 (21.85%)
05	Others	2,045 (01.09%)	211 (01.46%)	–	–	–	–	–	–	–	–	–	–
	Total	1,07,579 (100%)	14,415 (100%)	4,048 (100%)	36 (100%)	44 (100%)	42 (100%)	40 (100%)	40 (100%)	40 (100%)	30 (100%)	39 (100%)	284 (100%)

categorisation. The movement spread to every nook and corner of the state. The leader of Dandora, Mandhakrishna Madiga, walked for 1052 km starting from Naravaripalli, the native village of Chief Minister N. Chandrababu Naidu, to his official residence in Hyderabad in a padayathra.[23] This yathra revealed the massive response of the Madiga community to the call given by their leader. On the last day of the padayathra, 6 June 1997, he reached Hyderabad along with lakhs of Madigas and proved Dandora to be a pioneering social movement in contemporary India. After having witnessed the popular support to the Madigas, the TDP government issued orders categorising SCs into ABCD groups.

It is necessary to understand the struggle of Madigas with the spirit of Dr B.R. Ambedkar's social justice philosophy. He desired to break the monopoly of twice-born castes through the reservation policy. In the Constituent Assembly of India, he stated,

> there shall be reservations in favour of certain communities, which have not had a proper place in the administration. ... The administration for historical reasons been controlled by one community or few communities should disappear and other also must have an opportunity of getting into public services.[24]

He felt that no community should monopolize any opportunity even among the Scheduled Castes. Now the Madigas have been fighting for categorisation of SCs into groups to break the monopoly of one or two Scheduled Castes, which facilitates equal distribution of reservation benefits among 59 Scheduled Castes in AP. In fact the struggle of Madigas is a struggle for respectable identity, equality, and social Justice. It was argued that equal identity is equality. Identity cannot be diversed from equality, equality from social justice. Nor can equality and social justice can be diversed from identity as the equality and justice in precise identity.[25] The Dandora movement is a pioneering plural identity movement that triggered similar movements in AP.

Plural Identity and Principles of Social Justice

There are 59 sub-castes in the list of Scheduled Castes in AP. Every sub-caste has its own identity and existence. The first classification of SCs was done in 1931 by J. J. Hutton, Census Commissioner of India, who prepared a list of depressed classes from these sub-castes. This list was adopted by the Government of India Act of 1935 for providing special protection to the depressed classes. It is notable that the President of India promulgated the Scheduled Castes order in 1950 based on the list prepared by J. J. Hutton, following a number of tests to designate Scheduled Castes primarily based on the principles of commensality practices.[26] The Dandora movement demanded further categorisation of the castes as the list provided by President did not ensure equal distribution of reservation benefits among 59 Scheduled Castes. The logic that was followed by J.J. Hutton in the designation of depressed classes was taken to its logical end in the categorisation of SCs. The logic of categorisation of SCs in AP is based on the following principles.[27]

a) The principle of touchable groups: The caste system divided society into touchable and untouchable groups. The Panchamas have been untouchables to all four varnas. On the basis of the same traditional caste values, the Malas and Madigas are also divided into two untouchables groups. In other words, Brahmanic values of purity and pollution percolated down to SCs and divided them into touchable and untouchable groups. Madiga allied castes and Mala allied castes are touchable groups.

b) The principle of satellite living: Traditional caste values divided Scheduled Castes into Malas and Madigas and they are living together in Malapally (village) and Madiga gudem (collective residence), respectively. Bindla and Mala Ayyavaru are priestly castes of Madigas and Malas respectively. The respective priests believe that they have a common genesis and they share common sufferings and values. These two satellite castes are considered as groups and the quantum of reservations is decided on the principles of satellite living.

c) Principle of parallels: The caste system placed different castes at different places living in various parts of the country. Castes with equal status are brought under one group though they migrated from different States. The Mangs in Maharashtra Madigas in AP have equal status in the Panchama hierarchy by virtue of their traditional occupation. Such parallel castes are grouped together for the classification of SCs.

d) Principle of common name: Common name is the feature of a tribe of people. They have a common history, common God, etc. All those castes with prefixes or suffixes like Mala, Sale, Dakkal, and Madiga are recognised as groups and reservation benefits are distributed between these groups.

e) Principle of parity in traditional occupations: The traditional occupation of sub-castes has been the basis for caste hierarchy. Varna dharma allotted a particular traditional occupation, to each caste in society. The ritualistic pandits allotted particular grades to these occupations, and explain them in the terms of the notions of purity and pollution. On the basis of traditional occupations, the SCs are categorised into groups for the distribution of reservation benefits.

f) The principle of protection of group interest: The quantum of reservation has been decided in proportion to the population of SCs against the monopoly of one or two castes. Similarly, no single sub-caste should be allowed to corner reservation benefits disproportionate to their population. Methods should be adopted for the protection of the interests of each sub-caste. There are Scheduled Castes with a population ranging from thousand to lakhs of people in each group. A sub-caste in a group with a less percentage of the population should not be allowed to

corner the benefits that are due to other sub-caste. For the protection of
the interests of each caste, the un-represented, under-represented, and
adequately represented castes should be identified. The first and second
priority should be given to un-represented and underrepresented castes,
respectively, in the allotment of reservation benefits in each group. These
priorities should be given in alphabetical order of sub-castes in the respective ABCD groups (Table 7.2). The commission agreed to protect the
group interests of satellite committees. But it did not agree to protect the
interest of sub-castes within the group on the principle of priority. This
principle was not accepted by Inquiry Commission. The minority castes
with ABCD groups are demanding further categorisation of groups.

g) The more the insult and humiliation, the more should be protection:

> The Dakkals, Rellis, and Mehtars have been subjected to isolation and
> humiliation both by Chaturvarnas and by Panchams who treat them
> as the untouchables. The population of Dakkals, Rallis, and Mehtars
> is meager. But they deserve special protection by way of providing
> more benefits not necessarily proportionate proportion in their popu-
> lation. The commissioner after a thorough study of the underlined
> principles of social structure and traditional occupation recommended
> the categorisation of SCs into the following four groups.[28]

The Relli and Mehtar group of communities constitutes 1,33,689 (1/67%) of
SC population. They are categorised as Group "A" with 1% entitlement of
reservations in public appointments and educational institutions. The commission identified the "Madigas" group of communities, the leather workers,
as the next backward among SCs. They constitute 3737, 609 (46.94%) of
the SC population. They are categorised as "B" with 7% entitlement of reservation benefits. They constitute 32,63,675 (40.99%) of the SC population.
The Adi-Andhras are categorised as "D" with 1% entitlement of reservations. This is the most advanced group in terms of education and employment among the Scheduled Castes in Andhra Pradesh.

Sphere of State Authority

The categorisation policy formulated by the Government of Andhra
Pradesh brought forth controversy between states and central authority.
In a modern democratic system, the state government is a legal plural
authority while the central government represents monistic authority. In
the adjudication of categorisation policy, Madigas advanced pluralistic
arguments while the Malas, advanced monistic arguments. The Malas
under the auspices of "Mala Mahanadu" challenged GOs issued categorising 59 Scheduled Castes in the Honourable High Court of Andhra
Pradesh, stating that it is unconstitutional and that the categorisation
divides the Dalits.

Table 7.2 Group A: Relli Group

Sl. no.	Name of the caste	Traditional occupation	Total of sub-caste
1	Bavuri	Basket makers	756
2	Chachathi	Fruit selling and scavenging	5,244
3	Chandala	NA	184
4	Danadasi	Village watchman	5,410
5	Dom, Combara, Paidi	Weavers, musicians, drum beaters	23,214
6	Chasi, Haddi Relli Chachandi	Fruit and vegetable sellers Sweeping and scavenging	1,872
7	Godagali	Basket making, bamboo making	2,212
8	Mehtar	Scavenging	4,553
9	Paki, Mosti, Thoti	Scavenging	7,876
10	Pamidi	NA	5,647
11	Relli	Scavenging, fruit sellers	76,329
12	Sapru	Scavengers and fruit sellers	592
		Total	1,33,689 (1.68%)

Group B: Madiga Group

Sl. no.	Name of the caste	Traditional occupation	Total of sub-caste
1	Arundathiya	NA	78,496
2	Beda Jangam Budgajangam	Hunting, flowers, and Budgajangam cultivators	12,024
3	Bindia	Priests of Madigas, appeasers of Goddesses	13,589
4	Chamar, Mochi	Shoe makers and leathers	12,881
5	Chambar	Shoe makers and leather workers	519
6	Dakkal Madiga Dakkal war	Mendicants, bards of Madigas leather workers	1,598
7	Dhor	Leather and tanning works	2,452
8	Godari	Leather and shoe makers	834
9	Jaggali labourers	Leather workers and agriculture labourers	983
10	Jambavulu	Agricultural labourers	22,335
11	Kolupula Vandlu	Foretelling, appeasers of Goddesses	961
12	Madiga	Leather, tanning, chappal making	35,72,622
13	Madiga Dasu, Masteen	Spiritual advisers, acrobatics story tellers to Madigas	5,450
14	Mang	Drum beaters, basket, mat making, tanning, jugglers Snake charmers	8,007
15	Mang Garodi	Snake charming, buffalo shaving, acrobats, Jugglers	107
16	Matangi	Begging, singing, tanning	323
17	Samagara	Leather and tanning works	1,845
18	Sindhollu Chindlollu	Drama, dancing, and prostitution	2,583
		Total	37,37,609 (46.94%)

Group C: Mala Group

Sl. no.	Name of the caste	Traditional occupation	Total of sub-caste
1	Adi Dravida	NA	1,00,382
2	Anamukh	NA	76

(Continued)

Table 7.2 (Continued)

3	Arya Mala	NA	1,395
4	Arvamala	NA	22,937
5	Baniki	Village watchman, palanquin bearers, watchman	11,844
6	Byagara	Watchmen of graveyards, weaving	14,120
7	Chalvadi	Village watchman, weaving course cloth	1,740
8	Ellamalwaru Yallmmalwandlu	Vagrant caste	358
9	Gosangi	Mendicants	7,653
10	Holeya Weaving course cloth	Agriculture labourers, Serfs	665
11	Holeya Dasari	Begging	620
12	Madasi Kuruva	Sheep and goat rearing	3,550
13	Mahar	Weaving course cloth, village watch labourers	11,486
14	Mala	Watchman, labourers	28,94,643
15	Mala Dasari	Spiritual advisors to Malas, agricultural labourers	18,416
26	Mala Dasu	Spiritual advisers, acrobatics Story tellers	8,335
17	Mala hannai	Vagrant caste	120
18	Malajangam	Agriculture labourers	4,895
19	Mala Mashti	Acrobatics	474
20	Mala Sale Nethakani	Weavers, agricultural labourers	18,272
21	Malasanyai	NA	300
22	Manne	Village watchman	64,668
23	Mandala	Agricultural labourers	840
24	Pambada Pambanda	Devil dancers and musicians to Malas	2,333
25	Samban	NA	3,233
		Total	32,63,675 (40.99%)

Group D: Adhi-Andhra Group

Sl. no.	Name of the caste	Traditional occupation	Total of sub-caste
1	Adi-Andhra (Mala's and Madigas)	NA	6,98,860
2	Masthi	Dancers, Acrobatics Carpenters	2,922
3	Mitha Ayyalwar	Priests and spiritual advisors to Madigas and Malas	2,777
4	Panchama, Parish	NA	9,266
5	Unclassified in Census	1,12,933	8,26,757 (10.39%)
6		Grand total	79,61,780 (100%)

Data on traditional occupation is collected from ethnographic notes of India 1961 (1.67%) and classics like Thurston, S.S. Hasan.

The state government argued that it is competent to categorise Scheduled Castes into four groups for equal distribution of reservation benefits in the exercise of its power under Articles 15(4) and 16(4) of the Constitution of India to implement reservations in the field of education and employment as this power was allocated to states in the scheme of division of powers in our federal structure.

Malas argued reservation to SCs and STs is the subject matter of the Union Government alone as per the scheme of division of powers between the State and the Union Government of India. Under the Indian Constitution, powers are divided into three lists: Union list (97), State list (66), and the Concurrent list (47). State public services are included in list-II of the 7th Schedule at entry 41. Education was included in list-III of the schedule at entry 25 in the Concurrent list. The Malas took procedure for identification of SCs and STs, inclusion in and exclusion out of SCs and STs from the list to defend their argument. The Indian Constitution established a procedure for the identification of SCs and STs, for inclusion in or exclusion out of SCs and STs from the list for the purpose of reservations. Article 341(1) of our Constitution says that the President of India with respect to any State or Union Territory, after consultation with the Governor, thereafter by public notification, specifies the castes, races, or tribes or part of or groups within castes, races, or tribes which shall for the purpose of the Constitution be deemed to be Scheduled Caste. Article 341(2) states that parliament may by law include in or exclude from the list of Scheduled Castes specified in the notification issued under clause 341(1), any caste or race or any group within the caste. The Malas argued that the Government of Andhra Pradesh violated Article 341 of the Indian Constitution by categorising Scheduled Castes into four groups and further argued that the state government is not competent to formulate a policy for Scheduled Castes. The Government of AP and Madigas argued that the job of the President of India was over by identification and notification of 59 Scheduled Castes in Andhra Pradesh who can deem to be Scheduled Castes and that the state government is competent to categorise Scheduled Castes in the exercise of its power under the Article 15(4) and 16(4) of the Indian Constitution to implement reservations in the fields of education and employment and it is within the legislative competence of the states. Further, the Telugu Desam Party (TDP) Government argued that Article 341 does not diminish the state legislative competence for legislating with respect to education and state employment for this reason. And it was argued that Article 341 enables the President of India as a one-time measure to specify castes, races, tribes, or parts of or of groups within castes which shall be deemed to be Scheduled Castes for the purpose of the Constitution.

The Malas argued that the categorisation of SCs amounts to inclusion in or exclusion out of SCs from the list of Scheduled Castes which is unconstitutional and violative of Article 341(2) which empowers the Parliament of India to include in or exclude out of a caste or group from the list of Scheduled Castes. The state government argued that under the Articles 15

(4) and 16 (4) of the Indian Constitution, they are not going to change any caste or group from the list of the Scheduled Castes for the implementation of reservations. In the exercise of its power the state government proposed a resolution in the AP State Assembly on 22 April 1998 in favour of categorisation, and surprisingly the AP State Assembly unanimously passed a resolution supporting categorisation.

Malas advanced a true monistic argument against categorisation. They said, "all the specified and notified castes in the Schedule are one single unit called Scheduled Castes". They further argued "once a caste is specified in the list of Scheduled Castes they are equally entitled for attendant benefits unconditionally. Though they are heterogeneous by their caste, race or tribe they become homogeneous single unit when they are included in the schedule". The stand of Malas to ignore relative backwardness and heterogeneous occupational diversity is identical to that of the ruling class in general and Brahmanic in their partisan attitude. The Malas accepted the Schedule thus identified but refused to accept the categorisation of SCs when it takes the logic of identification of castes to the logical end for the realisation of social justice.

A Full Bench of Honourable High Court of AP after hearing the case declared that the G.O.s 68 and 69 categorising Scheduled Castes is unconstitutional and violative of Articles 338 and 341 of the Indian Constitution, on 18 September 1997. In its judgement, the High Court of AP came to these conclusions, i.e.: (1) the categorisation made by the state government amounts to identification of the most backward as notified under clause (1) of Article 341. (2). Any further clarification of SCs shall be permissible only in the manner as envisaged under Article 341 read with Article 338 of the Indian Constitution. (3) Sub-classification of SCs is a major policy matter affecting the Scheduled Castes and as envisaged under Article 338 (9) of the Constitution of India, and the state is obliged to consult the National Commission for SCs and STs.

Following the judgement of the High Court, the state government consulted the National Commission for Scheduled Castes and Scheduled Tribes. The Commission recommended having A relook at the working of reservations policy and development efforts that have to be made for Scheduled Castes and Scheduled Tribes. The Commission also recommended that the Government of India, being the custodian of the interests of SCs, come out with an appropriate national-level policy, which would take care of disparities within SCs and a new formula has to be evolved to reduce disparities between communities and families among the communities and finalise in consultation with National Commission for SCs and STs under Article 338(9) of the Constitution. After hearing from the National Commission, the state government issued an ordinance categorising SCs and sent it to the President of India seeking his opinion under Article 213 (1) of the Indian Constitution. The then President of India, K. R. Narayanan, assented to the ordinance categorisation of SCs as a step towards rationalisation of reservations.[29]

Thereafter the TDP Government passed an Act in the AP Legislative Assembly categorising SCs. Malas challenged the Act on the legislative competence of the state government. A larger bench of the High Court of AP heard the case and declared its judgement stating that categorisation was made intelligible and discernible grounds and argued that the rationalisation of reservation for Scheduled Castes as valid and constitutional. Mala Mahanadu challenged the categorisation in the Honourable Supreme Court of India. Now Madigas are fighting to protect categorisation of SCs, which ensures equal identity and the social justice in Supreme Court of India.

Division of powers is an element of pluralism and Indian federalism forms part of pluralist democracy. The federal structure in India created polyarchy where powers are exercised by multiple administrative units of states at the local level. The federal structure facilitates state governments to formulate and execute social policies as local authorities as they are in full knowledge of the social and economic problems of heterogeneous groups of people. The Government of Andhra Pradesh formulated a categorisation policy with this spirit of pluralism as the state government knew the relative social and economic backwardness of Madigas. The Malas advanced monistic arguments against categorisation ignoring spirit of social justice, pluralism, and federalism enshrined in the Constitution of India.

Divisions and Unity

Brahminism divided Indian people into various endogamous caste groups, placing them in a graded hierarchy and monopolised education, wealth, and political power in the hands of a few upper castes. This inequality produced the Dalit movement in India. As a result of the Dalit movement, the reservation policy came into being for providing equality of opportunities for SCs and STs. But this policy could not distribute reservation benefits equally among 59 Scheduled Castes in AP as the vertically structured system placed one Scheduled Caste below and above the other consequently new inequalities developed within Dalits in the form of reservation benefits in AP Brahminism produced the Dalit movement. Similarly Dalit Brahminism which believed in the monopoly of one or two Scheduled Castes produced the Dandora movement in AP, creating divisions in the Dalit movement. The Dalit movement is caught in a paradoxical situation of having to unite the Dalits against the upper castes and confront divisions within Dalits. In other words, the Dalit movement in AP is caught in dividing and uniting factors.

Varnadharma determined social distance between castes based on the gradation of occupations. The traditional occupation of Madigas is tanning the leather, making chappal, and leather goods production. The traditional occupation of Malas is weaving, and they are engaged as village watchmen and agricultural labourers. The occupation of Madigas was graded as unclean and of Malas was graded as clean occupations. It determined the distance between the residential quarters of Madigas and Malas, a symbol of their divisions. Notions of purity and pollution associated with their traditional occupation determined the social and physical distance between

Malas and Madigas. Living quarters of untouchables are constructed at a respectable distance from the living quarters of Savarnas and Sudras in AP. Malas live next to Sudras. Madigas live a little away from Malas, and Dakkals live a little away from Madiga's living quarters.[30] The geographical distance between residential quarters of various castes is designed in accordance with the strategy of Brahminism to separate one from another, indicating the cleavages between Malas and Madigas. The structural cleavages are responsible for the birth of the Dandora movement in Andhra Pradesh and necessitated the movement for a separate association for Madigas.

Leadership is a dividing factor of the Dalit movement in AP. Every caste has a distinct identity and its specific problems. The internal cleavages give ample scope for doubting the integrity of the leader of a particular caste by other castes. This lays a foundation for the other castes to develop their own leaders to attend their specific problems and to work for the development of their own caste. In the 1930s itself, the pioneering leader of Dalits Sri Bhagya Reddy Varma's pro-Mala leadership sowed the seeds of separate leadership culture for each sub-caste.[31] The leading personality of Arundhathiya Mahasabha, Mudigonda Laxmaiah, emerged as a leader of Madigas and carried on the separate leadership culture to the post-Independence period. Leadership of Arundhathiya Banduseva Mandali are the products of the same. Today, P. V. Rao of Mala Mahanadu and M. Krishna Madiga of MRPS represent the two sections of Bhagya Reddy Varma and Mudigonda Laxmaiah of pre-Independence Dalit wings. These two wings of Dalit movements are sharpening the idea of the need for separate associations. The emergence of sub-caste leadership on the foundation for separate identity on separate problems is unavoidable as long as these identities are continued in the hierarchically structured Indian society.

Dalits have been divided on party lines as well. A political party is rooted in social and economic systems. It also divided people as it represents various interests of different sections of society. We can see three types of divisions among the Dalits due to the mischief of party spirit: first, accommodations of Dalit leaders in political parties; second, encouraging Dalit associations as their sister organisations; third, splitting the Dalit organisations and converting them into their sister organisations. Mala leaders were the first beneficiaries in the accommodative politics of the Congress party. Dalit leaders who belong to the first generation stream of educated were accommodated into the Congress party during the 1930s itself. Ariga Rama Swamy and B.S. Venkat Rao were the first to join the Congress party. They continued in the Congress party even in the post-Independence period.[32] From the Madiga section, Shankar Deve and Mudigonda Laxmaiah were the prominent leaders who were accommodated by the Congress party as the leaders of Madigas. During the post-Independence period, the Madigas and Malas worked in different social organisations. The social organisations of Madigas carried on their activities with the blessings of Babu Jagjeevan Ram while the Mala social organisations carried on their activities with the blessings of the former Chief Minister of AP, the late Damodaram Sanjeeviah. It is viewed that the Congress party wanted separate organisations as it served the interests of the ruling party. Only in the 1980s, TDP made a clear policy to make the best use of already divided organisations for its political advantage and support Madigas' cause of categorisation. As against TDP the Congress party silently supported "Mala Mahanadu" against categorisation. Political parties clearly used the divisions among the Dalits to their own benefit. In the 1998 parliamentary elections Dandora supported TDP while Mala Mahanadu supported the Congress party.

Untouchability as a "touch me not" manifested itself in the form of social discrimination suffered by untouchables gives them a feeling "WE THE SUFFERERS OF UNTOUCHABILITY". Even after 50 years of independence Scheduled Castes are suffering from disabilities of untouchability in various forms in Andhra Pradesh. Dalit consciousness, the realisation of loss of prestige, societal benefits, and the need for togetherness to fight for lost rights exist among the Dalits in Andhra Pradesh. This consciousness is slowly growing to a stage where it breaks upper-caste hegemony due to the continuance of Brahminism within Dalits in form of separate wells, separate residence, and separate dining and wedding. The ideas of Phule, Periyar Ramasami Naiker, and Dr. B. R. Ambedkar are sowing the seeds of fraternity and unity among Dalits. In a way their ideas are providing an ideological umbrella for Dalit consciousness against casteism in Andhra Pradesh.

In a number of cases Dalits fought against upper-caste atrocities against the untouchables. Atrocities committed against them created a feeling of "WENESS" among Dalits. This feeling was witnessed in incidents like Karamchedu and Chunduru, the major atrocities on Dalits committed in the post-Independence period in Andhra Pradesh. In Karamchedue Madigas were killed by Kammas, while in Chunduru, Malas were killed by Reddys, forgetting their sub-caste feeling, which proved that they are one and can fight the upper castes whenever the occasion demands. There was an attempt to murder Gaddar, a Mala, popular singer, and prominent leader of People War Group in 1997. Dandora took the lead to oppose the ruling class and its attempt to murder Gaddar.[33] The Dalits have been proving their unity whenever atrocities are committed against them.

Conclusion

The respectable identity movement of Madigas launched by L. C. Guru Swamy eight decades ago entered the struggle phase with Dandora and succeeded in emboldening Madigas in using their caste name as a suffix to their names like Reddy, Rao, and Sharma. Once, the word Madiga was a term of abuse, symbol of pollution, and stigma, but today Madigas proudly say that they are Madigas, forgetting the word as abusive and the stigma attached to it. Slowly the word is turning to be a symbol of struggle and a source of political power. Inspired by the Dandora movement, Lambada, Koya, Tribes, Yadava, Gouda, and other backward castes came forward to fight for their rights using caste names as suffix in Andhra Pradesh.

Malas have been enjoying reservation benefits on the grounds of social and educational backwardness. But they have been opposing the demand of Madigas to take the same logic to the logical end and categorise SCs into ABCD groups for equitable distribution of the reservation benefits among 59 Scheduled Castes. The upper castes advance unity arguments whenever lower castes demand their due share. By advancing the same argument Malas proved themselves to be Dalit Brahmanic in their attitude to continue their monopoly in reservation benefits.

Triple identities – Arundhathi–Jambavantha, the Madiga, and Dandora – worked as an ideology for the mobilisation of mass people for all the public meetings organised by the Dandora movement. Through this movement, they have identified themselves as the rulers of this land. The Madigas today take pride that they are the descendants of Arundhati and Jambavantha and hereditary rulers of the land. Today, Common Madigas also feel that they were first born on Indian land reminding place of Arundhathi and Jambavantha in Indian mythology.

The schedule of Scheduled Castes is not a single caste; it is a list of castes. Every sub-caste in the list has an independent identity having its own place, privileges, and occupation in a structured plural society. Dandora won the battle in proving a need for the protection of rights of every sub-caste, by their categorisation on the lines of their inherited diverse occupations and backwardness. The argument of Malas in support of the singleness of Scheduled Castes proved to be a futile exercise in a plural democratic setup. It further established a precedent in formulating plural principles of social justice on the basis of plural identity.

The Madigas are successful in forcing the state government in conceding their demands as a plural legal authority and formulate a categorisation policy. The movement worked believing in the pluralistic principles that decentralised local authority is more competent to formulate a social policy since the state government is more informed of the socio-economic problems of deprived groups than the central government. It is a classic example to explain a political situation of how a developed community or caste makes use of existing law and machinery to defend its stand on a public policy for further development of the caste or group and advances monistic arguments.

The Dandora is a movement for equal identity and social justice. It believed that the rights of the weakest among the weak, rights of every caste whether it is minor caste or major caste, have to be protected equally. The Dandora demonstrates that monopoly is the foundation of inequality and emphasises that a monopoly of any form, whether it is the monopoly of Brahmins or monopoly of Scheduled Castes, has to be broken for realisation of equal identity and equal justice.

In a plural society every caste or group has to assert itself for the protection of its identity and rights. When a disadvantaged group questions the privileges of an advanced group, it naturally gives scope for divisions in the society. To resolve such problems, one needs to find remedies for the disproportionate distribution of reservation benefits.

The rejection of the Madiga leadership for the Mahajan Front tells the transitory nature of caste alliances in electoral politics in a caste-ridden Indian Society. The experiment of the Mahajan Front concludes that caste-based pluralistic politics continues with the emergence of new alliances like Mahajan Sangharashana Samithi and Mahajan Party till political consciousness of the electorate reaches the higher-level maturity to accept lower-caste leaders and sub-caste leaders committed to general interests or interests of all castes.

Notes

1 Published in *Social Action: A Quarterly Review of Social Trends* (April–June 2004).
2 Bharat Patnakar and Gail Omvedt. "Dalit Liberation Movement in Colonial Period", *Economic and Political Weekly,* Vol. XIV, No. 7, February 1979, p. 409.
3 Primary data was collected by the writer as participant observer of Madiga Movement.
4 *Eenadu* (Telugu Daily), March 27, 1999, p. 6.
5 *Frontline,* July 11, 1997, p. 44.
6 Pandit Jamisetti Appalaswamy. "Arundhathi" (Telugu), Sri. Ranga Printing Works, Vishaka, 1956, p. 2.
7 Namalakanti Jagannadham. "Arundhatheeyula Vamsha Vrukshamu" (Telugu), Jagjeevan Sahithi Kalaparishath, 1990, p. 27.
8 Chinthada Gouri Vara Prasad. "Madigalu Malkonnaru" (Telugu), 1996.
9 R. Akhileshwari. "A Battle Won", *Deccan Herald,* 18th June 1997, p. 8.
10 P.R. Venkataswamy. *Our Struggle for Emancipation*, Vol. I, 1995, p. 60.
11 Ibid., p. 33.
12 Interviewed with Dr. Kishan Lal.
13 "Status of Arundhateeyas in Andhra Pradesh and Need for Review of the Rule of Reservations", 1982, p. 10, published by Bandhu Seva Mandali.
14 Interview with Dr Vidyakumar A Medical Doctor, made it clear, that there was no need to hide the name of caste as others are using our caste identity for their political advantage.
15 *The Hindu,* July 27, 1982, p. 12.
16 Adi-Jambhava/Arundhatheeya Samakhya: Its Programmes and Achievements, p. 1.
17 *Udyam* (Telugu Daily), June 13, 1992, p. 1.
18 *Deccan Chornicle* (English Daily), May 30, 1994.
19 The writer as sympathizer of Marxism observed negation of Ambedkar's caste annihilation theory in the students' organisations like PDSU, RUS, SFI and their political parties prior to Mandalisation of political process.
20 M.P. Kumar. "Dandora" Bulletin, M.R.P.S. Publication, March 2, 1996.
21 Sisir Bhattacharya. "Social Darvinism", in *India's Welfare State*, M. Venkata Rangaiah Foundation, 1984, p. 235.

22 Data on educational development of SCs is collected from Special Tables for SCs and STs, Census of India, 1981. There was no caste-based census after 1981.

23 "Dalit Classification in A.P.", *Frontline*, July 11, 1997, p. 43.

24 7, Constituent Assembly of India Debate, p. 702.

25 P. Muthaiah. "Reservations and Recruitment: A Study with Special References to SCs in A.P.", 1993, p. 200.

26 Marc Galaner. *Competing Equalities*, Oxford University Press, 1984, p. 132.

27 The writer proposed these principles of categorization of Scheduled Castes into four groups for equitable distribution of reservation benefits within 59 Scheduled Castes in A.P.

28 Justice P. Rama Chander Raju, Commission of Inquiry based on census of India, 1981 for population particulars. There was no caste-based census after 1981.

29 Memorandum against categorization of SCs in A.P., published by Mala Mahanadu, 1998. *The Hindu*, December 3, 1991, p. 1.

30 *Census of India*, 1961, Vol. II part V-B (10) Ethnography notes, A.P., p. 45.

31 *Census of India*, 1931, p. 256.

32 P.R. Venkataswamy. *Our Struggle for Emancipation*, Vol. II, Universal Art Printers, 1955, p. 656.

33 Interview with Mr Krishna Madiga, President of MRPS, who stated that MRPS took lead in exposing the TDP government's attempt to murder Gaddar, a popular singer of PWG (ML).

8 Post-Ambedkar Scheduled Castes' Agitations and Social Exclusion in Andhra Pradesh[1]

K.S. Chalam

Andhra Pradesh was formed as a separate state in 1956, the year in which Babasaheb Ambedkar passed away. Therefore, the SC agitations in the state need to be viewed as post-Ambedkar agitations. (Some of the Dalit movements in the State before Dr Ambedkar and contemporary to Dr Ambedkar are ignored here for the time being as they are associated with other regions also.) Though Andhra Pradesh administratively emerged as an independent entity, it consisted of four distinct regions. Each region has its own socio-economic, cultural, and geographical identity. But, in the mainstream literature, the dominant region of coastal Andhra is projected as Andhra Pradesh. This has inhibited the unique nature of SC problems in Telangana, Rayalaseema, and North Andhra. The so-called social movements and protest movements of Andhra Pradesh as depicted and explained by scholars relate to coastal Andhra Pradesh only. In fact, the region had a unique advantage of conversions by 1931. It was estimated by Forrester D.B. that 20 per cent of the depressed classes in Godavari districts, 32 per cent in Krishna, and 57 per cent in Guntur have been converted to Christianity by 1931. It was in this region that the Ambedkar movement originated. Except in the studies of Gail Omvedt who has studied the Ambedkar movement separately for Telangana (Hyderabad) and coastal Andhra, none of the scholars paid any attention to the diversity in the problems of Scheduled Castes in different parts of the state. The social movements in the Telangana region are absorbed in the left and radical left struggles from 1950, before the formation of the state. The Rayalaseema region has a unique problem of factionalism, and the Scheduled Castes are the active players in this game. The north coastal Andhra is the most neglected and marginalised region and therefore the agitations and events have never been brought to the attention of the scholars except as a part of the Srikakulam struggle. It is, therefore, now clear that a study of the agitations of the Scheduled Castes in Andhra Pradesh is expected to pay attention to the different aspects of the struggles unique to each region. A blanket generalisation may not help the scholar to comprehend the problem.

DOI: 10.4324/9781003317173-12

Methodologies

There appears to be no unanimity in the use of a single method to study the agitations, struggles, and movements of the Scheduled Castes in Andhra Pradesh in particular and social movements in general. Several approaches have been employed by scholars to study social movements. There are broadly three approaches that are popular in the study of SC movements.

1. Gail Omvedt in her study on Dalits and the Democratic Revolution discussed the revised idea of historical materialism wherein the dialectical nature of caste has been identified as class-caste. She[2] has analysed the ideology and organisation of a movement as an anti-caste and class struggle with its interactions with the freedom struggle. She has used the Marxist categories of class, dialectics, and ideology of base and super structure in her analysis of the social movements.
2. The institutional process of M.S. Gore who has developed a theory of social context to place Ambedkar and his movement in an ideological perspective.
3. Relative Deprivation or social exclusion approach as a new theory of social development in the context of globalisation. This is a revised theory of capability approach developed by Amartya Sen, mostly bringing economic categories for analysis rather than the social classes of castes in India. But it can be productively used to study the Dalit situation in the global context.

Agitations in Andhra Pradesh

It is observed from the literature that the approaches used by scholars to study the social movements or struggles or agitations of SCs are not uniform. Further, most of the studies undertaken on Scheduled Castes or Dalits in Andhra Pradesh are related to the Ambedkar period, prior to 1956, before the formation of the state. Therefore, the studies do not focus on the process of change and the issues that are generated from these struggles to resolve those problems. Most of the studies do concentrate on the Ambedkar movement as an extended ideology of all India characters without considering the specific nature of each state and region. As a result, they have failed to bring out the shortcomings of the movements to provide insights into the problems.

The following important events are identified here around which the SC agitations or struggles in Andhra Pradesh are concentrated.

1. 1962   Sanjivaiah became the first Dalit Chief Minister of Andhra Pradesh
2. 1969   Kanchikacherla Kotesu was burnt alive in Krishna District
3. 1983   Burning of four persons in Padiri Kuppam in Chittor district

4. 1985   The Karamchedu massacre took place on 17 July in Prakasam District, resulting in the formation of Dalit Mahasabha
5. 1991   Chunduru carnage took place on 6 August in Guntur district. The breaking of Dalit Mahasabha
6. 1992   A Dalit writers, artists, and intellectuals collective formed in Hyderabad
7. 1995   Madiga Dandora was formed in the coastal districts of Andhra Pradesh
8. 1998   Vempenta incident in Kurnool district where Dalits were brutally killed through the alleged involvement of Naxalite groups
9. 2001   Dalit human rights organisation as an NGO initiative formed to represent the Dalit issue at WCAR at Durban
10. 2003   SC reservations were categorised by the government as ABC &D

The Context of the Struggles

The ten important events identified in the history of SC struggles in Andhra Pradesh took place over a period of four decades. This covers the major part of the period after the formation of the state in 1956. In all the events, the significant factor of dispute appears to be social exploitation and the protest against caste discrimination. It is further noticed that the first events in the beginning of the agitations have shown the SC upsurge, symbolically resulting in the capture of the coveted post of chief minister of a state first time in the country. The major content of the protest movements, which are an extension of the anti-Brahmin struggles from the combined Madras Presidency, appears to be social equality. This has facilitated the emergence of the leadership of Dr Sanjivaiah, a scholar politician.

The Kanchikacharla Kotesu case became a landmark in the history of Dalit struggles in Andhra Pradesh. This incident helped the ruling castes to become conscious of their hegemony over the Dalits in the advanced districts of Andhra Pradesh. The Padiri Kuppam case is the beginning of a new political regime based on anti-Brahmin struggle and consolidation of caste power of a Sudra caste in Andhra Pradesh. Caste is always seen in India or in Andhra in its practice; otherwise, it has no meaning. Therefore, when a particular caste becomes strong, it tries to show its power in relation to another caste, mostly the deprived castes like Scheduled Castes. This is what has happened in Padiri Kuppam and in Karamchedu. The Karamchedu massacre was so brutal that two Dalit minor girls were raped, and their private parts mutilated (same as in Khairlangi in 2006). The brutal massacre gave conscious development of an organisation to protest against the incident. The formation of the Dalitha Mahasabha was a long-felt need of the Dalits in the state, as the mainstream Dalit struggles in the state were confined to job reservation by the organised few till the incident happened in Karamchedu. Within five years after the Karamchedu incident, the Chunduru incident took place in the neighbouring district of Guntur. But the usual Daliting, i.e., breaking into pieces, has taken place within the Dalith Mahasabha when the Chunduru issue came up for agitation. However, these two important events moved the intellectuals and writers belonging to the Scheduled Castes and some backward castes to form an organisation to reflect on the woes of Dalits in Andhra Pradesh.

The Madigas of Andhra Pradesh, the victims of Karamchedu, became conscious of their conditions and rights. They perceived that injustice was done to them by Malas within the SC group and therefore wanted a separate identity for their group. This helped to form a separate organisation called Madiga Dandora. The Malas protested against this and formed a separate organisation called Mala Mahanadu. The ghastly incident in Vempenta where about a half a dozen Dalits were killed passed off without any significant attention in the melee of internal bickerings. Keeping the world conference against racism, the NGO sector reacted positively to take the "Dalit" issue to the international forum through the formation of a Dalit human rights group. The government of Andhra Pradesh passed an order dividing the Scheduled Castes into ABCD groups in 2003. The Malas challenged it in the Supreme Court, and it was struck down by the Supreme Court as unconstitutional. Interestingly all the struggles in the state moved around the above issues and took place in the advanced districts of coastal Andhra Pradesh.

An Evaluation of the Struggles

We have presented the incidents and data on the SC struggles, which are basically caste-related issues in Andhra Pradesh. It is now difficult to evaluate the struggles in terms of any of the methodologies that have been so far used by scholars. We have not been able to develop a political economy of Dalit movements in India. Marxist scholars have used the European categories to study and evaluate caste struggles with little success. Therefore, an attempt is made here to evaluate the struggles in terms of the empirical data in relation to other major events in the Andhra society, so as to get some meaningful conclusions. We are trying to relate the incidents and events in the context of the overall change and development in Andhra society in a comparative perspective. If the events are not related to the overall development in the state, they become autonomous without any substantial meaning in it for others. In fact, a situation has already set in Andhra Pradesh where the SC struggles and agitations are viewed as independent and autonomous without any active participation or relation with other contemporary struggles. The SCs and their agitations are slowly excluded from the mainstream Dalits? How are the SCs/Dalits trying to build up their movements or agitations in an era of economic globalisation where events are interdependent?

It is very significant to find that all major events in the SC struggles took place in the developed coastal Andhra Pradesh. Social scientists have identified people of these districts as beneficiaries of the green revolution with new inputs both from the government and other institutional structures. This green revolution has brought in new social relations in these districts that the social scientists have recorded and analysed as a part of the general development model. No attention is, however, paid by the scholars to the issues of caste relations in the process of agrarian change. Some scholars have analysed the events as a part of class struggle or agrarian class conflicts with some attention on caste conflicts. But this may not help Dalit activists to arrive at meaningful conclusions for the continuation of his work with people. It is our view that so far the SC struggles were burdened with social and psychological issues without paying much attention to the economic issues, which is perhaps one of the factors responsible for the alienation that we have identified already. This does not mean there is a base–super structure relationship here. Gail Omvedt and others have employed those categories in the past and they are now disappointed. Therefore, without going into the methodological questions, (which is beyond the scope of the chapter though we have used some variant of comparative method), we present here the three phases of the agitations/struggles in Andhra Pradesh after the formation of the state.

Self-Respect Movement: Phase I

The Telugu-speaking people of the Andhra region inherited the self-respect movement of the Madras Presidency when a separate state was formed in 1956. The Adidravida and Adi Andhra movements initiated in Hyderabad state by Bhagya Reddy Varma had also its impact on the coastal districts of Andhra. Dr Ambedkar had also toured the districts in the early 1940s and enthused the Dalit masses. All these have culminated in the self-respect and anti-untouchability struggles in Andhra Pradesh. The Scheduled Castes were slowly consolidating themselves as a cohesive group. The leaders among the Scheduled Castes have started management (Welfare) hostels for the educational development of the Scheduled Castes with state aid. This has given opportunities to some of the ex-untouchables to enter higher educational institutions and civil service. A separate "Harijan elite" started emerging in Andhra Pradesh.

Social Equality Struggles: Phase II

The emergence of a few educated SCs in the civil society as a pressure group helped them to enter public sector jobs. The jobholders started organising the Scheduled Castes Welfare Organisations when they started facing discrimination, humiliation, and punishment in their places of work. In order to protect their self-respect and constitutional rights in the area of promotion, transfer and appointments of their kin, these groups have slowly formed Ambedkar organisations to incorporate the support of the local Dalits. The formation of the Ambedkar associations at the district headquarters along with the employees' organisations helped to form a network of SCs in the state. This helped the Dalit organisations to put forward certain demands before the government. The government has to yield to these demands and allocate funds in the plan budgets of social welfare departments. Most of the demands relate to the enhancement of scholarships, opening up of new residential schools, and so on. By the end of the second term of NTR, the government seemed to have realised that it is too expensive to meet the demands of the organised SCs. However, except a few SC organisations, the majority of them have raised issues relating to social equality, abolition of untouchability, etc., and not about the amelioration of poverty. We have not made any content analysis of the demands here. But a cursory look into the protest literature created during the period contains mostly social issues. And most of the issues are addressed to the government for a solution.

The literacy rate of the people of Andhra Pradesh is one of the lowest in the country and that of the Scheduled Castes much lower than the national average. In the 50th NSS Report (1999–2000), it is reported that out of every 1,000 households in the age group of 15 years and above, 522 among males and 772 among females are illiterate among Scheduled Castes in Andhra Pradesh. This is one of the highest rates in India. Though Ambedkar and SC organisations are very active in social life, the attention paid by these groups to the development of literacy in rural areas is negligible.

Determinants of Caste Discrimination in Phase III

The caste system in India ascribes different values to different castes. This can be found across all castes. Some castes are discriminated in the private sphere, some are in public life, and SCs are discriminated everywhere. This is because of the low value attributed to the life of an SC. This discrimination is practised in several ways. The SCs are discriminated against even in simple human gestures such as giving drinking water and treating all human beings as equal before God. In order to find out how the Dalits are discriminated against on the basis of their birth, a statistical estimate is made on the basis of the data culled out from Punnayya Commission report. As the number of cases in each item of discrimination is not uniform and the severity of injury varies from one incident of discrimination to another, we thought of estimating a composite index of discrimination. Out of the four events of discrimination reported in the Report, we have taken two important events, temple entry and two-glass system, to represent discrimination across districts. These two events are reported in all the districts in the state. We have assigned 2/3 weight to temple entry and 1/3 weight to two glasses system to estimate the composite index. The indices are presented in Table 8.1 along with the illiteracy rates and incidence of general poverty and agriculture labourers among SCs in each district. The value of composite index shows the magnitude of discrimination. It is found that the composite index is not uniform across the districts. It may be related to the economic status of the people represented by their poverty and economic calling. Therefore, we have run the following regression to test the determinants of discrimination.

Table 8.1 Composite index of caste discrimination

Sl. no.	District of discrimination	Composite index (%)	SC illiteracy poverty (%)	General (%)	SC ag. lab
1.	Adilabad	11.33	75.74	77.00	23.51
2.	Anantapur	211.33	74.32	62.00	35.43
3.	Chittoor	209.33	64.72	62.40	35.97
4.	Cuddapah	23.33	67.65	54.00	37.87
5.	East Godavari	23.67	60.11	51.00	35.44
6.	Guntur	143.33	62.51	56.60	42.14
7.	Karimnagar	6.33	75.1	53.00	36.17
8.	Khammam	66.33	68.39	58.00	35.47
9.	Krishna	5.00	59.84	47.00	40.43
10.	Kurnool	290.67	71.92	50.50	37.23
11.	Mahbubnagar	754.00	85.49	65.00	47.97
12.	Medak	74.33	82.73	58.00	25.72
13.	Nalgonda	165.00	75.4	58.50	37.65
14.	Nellore	43.00	64.94	48.00	37.54
15.	Nizamabad	15.67	80.46	42.00	32.98
16.	Prakasam	81.33	68.61	53.00	43.36
17.	Ranga Reddy	244.67	69.94	58.00	26.01
18.	Srikakulam	65.33	68.99	60.00	34.85
19.	Visakhapatnam	61.00	55.27	58.80	19.37
20.	Vizianagaram	61.33	71.46	55.00	31.81
21.	Warangal	41.00	72.74	48.50	25.85
22.	West Godavari	15.33	59.26	46.90	42.57

Source: Chalam KS; "Offences and Atrocities against Scheduled Castes in Andhra Pradesh: An Empirical Investigation" Social Action, Jan–March 2004.
The determinants of discrimination
$CID = \beta_0 + \beta_1 \, ill + \beta_2 Pov + \beta_3 Aglab$
Where CID = Composite index of caste discrimination
Ilt. = rate of illiteracy among SCs
Pov = % of population below poverty line
Aglab = % of Agriculture Labour among SCs
$\beta_1 \beta_2 \beta_3$ are coefficients to be estimated.
We have obtained the following results.
$CID = \beta_0 + 0.331 \, \beta_1 + 0.440 \, \beta_2 + 0.445 \, \beta_3 \quad r^2 = 0.45$
    (1.82)   (2.14)   (2.46)
Figures in brackets are t values. They are statistically found significant

The above results show that the model is found to be statistically significant as it is explaining 45 per cent of the variations. Out of the three
variables, poverty among the people and incidence of agricultural labourers
among Scheduled Castes are explaining the prevalence of caste discrimination much stronger than illiteracy. They are also found to be statistically
significant. It is interesting to observe from these results that economic
factors are still contributing to the prevalence of caste discrimination in
Andhra Pradesh. We have also estimated correlation coefficients between
CID and the percentage of the Christian population as an alleged stimulant

for discrimination. We found that there is no relation between the two. The correlation coefficient between CID and the percentage of the SC population in a district is found to be 0.52. Therefore, we are of the opinion that the above model of regression is valid in explaining the determinants of caste discrimination.

Social Exclusion and Alienation: The Present Situation

The data on land holdings and the levels of poverty among the SCs clearly indicate that there is a relationship between the overall development of the state and the development of the SCs. The caste-related development index developed by the author and presented in Table 8.2 shows the index of development achieved by the Scheduled Castes in Andhra Pradesh. Though the rate of growth of the CDI among the Scheduled Castes is lower than the HDI between 1971 and 1991, it is found that it is increasing over a period of time. As pointed out earlier, the development of the Scheduled Castes is related to the overall development of the state. Interestingly, several commentators observed that SCs are socially excluded from all developmental activities today. It is because of the economic globalisation process, which is structurally exclusive in nature. Scholars like Amartya Sen and even UNDP experts are pointing out the phenomenon of social exclusion as a dangerous trend that will lead to deprivation and capability failure.

The phenomenon of social exclusion in India in general and in Andhra in particular consists of inequalities, labour market, gender, food market, etc., exclusion of Scheduled Castes from the mainstream. This exclusion will further accentuate the misery of the Scheduled Castes who are already structurally excluded from the mainstream society. The society appears to care less for these groups as long as they are raising issues of discrimination, without bringing issues with which others are equally interested. The spontaneous nature with which non-Dalit groups ignore the issue of untouchability and discrimination in their discourse is a significant phenomenon. It has gone to such an extent that both scholars and policymakers are impalpable of the declining trend of urbanisation among the Scheduled Castes.

Table 8.2 Caste-related development index for Andhra Pradesh

S. No.		1971	1981	1991
1.	Life expectancy index	0.367	0.500	0.583
2.	Educational attainment index	0.177	0.341	0.521
3.	Income index	0.046	0.108	0.145
	CDI	0.197	0.316	0.416
	AP HDI	–	0.466	0.592

Source: Chalam K.S. South India Journal of Social Sciences, June 2004.

The SC urban population is declining in Andhra Pradesh compared to the overall increase in the proportion of people who are living in urban areas. In Table 8.3, the SC urban population for the years 1991 and 2001 is presented. It is clear that the proportion of the SC urban population in the state has declined from 17.31 per cent in 1991 to 17.18 per cent in 2001. Except in the districts of Adilabad, Ranga Reddy, Vizianagaram, Anantapur, and Chittor where a marginal increase is found, in all the remaining districts (mostly in coastal) SC urban population has declined. It is a known fact that the opportunities for employment, income, and power are concentrated in urban centres, particularly after liberalisation. But the data suggest that Scheduled Castes in Andhra Pradesh are excluded from the trend. This is an expected outcome of the process of globalisation where the Scheduled Castes are not considered as (important) players at all. They are unwanted. The SC organisations have also failed to prepare the Dalits for the limited opportunities in urban centres or even to fight against such discrimination and exclusion. Already the educated employees seem to have formed into a separate group as a federation without considering the serious economic issues of the SCs in general. The elite

Table 8.3 Scheduled Castes urban population to total in Andhra Pradesh (%)

Districts	Year	
	1991	2001
Andhra Pradesh	17.31	17.18
Adilabad	19.20	23.45
Nizamabad	10.88	9.34
Karimnagar	13.11	12.87
Medak	8.25	8.2
Ranga Reddy	32.36	35.19
Mahabubnagar	5.51	4.84
Nalgonda	7.37	8.64
Warangal	14.74	14.55
Khammam	16.44	16.98
Srikakulam	12.03	10.47
Vizianagaram	18.46	20.54
Visakhapatnam	45.94	43.54
East Godavari	15.99	15.36
West Godavari	11.73	11.84
Krishna	18.90	15.72
Guntur	18.39	17.28
Prakasam	8.48	8.22
Nellore	13.0	12.31
Cuddapah	13.62	12.41
Kurnool	19.76	18.60
Anantapur	14.56	15.33
Chittor	9.79	11.77

organisations are trying to perpetuate and bargain for perks and power for the few families that they represent. This phenomenon is also responsible for the social exclusion of the majority of the SCs who are poor, ignorant, and unorganised. This process of exclusion seems to have two dimensions. One, the majority of the poor and ignorant among the Scheduled Castes are excluded from the overall development of the economy and society. Two, the so-called elite among the Scheduled Castes, however small they may be, are alienated from the mainstream. On the other hand, there is some kind of an inclusion process started (both conscious and unconscious) among the upper castes. This process of inclusion is found to be both internal and external to the country. These groups are internally cohesive and adaptive to changing situations and can manipulate their caste orientation to form social networks. The networks have been in existence for a long time even before independence but strongly manifested after globalisation by extending their tentacles beyond the boundaries of the country. The phenomenon of multi-caste corporations (MCC) in place of MNCs is a part of this trend (Chalam, 1998). The Scheduled Castes, including the so-called creamy layer, are banned from this new formation. Some of the manifestations of this trend are not amenable to the concepts of poverty, deprivation, etc. Therefore, our social scientists have paid very little attention to this phenomenon.

Conclusion

The Scheduled Castes of Andhra Pradesh were one of the earliest groups to participate in the Ambedkar movement. Though the Ambedkar movement was confined to the awakened coastal districts due to mass conversions by 1931, it became a state-level upsurge by the 1970s. The Ambedkar movement was taken up in Andhra as a social upliftment and anti-untouchability struggle as a constituent of the missionary agenda. In fact, the ruling castes have been very sensitive to the demands of the organised Scheduled Castes and, therefore, introduced several schemes and programmes such as IRDP and food for work as a part of the development agenda to co-opt the Dalits. Though Ambedkar realised the lacunae in his struggles and brought out the document "States and Minorities" as an economic agenda, the majority of the SC organisations have not taken up economic issues, including privatisation, seriously. Now they are excluded and alienated from the mainstream. (Some critics say that there is only one movement that is permanent and strong; it is conversions, as seen from the massive gatherings in all important towns and cities in Andhra Pradesh.) Unless the Scheduled Castes start organising a reform process within each group through self-help and other means to strengthen their solidarity, the social exclusion with which they are suffering now will become a permanent feature in future.

Notes

1 Published in *Social Action: A Quarterly Review of Social Trends* (July–September 2007).
2 Gail Omvedt, *Dalits and the Democratic Revolution*, Sage Publications, Delhi, 1994.

References

Chalam, K.S. (2004). "Economic Development of Scheduled Castes in Andhra Pradesh 1956–2001", South India Journal of Social Sciences.
Chalam, K.S. (2004). "Offences and Atrocities against Scheduled Castes in Andhra Pradesh: An Empirical Investigation", Social Action, Jan-March.
Chalam, K.S. (1998). "Caste and Economic Reforms", Seminar November.
Sen, A. (2004). *Social Exclusion: Concept Application and Scrutiny*, Delhi: Critical Quest.

9 Caste Conflict and Dalit Identity in Rural Punjab[1]

Significance of Talhan

Prakash Louis and Surinder S. Jodhka

The recent case of conflict involving members of Dalit[2] caste of *Ad-Dharmis* and the dominant landowner Jats over the participation in the management of a local shrine in a village called Talhan in Punjab points to some very interesting trends in the nature of caste conflict in the region. Though caste has always been a fact of life in Punjab, it never led to any major cases of violence as frequently reported from some other parts of India. Caste has also not been an idiom of the political discourse in the state. State politics in Punjab has revolved around questions such as regional interests of Punjab vis-à-vis other states, identity politics of religious communities, or class interests of peasantry and other sections of the Punjabi society.

Socially also the relations between the underprivileged castes or Dalits and the traditionally dominant or upper castes have generally been, relatively speaking, cordial. Caste divisions are not too visible in Punjab. Though caste survives as an endogamous group for fixing marital alliances, one can observe the presence of "prejudice" against Dalits among the upper castes or the practice of "pollution" or "untouchability" is rare even at the village level in much of Punjab. However, the most important aspect of caste in Punjab is that it remains the major source of social inequality. A large proportion of the Dalits continue to be among the poorest in Punjab. On the other end, the rich and powerful are predominantly from the upper castes. Further, Punjab has also not been free from cases of atrocities against Dalits committed mostly by locally dominant castes or the state agencies.

Though it has its own complexities, the story of Talhan, in a sense, reminds us of the continuing presence of caste in the region. Perhaps the most deplorable fact that comes out from Talhan is that even in a region that has seen vibrant Dalit movements and considerable social and economic mobility among Dalits, a social boycott can be still imposed on them by the locally dominant castes.

The incidents that unfolded in Talhan village from January to June 2003 reveal the nature of caste relations in the state of Punjab. They also provide us with a good idea of the growing aspirations of Dalits and point to the emerging patterns of caste conflict in the region. The demand by the *Ad-Dhramis*, or the Dalits or the erstwhile untouchable castes, for representation in the Management Committee of Baba *Nihal Singh Smadh-Gurudwara* is not just

DOI: 10.4324/9781003317173-13

a demand for equal share in the cake but it is an indication of Dalit assertion for equality and equal rights. It questions the age-old assumption that the
landowning dominant castes of Jats have the right to exclusive control over the
economy and sociocultural resources of the village. It has also highlighted their
resolve to determine their course of action in day-to-day life as well as in crisis
situations. Hence, change in the caste system is in the offing in rural Punjab.

Dalit assertion in Talhan has also exposed the political parties and the
limited scope of their electoral politics for not only the Dalit assertion and
emancipation but for restructuring the Indian social order. Identity formation of the Dalits has been going on unabated in various parts of India, and
the recent Dalit assertion in Talhan has once again provided scope and space
for discourse on restructuring the Indian social order. Social scientists and
political activists are called upon seriously to pay attention to the emerging
Dalit assertion for emancipation.

The Social Composition of Dalits of Punjab

The Scheduled Castes of Punjab constituted over 28.3 per cent of the total
population of Punjab in 1991, which is much higher than the national average
16.48 per cent. They are divided into 37 sub-castes (Table 9.1). Among the
37 sub-castes, the Ravidasi-Chamar (Ad-Dharmi and Ramdasi) and Chuhras
(Mazhabis and Balmikis) are numerically the most dominant groups. Most
of the Scheduled Castes live in rural areas (79.45%), and only about 20.55%
live in urban centres of Punjab. The Scheduled Castes of Punjab, like their
counterparts in other parts of the country, are treated as untouchables,
though the level of untouchability practiced might have differed in the state.

It has been reported that Punjab was a notable exception to the caste
system in India. There are many factors which contributed to this phenomenon. Compared to other parts of India, Brahmins have not occupied any
position of influence and power in Punjab. The Sikh Gurus' opposition to
Brahmanical orthodoxy and caste system reduced the oppressive nature of
casteism in Punjab. In positive terms the Sikh Gurus advocated sangat, kir-
tan, and langar (congregational worship, corporate singing, and common
dining). At the economic realm, the growing demand of leather goods such
as boots and shoes for the British army had brought some prosperity to some
of the enterprising members of the Chamar caste during the 19th century.
Some of the Chamars and Ad-Dharmis have also been extremely successful entrepreneurs. They have a considerable of share in the surgical goods
industry in the town of Jalandhar (Jodhka, 2000 and Puri, 2003). Education
and reservation also contributed in enabling the individuals and communities
to resist caste oppression. All these contributed in moving away from traditional occupation, which were considered to be menial and impure occupations. Significantly this mobility was particularly well pronounced in the
Doaba region of Punjab. Jalandhar district, in which the Talhan village falls,
is a part of the Doaba region.

Table 9.1 Scheduled Caste population breakup 1991 (%)

Sl. no.	Caste	Jalandar	Punjab
1.	Ad-Dharmi	60.18	15.34
2.	Balmiki, Chuhra	21.34	21.34
3.	Bangali	0.06	0.07
4.	Barar, Burar	0.27	0.18
5.	Batwal	0.06	0.24
6.	Bauria, Bawaria	0.06	1.37
7.	Bazigar	1.49	2.84
8.	Bhanjra	0.13	0.08
9.	Chamar	5.29	25.85
10.	Chanal	0.0	0.01
11.	Dagi	0.0	0.01
12.	Darain	0.0	0.02
13.	Deha, Dhaya, Dhea	0.0	0.12
14.	Dhanak	0.05	1.01
15.	Dhogri, Dhangri	0.0	0.01
16.	Dhumna, Doom	0.18	2.76
17.	Gagra	0.0	0.01
18.	Gandhila, Gandhil,	0.10	0.06
19.	Kabirpanthi, Julha	0.40	1.13
20.	Khatik	0.14	0.18
21.	Kori, Koti	0.09	0.11
22.	Marija, Marecha	0.01	0.03
23.	Mazhabi	2.13	30.75
24.	Megh	3.98	1.83
25.	Nat	0.0	0.02
26.	Od	0.0	0.23
27.	Pasi	0.08	0.16
28.	Perna	0.0	0.0
29.	Pherera	0.01	0.01
30.	Sanhai	0.0	0.01
31.	Sanhal	0.01	0.01
32.	Sanai, Bhedkut	1.02	1.41
33.	Sansoi	0.01	0.01
34.	Sapela	0.01	0.04
35.	Sarera	0.09	0.21
36.	Siligar	0.09	0.15
37.	Sirkiban	0.56	0.50

Source: Census Report 1991. CD Version.

Though the above facts are true about the Dalits of Punjab, due to the iron grip of the caste system they were not fully liberated from its oppressive practices and attitudes. Mark Juergensmeyer, in his pioneering work *Religion as Social Vision*, argues,

> In the Punjab the experience of the untouchables is widely varied. They live in the villages, and they live in the cities. They are mired in bitter poverty, and they relax in financial comfort. They profess variously to

be Muslim, Sikh, Hindu and Christian, and some deny any religious affiliation at all. Most members of the lower castes, however, share the stigma of untouchability: they are frequently denied the chance to eat, smoke, or even sit with members of the upper castes, and they often must use separate wells from the those maintained for the use of others. These injustices are sanctioned more or less by religion, but there are others, more extreme, that go entirely beyond religious approval; beggar – forced labour – for instance, and the sexual abuse to which many lower caste wives and daughters are subjected.

(Juergensmeyer, 1982)

Talhan, Jalandhar, and Punjab

The social indicators of the Dalits in Jalandhar are comparatively much better than that of the Dalits in the rest of Punjab and India. It is a fact that 25.44 per cent of the Dalits are returned as cultivators at the all-India level, while in Punjab the rate is just 4.8 per cent (Table 9.2). In Jalandhar district the cultivators among the Dalits are fewer in number. There is a sizeable population of Dalits who are returned as agricultural labourers. The percentage of agricultural labourers in Jalandhar is lower (48.65) than Punjab (59.83) and national average (49.06). This goes to state that in Punjab many Dalits are engaged as agricultural labourers. But if one examines manufacturing, servicing, and other services, the Dalits of Jalandhar and Punjab are far ahead than their counterparts in other parts of India. Especially the Dalits of Jalandhar district are engaged in manufacturing and other services in a big way. This explains the social fact as to why the process of distancing, differentiation, and autonomy has become a success with regard to the Dalits of Punjab.

Table 9.2 Profile of Scheduled Castes (1991)

Item	Jalandhar	Punjab	India
Total population[a]	6,11,399	57,42,528	13,82,23,277
Male population	3,29,007	30,65,671	7,19,28,960
Female population	2,82,392	26,76,857	6,62,94,317
Total literacy rate	50.43	41.08	37.41
Male literacy rate	59.52	49.82	49.91
Female literacy rate	39.33	31.03	23.76
Main workers	29.39	29.66	36.08
Cultivator	3.62	4.80	25.44
Agricultural labourers	48.65	59.83	49.06
Manufacturing, servicing in other than			
Household services	14.75	8.14	5.13
Other services	15.08	13.15	7.97

Source: 1991 Census Report.
[a]Rows dealing with population are absolute numbers while the rest are in percentage.

It is also reported that many from the Dalit communities are making a better living not only in other parts of the country but in other parts of the world.

As has been widely reported in the media, the conflict between Ad-Dharmis and Jats in Talhan village emanated from the former demanding representation in the management of a local religious shrine. Though the locally dominant Jats were trying to convert this shrine into a "proper" Gurudwara with help from some outside Sikh religious organisations, it was originally a *smadh* (or *samadhi*), a shrine where the bodies of one Baba Nihal Singh and his aide were laid to rest. The history and nature of this shrine reflects very interestingly on the synergetic religious traditions of the region. Simultaneously, it also highlights the conflicts that are emerging between various caste groups who want a share in the economy of religious centres.

As the story goes, Baba Nihal Singh was a Sikh from the artisan caste of Ramgarhia who lived in a neighbouring village called Dakoha. He was no saint or fakir while he was alive. He made and fixed pulleys, the wheel-like structures, for the newly dug drinking water wells in the area. These wheels are kept at the base of the wells in order to stabilise water supply. Villagers of the area had deep faith in the skills of Nihal Singh. "If he put wheel in the well, it would never dry, and its water would always be sweet".

However, one day while fixing a wheel in a newly dug well near Talhan, Baba Nihal Singh died. For the common villagers this was a sacrifice he made for the village, and he consequently was declared a *Shahid*, that is, martyr. Out of respect for Nihal Singh and in order to preserve his memory, they decided to make a separate structure where his body was laid to rest in the village land near Talhan. Close to the *smadh*, a flame too was kept burning. Harnam Singh, who used to be an aide of Nihal Singh, took care of the *smadh* all his life and kept the flame burning. When Harnam Singh died, another *smadh* was built close to the earlier structure. Over the years these *smadhs* began to attract devotees, who also brought offerings, mostly in the form of cash. These two small structures were slowly converted into a shrine. In due course another structure came up in the middle of these two *smadhs* where the Sikh holy book, Guru Granth, was kept and it began to be read as per the Sikh rituals. To mark the death anniversary of Shahid Baba Nihal Singh, his devotees from Talhan and neighbouring villages started organising an annual fair (*mela*) at the shrine. With the growing prosperity of the region and of Baba's devotees, offerings grew. According to available estimates, the current annual amount of offerings at the shrine is anywhere between three and five crore rupees. As the shrine grew in stature, its management shifted to a committee of "powerful" individuals from Talhan and neighbouring villages. They also controlled all the money and decided on how to spend it. Elections to the 13 members committee were held every year on the evening of Maghi (a local festival that falls around the 14th of January). However, not everyone from the village could participate in these elections.

Apart from the shrine of Baba Nihal Singh, the village also has three regular Gurudwaras. One is called the village Gurudwara, which was built by the dominant Jats. Second is the Gurudwara of Ramgarhias and the third is a Ravidas Gurudwara/Mandir,[3] which has been recently built by the Ad-Dharmis. Though in principle Gurudwaras are open to all, different caste communities have tended to build their own Gurudwaras, generally to assert their separate identity (Jodhka, 2002) in a caste divided set-up of rural Punjab.[4]

While for regular religious/ritual functions, different caste groups have their separate Gurudwaras, all villagers visit the shrine of Shahid Baba Nihal Singh and participate in the organisation of the annual *mela*. However, the committee that manages the shrine and deals with the finances is fully dominated by the landowning Jats.

Talhan is about 10 kilometres from Jalandhar district headquarters. Talhan has a population of around 4,500, out of which only around 20 per cent are Jats while nearly 70 per cent belong to Ad-Dharmi caste. The rest are from other "servicing castes" such as Ramgarhias, Lohars, and Jheers. Except for Ad-Dharmis there are no other Scheduled Castes in the village. Interestingly though some other caste communities of villages in the area have been given representation, no Ad-Dharmi was ever represented in the managing committee.

The Ad-Dharmis are not only numerically predominant in the village, but over the last several decades they have also experienced a considerable degree of mobility and autonomy. Though they were originally Chamars, their long history of mobilisation and cultural awakening has transformed them into a well-to-do community. The Ad-Dharmis of the Doaba sub-region of Punjab hardly resemble their counterparts elsewhere in India. While they do not mind being identified as a Scheduled Caste, some of them dislike being called Dalits. Despite the fact that very few among them own agricultural land, a large majority of them live in well-built pucca houses and there would be hardly any Ad-Dharmi whose children did not go to school. Many of them have urban jobs and at least one person from every alternative household is abroad, either somewhere in the West or in the Gulf.

The genesis of their prosperity goes back to the establishment of the cantonment by the British colonial rulers in Jalandhar in the second half of the nineteenth century after they established their rule in the region. The sudden spurt in demand for leather boots brought riches to the local Chamars. Mangoo Ram, who spearheaded the Ad-Dharmi movement, was the son of one such Chamar who earned enough wealth by supplying boots to the British army to send his son to California for better employment. However, Mangoo Ram came back and began to mobilise his people against caste discrimination and untouchability. He tried working with the Arya Samaj but soon realised that Dalits had no future within Hinduism and demanded from the colonial rulers that the Ad-Dharmis be listed as a separate religious community and should not be clubbed either with the Hindus or the Sikhs (Mark Juergensmeyer: ibid.).

While the British conceded to the demand and they were actually listed separately in the 1931 Census, the post-independence Indian state once again put them in the list of Hindu Scheduled Castes. Notwithstanding their "legal" religious status, the everyday practices of the Ad-Dharmis are closer to Sikhism. They worship Guru Granth (which also contains the writings of Guru Ravidas, who too was a Chamar by caste). They also perform their weddings and other rituals according to Sikh tradition. Very few among them, however, have long hair or tie turbans. Their names too are like those of the Punjabi Hindus. In the local traditions, they could easily be called *sahijdhari* Sikhs.[5]

Over the last four or five decades, the caste scene in Punjab has undergone many changes. The traditional *jajmani* relations have nearly completely disappeared from the region. These changes have been greatest in the Doaba sub-region. The rural Dalits of Doaba have nearly completely distanced themselves from the local agrarian economy. In Talhan, for example, not even a single Ad-Dharmi worked on a farm as a servant with the landowning Jats, something that they regularly did in the past. Migrants from Uttar Pradesh and Bihar do virtually all the agricultural labour work. The Ad-Dharmis have also acquired a sense of autonomy as regards their cultural resources and employment (Jodhka, 2002). Thanks to the growing hegemony of the Sikh movement, Brahminism is virtually dead in rural Punjab (Jodhka, 2001). Given their numbers, Ad-Dharmis have also become much more influential in local politics. Though the current sarpanch in the village is a Jat, no one could win the panchayat elections without the support of Ad-Dharmis. Some Ad-Dharmis claimed that the current Sarpanch was their candidate. The Ad-Dharmis in Talhan and the neighbouring villages are clearly not easily susceptible to pressures from the dominant caste.

However, despite their overall empowerment and near complete absence of a Brahmanical social setup, rural Punjab has not forgotten caste and the fact that it means inequality. In other words, while *pollution* has nearly disappeared, the upper-caste *prejudice* vis-à-vis Dalits remains.

As mentioned above, the Ad-Dharmis revered Baba Nihal Singh almost as much as the Jats did and participated in all events at the shrine with similar enthusiasm. However, when they demanded representation in the committee that looked after the affairs of the shrine, the Jats did not even take their claim seriously. This happened for the first time some four or five years back, and since then caste relations in Talhan have not been cordial.

Perhaps the most contentious issue in this whole struggle has been the money that comes to the shrine as offerings. The Jat members of the committee claim that a large proportion of the money went into the upkeep of the shrine and development activities that the committee had initiated for the whole village. Over the last five years or so they have spent a large amount of money on the construction of a hospital and a telephone exchange in the village. The money has also been spent on schools and streets. The Jat members of the committee claimed that even the Ad-Dharmis were given 2.5 lakhs of rupees for the construction of their Gurudwara/Ravidas Mandir. Moreover, the Jat members of the committee we spoke to argued, "Since *Ad-Dharmis* were anyway not proper Sikhs, how could they be made members of the managing committee of a Sikh shrine".[7]

The Ad-Dharmis, on the other hand, question such arguments. *Smadh Baba Nihal Singh* was never a proper Gurudwara; and if clean-shaven Jats could become members of the committee, why couldn't they? They too worshiped Guru Granth and conducted their ritual life as other Sikhs did. The Ad-Dharmis also accused the Jats in the committee of corruption and bungling. "It is because they make huge amount of money by being members of the committee that they do not want us to be members", argued most Ad-Dharmis we spoke to.

In course of time, not receiving any positive response from the Jats, the Ad-Dharmis decided to go to court in 1999 with a petition challenging the manner in which elections to the managing committee were held. While the court did not give a clear verdict, it directed that a few Ad-Dharmi observers be allowed to be present at the time of the annual elections of the committee.

However, when they went to the shrine for attending the meeting on 14 January 2003 with the order from the court, the Jats did not turn up for the election meeting. The elections were finally held on the evening of 19 January 2003. However, the Jats refused to concede to the demand of Ad-Dharmis for representation in the committee. The Ad-Dharmis claim that the Jats had called the police, who chased them away and beat them up when they insisted on their representation in the committee. The Jats also issued a letter to the non-Ad Dharmi residents of the village to not keep any social or economic relations with them. They stopped going to the shops run by Ad-Dharmis in the village and banned the poorer Ad-Dharmis from collecting fodder from their farms. They had to either bring fodder from the town or had to collect it from neighbouring villages. Even the use of village fields for defecating was disallowed. A portrait of Guru Ravidas that hanged in the shrine was also torn.

Though the Ad-Dharmis of Doaba do not depend much on the local agrarian economy for employment, their "social boycott" was quite a shock for most of them. "Though it did not matter much to us, our ego was terribly hurt", said a retired employee of the Punjab government who lived in Talhan and led the mobilisation by Ad-Dharmis. Similarly, Lahauri Ram Bali, an aged Ambedkarite, editor of a monthly paper called *Bheem Patrika*, said that such a thing had not happened in Doaba in the recent past. "What has been the use of all our struggle, education and mobility if our people have to still face such humiliation", he said in despair and anger. He took upon himself to organise the local Ad-Dharmis against the "social boycott" and for representation in the management of the local shrine. A Dalit Action Committee (DAC) consisting mostly of the local Ad-Dharmis was formed to spearhead the movement.

The Dalit Action Committee gave a representation to the SC/ST Commission and organised dharnas in the town. A team from the Commission came to the village on 5 February 2003 and found that the "social boycott" was indeed in place. Though they asked the local administration to intervene immediately, nothing happened. Meanwhile DAC continued its protest in Jalandhar town and in the village. They did not get much support from any of the political parties. The then Congress government had five Dalit ministers, three of whom live in Jalandhar, but they did nothing to help the Ad-Dharmis in Talhan. The Bahujan Samaj Party (BSP) also did not come to their support. According to Mr. Bali the only political party that supported their cause was the Akali Dal (Amritsar). Some left-wing leaders and a few Sikh organisations also gave statements against the social boycott and in favour of Dalit representation in the committee, but to no effect.

However, DAC continued its agitation and finally some officers in the district administration called a meeting of both parties and a compromise was worked out on 3 June 2003. The Jats agreed to include two Ad-Dharmis in the committee provided they wore turban. The other terms of the agreement included a public apology by all parties involved, lifting of the social boycott, and restoration of the picture of Guru Ravidas. However, two days after the agreement, members of the two castes again clashed each other during the annual *mela* at the Mazhar of Peer Baba Fateh Shah. It was after this clash that violence erupted in Jalandhar, resulting in police firing in which one person was killed. After nearly two weeks of tension, the two groups were brought back on the negotiating table by the administration and the same compromise was made effective.

Dalits, Jat Sikhs, and Identity formation

In terms of religious principles and practices it has been repeatedly argued that Sikhism seems to have provided avenues for escape from caste atrocities. Harish Puri argues,

> Sikhism appears to have exercised a significant liberating influence on the dalits (former untouchable castes) in Punjab. The teachings of the Sikh Gurus, the religious institutions of "sangat" and "langar", the absence of a caste-based priesthood, and the respect for manual labour, all these were together aimed at creating a caste-free *Khalsa* Brotherhood. When the Singh Sabha leadership chose to assert a separate and distinct identity to underline their boundary demarcation from the Hindus – "*Hum Hindu Nahin*" – (We are not Hindus) at the beginning of 20th century, the key differentiating factor they referred to was rejection of "*varnashram*" and purity-pollution syndrome which were central to Hinduism. The people of the untouchable castes in the region converted to Sikh religion in large numbers with a view to improve their status. Their gain was not small. However, there was a wide gap between the doctrinal principles and social practice.
>
> (Puri, 2003)

While conversion to Sikhism seems to have reduced the stigma and discrimination suffered by the Dalits, other forms of marginalisation continued in Punjab. Denial of access over resources, especially land, was one such prohibition imposed on the Dalits. "Given its commitment to the 'sound principle'" – "not to upset the existing social and economic order" – the British government ensured that tenants, labourers, and other landless men should not, as a rule, be chosen for allotment of level. The land was allocated to the "dominant castes", as per the scale of already existing landholding status. In the customary scheme, outcastes such as mazhabis, balmikis, and ramdaisas/ravidasias were not allowed to own land. In fact even access to *shamlaat land* (village commons) could be shared only among hereditary landowning communities. Consequently, as Ambedkar told the Rajya Sabha in 1954, the untouchables or *kamins* were not entitled to build their houses in a *pucca* form on the land on which they stayed. They are always afraid lest the zamindars of Punjab may, at any time, turn them out. Another development, more significant to this effect was the Punjab Land Alienation Act 1901. According to this (which was enacted primarily to save the indebted farmers from the rapacious moneylenders of the Khatri, Arora, or Brahmin castes), agricultural land could be purchased or acquired only by people belonging to the defined "agricultural castes". All those belonging to the lower castes, not included among the "agricultural tribes", were debarred from owning land even if a few had the means to purchase land for cultivation. (It was only after Independence that B.R. Ambedkar, as law minister, moved to repeal the Act in 1952 to remove the invidious disability.) "This extraordinary privileging of the Jat agriculturalist (80 per cent of whom turned to Sikhism in central Punjab districts by 1921) contributed further to their caste domination and arrogance of privilege" (H.K. Puri: ibid.).

In Punjab caste, access over resources and religion provided basis for identity formation. According to B.L. Abbi and Kesar Singh,

> Among the urban Sikhs, the trading castes of, Kahtris and Aroras were very strongly represented as against Jats who constituted the dominant element in the countryside. The urban Sikhs from these trading castes who were mainly migrants from the western Punjab faced intense competition from the already entrenched local Hindu traders as well as Hindu migrant traders, though the local Hindu traders and the migrants did not necessarily constitute a cohesive group. The urban Sikh's attempts to promote their trading and other interests by seeking to mobilise as Sikhs, the rural Sikh folks were to become an important element of state politics. Most of the converts to Sikhism have come from the Hindu fold and there have always been commensal relations as well as ties of kinship and affinity, particularly between persons of the same caste. There are a number of sectarian groups, such as Radha Soami, Nirankari, Nirmalas, Udasis, etc., which eclectically incorporate some of the features of the two religious and draw

members from both. Further, there are a large number of Sikhs who are *sahijdharis*, that is, those who are not baptized within the Khalsa Panth and do not adhere to the observance of the five Sikh symbols or five Ks (*kesh, kangha, kara (steel bracelet), kirpan (sword), kachh (shorts)* but regard themselves Sikhs.

(Abbi and Singh, 1997)

Paul Hershman, while analysing some of the studies on the social milieu of Punjab, points out to some of the wrong notions about caste, honour, pride, etc. According to Paul Hershman, Pettigrew, in her recent study of political system of the Sikh Jats, writes,

The social organisation and value system especially of the rural Punjab, differ from that of Hindu India. The prevailing form of social cooperation and the type of political solidarity bear no reference to 'caste' and to rules of purity and pollution, but rather to the family unit and to the values pertaining to that unit, namely honour, pride and equality, reputation, shame and insult.

Hershman, while agreeing with Pettigrew about the nature of family honour among Punjabis, says it is difficult to come to terms with her contention that there is no such thing as "caste" in Punjab (Hershman, 1981). Interestingly, the Sikhs are also constituted of the following groups: Jat, Ramgarhi as Aroras and Khatris, Mazhabis, Ramdasis, etc.

If we examine the religious adherence of various segments of the population of Punjab and Jalandhar, it becomes clear that there is no uniformity. According to the 1991 census, Hindus are only 34.45 per cent in Punjab, which is much lower than the national average 82.14 per cent (Table 9.3). Sikhs are over 62.95 per cent, while their national average is only 1.99 per cent. When we look at the population size of the Hindus in Jalandhar district, we notice that they constitute 53.37 per cent, and out of this about half of the population lives in urban areas. In contrast to this, the Sikhs

Table 9.3 Religious breakup of Punjab and Jalandhar

Area	Total	Hindus	Muslims	Christians	Sikhs	Buddhists
Punjab	2,02,81,969	34.45	1.18	1.11	62.95	0.12
Rural	70.45	48.16	60.51	79.44	82.78	66.69
Urban	29.55	51.84	39.49	20.56	17.22	33.31
Jalandhar	20,26,787	53.37	0.42	0.73	44.01	0.67
Rural	64.04	51.47	75.87	65.51	79.42	70.68
Urban	35.96	48.53	24.13	38.48	20.58	29.32

Source: 1991 Census Report; Religion.

constitute only 44.01 per cent but out of them over 79.42 per cent reside in rural areas. The other minority communities like the Muslims, Christians, and Buddhists do not have any sizeable population. But some sociologically significant facts need to be highlighted here. About 24,930 were returned as Buddhists in Punjab in the 1991 census. Out of this over 13,623, that is, 54.65 per cent, are in Jalandhar itself. Secondly a sizeable population among the Sikhs, Muslims, Christians, and Buddhists live in urban areas. Many of the Dalits were converted to these religions, and those among them who are socially mobile moved to urban centres and have escaped the manifest and latent forms of exclusion and discrimination.

The literacy rate among the Scheduled Castes of Punjab in comparison to general population of Punjab is low (Table 9.4). This goes to state that they are further disadvantaged since they have not progressed with education and literacy and since lack of education denies access to gainful employment. This further curtails social mobility. But the Scheduled Castes of Punjab are comparatively better off than their counter parts in India. The literacy rate of Scheduled Castes of Punjab is 41.09 while the national average is 37.41 per cent. Similarly, the literacy rate of Scheduled Caste women in Punjab is 31.03, which are higher than the national average 23.76 per cent. This goes to explain why they are socially mobile.

If the Dalits of Punjab have fared in education, it is pertinent to look at the usage of affirmative action for social mobility by the Dalits. The quantum of reservation prescribed for the Scheduled Castes and Scheduled Tribes was fixed on the basis of the percentage of their population. But this percentage has not been further revised while the population of these weaker sections have increased. For instance, the Scheduled Castes of Punjab constituted 26.87 per cent in 1981, and the percentage of reservation was 25. Even when the Scheduled Caste population moved to 28.3 in 1991, the proportion of reservation remained at 25 per cent.[6] It is estimated that the Scheduled Caste population of Punjab has gone up to 30 per cent in the 2001 census, but the proportion of reservation remains the same. But more important point of conflict is that even this 25 per cent of reservation has not been implemented

Table 9.4 Literacy among the Scheduled Castes (% 1971, 1981, 1991)

India					Punjab			
Year	Total	SCs	SC (men)	SC (women)	Total	SCs	SC (men)	SC (women)
1971	29.45	12.77	20.04	5.06	33.67	1600	22.95	8.10
1981	36.17	21.38	31.12	10.93	49.12	23.86	33.96	16.67
1991	52.21	37.41	49.91	23.76	58.12	41.09	49.82	31.03

Source: Census of India 1971, 1981, 1991; as calculated by B. Yadav and A.M. Sharma. Economic Uplift of Scheduled Castes. Unpublished report. P.5. (Quoted in S.S.Jodhka: 2000: 393).

fully. According to the National Commission for Scheduled Castes and Scheduled Tribes, out of the 25 per cent only 9.23, 12.39, 9.56, and 14.38 per cent of seats have been filled in Groups A, B, C, and D, respectively, in Punjab (Louis, 2003). Again, in Punjab, the representation of the Dalits in reserved posts is comparatively better than other regions of India.

B.L. Abbi and Kesar Singh, in their empirical study of Barwali Khurd a village in Punjab, identify a process of identity formation among the Dalits.

> The famous Singh Sabha leader Giani Ditt Singh was a Weaver from the village Nandpur Kalaur about 20 kms away and a number of local Weaver men were in contact with him and influenced by his religious teachings. From among them, Mangal Singh was the first one to learn to read and write Gurmukhi. He was from one of an initial batch of teachers who after having been given some training in reading and teaching religious literature in Gurmukhi were sent by the Singh Sabha to impart religious instruction in the villages. Through his efforts a number of the village Weavers became literate in Gurmukhi. Mangal Singh and his group later started holding regular religious meetings and exhorting people to have a regular gurudwara established in the village. He later went away to Amritsar to become a *granthi* of the *Shiromani Gurdwara Parbandhak Committee* (SGPC). He got his son educated at Khalsa College Amritsar and also helped a number of village boys both Weaver and Jats to get educated at Amritsar. His son later qualified for the Punjab Civil Services and became the first one to become a Magistrate from this village... Later the Weavers built a Gurudwara in the village, the Jats would not cross the untouchability barrier to worship there. The Mazhabis were considered to be too low by the Weavers to extend them welcome... Following the setting up of a primary school in the village in 1957-58 an increasing number of Weaver girls also started attending the school... In this way, apart from taking up various skilled occupations, a number of Weavers came to have sufficient qualifications to take up teaching, clerical, military, administrative and professional jobs.
>
> (Abbi and Singh, 1997)

Land Ownership and Identity Formation

Moving from these sectors let us examine the level of land ownership among the different communities, the progress of land reforms and the results of these especially from the point of view of identity formation of the Dalits and the Sikhs. Nonica Datta states,

> Jats were not only regarded as an important community represent-ing the interests of the "agricultural classes" but whose interests

were safeguarded in the Punjab Land Alienation Act of 1901, the lynchpin of the imperial system. With the Jats emerging as stable agriculturists and soldiers, the British decided to establish a system of imperial patronage and control in rural southeast Punjab..... In addition, the Land Alienation Act of 1901, which sought to prevent sale of agricultural land from "agriculturalists" to "non-agricultur-alists", marked the peasant proprietors as members of one of the most important "agricultural tribes". One of its principal aims was to protect the "agricultural tribes" of "political importance, who were being displaced by the Bania". The 'agricultural identity of the Jats and other rural groups that developed in early twentieth century was rooted in this legislation.

(Datta, 1999)

In the same vein Sucha Singh Gill and R.S. Ghuman argue,

Several Acts were passed in Punjab and PEPSU between 1948 and 1955 as measures of land reforms. To be precise, seven major Acts in Punjab and six in PEPSU. The main objectives of these measures were to provide security to tenants, particularly the tenants-at-will, to abolish intermediaries between the state and the actual cultivators; to confer proprietary rights to occupancy tenants; to consolidate the fragmented holdings; to fix the upper ceiling on operational/owner-ship holdings and distribute surplus land among the tillers; and to fix and regulate rent on tenanted land. It may be pointed out that the Punjab area did not have any ceiling Act on ownership holdings till 1972, though ceiling on owned operational holdings came into force right from 1950.

(Gill and Ghuman, 2001)

In Punjab ceiling on ownership holdings of the individual was fixed at 17.5 acres for double crop irrigated land, 27 acres for irrigated one crop and 51 acres for dry land for a family of five. The limit was extendable by one-fifth for every additional family member to the maximum limit of three (beyond a family of eight, the exemption limit was not extendable).... Up to December 1994, the area declared sur-plus was 132,600 acres out of which 102,500 acres were distributed among 26,700 beneficiaries. The remaining area (30,100) was under litigation.... This position is however, questioned by several scholars. Land owners have bypassed the ceiling laws through manipulation of land records showing double cropped irrigated land as dry land, procuring fake age certificates of minor children and showing them as independent and separate cultivators, and through *benami* transfers ... the landlords used their political clout to influence revenue officials and the police and prolonged litigation to exhaust the poor tenants, exert pressure on the allottees for voluntary surrender or to ensure benami transfers. In some cases, violence has been resorted to, to get back possession of the land and secure benami transfers.... Only in few cases where landlords were weak, not well connected or illiterate, the land could be allotted and physical possession be given to poor cultivators.

(Singh and Ghuman, 2000)

Thus, it is argued here that if land reform policies were put into practice, the Dalits who are supposed to be the principal beneficiaries of land reform measures would have further improved their lot in rural Punjab.

A strong nexus between ruling class influential public men, bureaucrats, revenue officials, and police has been documented vividly in Punjab by the Harchand Singh Committee. This committee was set up by the Punjab Legislative Assembly in 1972 to enquire into the setting up of sizeable agricultural farms on evacuee lands by officers, their relatives, and other influential public men. The victims were those poor tenants who illegally occupied the *banjar* and *gairmumkin* lands and with their sweat converted them into fertile farms along the riverbeds. This land was transferred to the Government of Punjab by the Government of India, in April 1961. The modus operandi to dispose of this land adopted by the Government of Punjab was through open auction, in which anybody could participate, and restricted option in which only Scheduled Castes including government servants could participate at a reserved price set at 1961–1962 land prices. The committee pointed out that these prices were very low. In many cases, the auctions were just a formality. In fact, under the guise of auction, it was a "stage managed show" to help the officials and public men. It was an equal competition among unequals. In all, the committee investigated 126 cases involving ministers, ex-ministers, MPs, ex-MPs, MLAs, ex-MLAs, other public men, IAS officers, IPS officers, PCS officers, and other officers. Out of these, 61 have been cleared, mainly for observing the "laid down procedure", and 65 have been recommended for setting aside of the sales or such other action as is warranted by the circumstances. The committee observed,

These persons, men with means as they are, had an edge over the poor tillers, who could not mobilize requisite resources to compete with them. Even otherwise, they had the goodwill and patronage of the auctioning officers on their side. As a result, the poor and needy persons depending upon agriculture alone had been deprived of opportunity of purchasing these lands and such actual landless tillers of land as occupy the same, of course, unauthorisedly, had been uprooted. This was a tragic outcome of the policy of open auctions; it frustrated the cherished ideology of "land for the landless tillers". These are the officers and public men, who have taken law in their own hands; misuse their authority and influence and have occupied large areas by terrorizing the local population, forcibly evicting the existing tenants and occupants in collusion with the police and the field revenue staff.

As per the norms laid down by the Government of India, priority should be accorded in matters of distribution to the weaker sections of society, such as Scheduled Castes and the Scheduled Tribes. Since there is no Scheduled Tribe population in Punjab, priority has to be given to the Scheduled Castes in the assignment of land. The micro data indicates that of the total beneficiaries, only 38.24 per cent belong to the Scheduled Castes and of the total area, only 40.96 per cent has been allotted to them. This is a gross violation of the norms of allotment, as not even 50 per cent of the beneficiaries and allotted land are made in favour of the Scheduled Castes.

The implementation of land reforms measures, passed in Punjab and PEPSU in the 1950s, led to the initiation of the process of changes in land relations. The changes began to undermine the prevailing law resulting in self-cultivating peasants as the dominant producers in Punjab. The occupancy tenants became owners of land and tenants-at-will were largely ejected. But tenancy existed in a camouflaged manner, the landlords preventing the entry of tenant's name in the record for fear of losing land. The early completion of consolidation of land holdings by the Punjab government eradicated the problem of fragmentation to a great extent and, thereby, created the objective possibility of investment by individual farmers on land improvement and irrigation facilities. The massive state investment in canal irrigation, rural electrification, development of regulated marketing system, and other infrastructure facilities prepared the grounds for the quick adoption of green revolution technology when it became available in the mid-1960s (Singh and Ghuman, 2001).

The arrival of the green revolution in the state brought about major changes in the mode of cultivation. The production process became investment intensive. It required a large investment in fixed assets in the form of mechanical inputs and huge expenditure of working capital on crop inputs, such as fertilizers and other chemical inputs, new varieties of seeds, and fuel for operating mechanical inputs; at the same time, it increased the output manifold and farmers started producing a large quantity of marketable surpluses. Year after year, the cycle of production expanded and manifestation of capitalism in agriculture appeared on the scene. The capitalist farmers increasingly consolidated their position, though the poor peasants too registered some gains in their economic status. The persons who entered farming included former industrialists, moneylenders, civil servants, army officers, doctors, lawyers, and similar persons of high economic status and castes.

There are also studies which go over board and present a well-developed and well-distributed Punjab but fail to take into account many contradictions. For instance, Himmat Singh portrays the following picture:

There was a corresponding rise in real wages and incomes of both landowners and laboures. This was accompanied by the steady upgradation of the rural civic and educational infrastructure. By the late 1960s, Punjab, for example, had already implemented the land reforms, had furnished irrigation to the majority of its agricultural land and was in the process of linking all its villages with macadamized, all-weather roads. By the early 1970s it became the first state in India to have electricity available in all its villages. By 1980s rural Punjab had generated sufficient employment opportunities to attract migrant agricultural labourers from other parts of the country. Its own small farmers were developing into agrarian entrepreneurs subcontracting the cultivation of farms. Above all, rural Punjab had also become prosperous enough to finance the maintenance and expansion of its infrastructure.

(Singh, 2001)

Anyone who travels in rural Punjab would be overwhelmed by the progress made by many of the villages. But it would be far from the truth to claim that all the villages and all the social groups in these villages have benefitted in the same measure from development.

There are other social scientists who have tried to present the realistic picture of caste, class, and religious realities of Punjab. Among the Sikhs, the *langar*– the community kitchen – as an institution is meant to display the equality of all. In caste society, where the rules of purity and pollution combined with those of hierarchy govern the eating of food, the *langar* was a revolutionary institution. While the *langar* may grant symbolic equality, it is in no way capable of granting real or actual equality. To the "outside" world, the group can symbolically and actually present the "common interests" of its members: what this makes possible is the scope for hiding dissent within the community, from the view of outsiders, and hence not damaging the community in anyway. Community is thus Janus-faced; one face is presented to the outsider and the other to its own members; the public and the private face; the consensual face and its often contested idiosyncratic content (Kaur, 2001).

Further, while the green revolution and small-scale industries flourished in Punjab, economic development was not even in all the regions of Punjab. Once again it is the poor who in class terms are the landless agricultural class and in caste terms Dalits who are deprived of the benefits of economic development. Gopal Iyer and M.S. Manick, in their study of *Indebtedness, Impoverishment and Suicides in Rural Punjab*, argue that the percentage of rural families below the poverty line in Sangrur district was 45.65 per cent during 1991–1992. Of the total families below the poverty line the agricultural labourers constituted 71 per cent, marginal farmers 22 per cent, small farmers 2 per cent, and rural artisans 5 per cent (Table 9.5).

Table 9.5 Families living below poverty line in Sangrur District 1991–92

Sl. No.	Category	Number	% Below Poverty Line
1	Total rural population	1283,808	
2	Total rural families	2,56,762	
3	Number of families below poverty line		
	Up to Rs 4,000	51,009	19.87
	Rs 4,000 to Rs 8,500	41,817	17.45
	Rs 6,000 to Rs 8,500	13,925	5.42
	Rs 8,500 to Rs 11,000	7,467	2.91
	Total	1,17,218	45.65
	Classification of families below poverty line		
4	Small farmers	2,344	2.00
	Marginal farmers	25.787	22.00
	Agricultural labour	83,234	71.00
	Non-agricultural labour	0	0
	Rural artisans	5,863	5.00
	Others	0	0
	Total	1,17,218	1,000.00

Source: Additional Deputy Commissioner, Rural Development Agency, Sangrur.

Issues Raised in Talhan

As has been stated above, caste is not the main idiom of Punjab like other parts of India. But from the point of view of the Dalits, untouchability is practiced in some form or the other. Further, Sikhism is supposed to have been one of the liberative aspects in the lives of the Dalits of Punjab. The unprecedented economic development that unfolded in Punjab also provided enormous scope for Dalit identity formation and assertion. From this background one can identify some issues that are raised by the Talhan incident.

Casteism and untouchability that are widely practiced in other parts of India do not exist in its cruel form in Punjab. But prejudice against Dalits and the mindset that goes with the age-old caste system exist and operate here too. For an external observer everything seems to be normal but caste hatred is hidden beneath. This caste oppression shows its ugly head at different times. In the same vein, it needs to be stated that a careful reading into the Talhan incident reveals that unlike the past, at the present circumstances, injustice and atrocities cannot be perpetuated on the Dalits. They retort back and are ready to assert their rights and dignity. When the dominant castes do not tolerate resistance of the Dalits and downtrodden, conflict and violence becomes a common phenomenon.

Another sociologically pertinent issue is the imposition of a social boycott. Whether it is the Talhan incident or the Pankhan incident[7] imposing social boycott continues even today. This goes directly against the provisions made in the Scheduled Castes and Scheduled Tribes Prevention of Atrocities

Act 1955. The local and state administration pretends to be unaware of this practice. But now the dominant castes cannot adhere to this practice as Dalits resist it and engage in countering it with all their might. In this regard, as argued by Mr. Lahauri Ram Bali, the Talhan incident has hit the Jat pride in two senses: (a) due to the demand made by the Dalits for representation in the committee; (b) but more important than this is the fact that the Dalits challenged the social boycott imposed on them by the Jats. Hence, there was every chance of retaliation by the Jats. But since the Dalits were well mobilised and organised in the village and region, this could not be carried out.[8]

The Dalits' demand for representation in the *Smadh-Gurudwara Prbandak Committee* in a sense is a claim for equal share in the economic resources. But this claim does not stop there. It is also seeking equality with the Jats and other dominant castes of the region. The Dalits in general and the Ad-Dharmis in particular have slowly and steadily moved away from traditional occupations and agricultural sector. As landless agricultural labourers, their dependence on Jats was very high. But since they have diversified and have moved to other occupations, they are independent and thus can challenge the caste atrocities and the caste system itself.

Political parties tried to exploit the Talhan issue for electoral gains. It is reported that the BSP has been trying to continue the simmering to make the best out of the situation. The BJP attempted to communalise the issue between Sikhs and Hindus, that is, Jat Sikhs and Dalit Ad-Dharmis or Hindus. The Congress party, which was in power in the state, did not try to examine the issue in its totality and the government did not direct the administration to ease the tension and work out an amicable solution with the consent of all the groups, especially from the perspective of the victims, the Dalits. In the panchayat elections that commenced after the Talhan incident, it is reported that in some places the BSP candidates lost. This goes to state that the Dalits are not simply attracted by electoral politics. They have once again communicated the message to the mainline political parties as well as to Dalit political parties that their struggle for emancipation is the ultimate objective.

Sikhism is a compassionate religion. It also propagated equality and community sense. This was not limited to religious principles alone but found in day-to-day practices too. As stated by some people in Jalandhar, Sikhism itself had to face violence, but it continued to adhere to equality, compassion, and *bhaichara* (brotherhood). If this is true Talhan has raised the following questions: How could the followers of Sikhism engage in exclusion of the Dalits? Is this individual aberration or part of the social reality? If Sikhism is a religion that preaches and practices compassion, community living, collective enterprise, the demand of the Dalits seems to be genuine and this would result in "including the excluded".

A careful analysis of the religious traditions of Punjab unravels the fact that the Ad-Dharmis are closer to Sikhism than Hinduism. Based on the investigation conducted by us, it can be stated that Sangh Parivar is waiting in the wings to exploit the situation. And hence the Jat Sikhs and the Dalit Sikhs have to understand the impending threat posed by fascist forces and engage in dialogue and reconciliatory exercise. This exercise should be undertaken not only to ensure the common religious tradition, namely Sikhism, but to oppose every form of communal, fascist, and oppressive forces. Above all it is also to ensure equity and justice.

Finally, it needs to be stated that Dalit assertion has come to stay not only in the urban centres of Punjab but also in rural Punjab. As stated above, the demands of the Dalits are not limited to annihilation of caste system and the evil practice of untouchability. But the demand goes further and calls for restructuring the Indian social order where all the downtrodden masses would have equal share in resources, power structure, social dignity, and religious traditions. One has to wait and see if the political establishment of the dominant castes takes this assertion seriously or not. Whatever may be the response of the ruling castes and classes, Talhan has once again shown the way that only a long drawn out struggle would provide the space and scope for the Dalits to continue their struggle for building an egalitarian, democratic, plural society.

Notes

1 Published in *Social Action: A Quarterly Review of Social Trends* (October–December 2003).
2 The term "Dalit" is and has been defined exclusively and inclusively. There are some Dalits and non-Dalits, who under exclusive definition refer only to the Scheduled Castes or erstwhile untouchables. There is another group of Dalits and non-Dalits which include Scheduled Castes and Scheduled Tribes under the category Dalits. Thus, 160 million Scheduled Castes and 80 million Scheduled Tribes are at times clubbed together and called Dalits. This group of people at times in extension also includes all the exploited masses within the fold of Dalit. While the term Dalit is evolved by the Dalits as part of their identity formation, the term Scheduled Caste is an administrative term. In this paper the term Dalit has been used to refer to the Scheduled Castes or the untouchables.
3 Though they are locally called Ravidas Mandirs, their structure is more or less like Sikh Gurudwara. The only major difference is that beside the Sikh holy book, the Ad-Dharmis also keep a picture of Guru Ravidas. In the Talhan Gurudwara they also had a picture of B.R. Ambedkar inside the main hall.
4 The village also has a Mazhar of a Sufi Peer Baba Fateh Shah. Though there is no Muslim family currently living in the village, the Mazhar is well looked after by an aged Ad-Dharmi. An emigrant Jat Sikh from Talhan also organises a fair at the Mazhar every year on the 5th of June when he visits the village. No caste distinctions are practiced at the *mela*, which is more of a cultural festival than a religious affair and almost everyone from the village participates in it. Some reports have tended to confuse the Sufi shrine with the shrine of Baba Nihal Singh. The later was a Sikh and not a Sufi. Sufis are by faith generally Muslims.
5 The word Sahijdhari means slow adopters and was traditionally used for upper-caste Khatris and Aroras who believed in Sikhism but did not confirm to the Khalsa tradition of keeping five symbols of the Sikhs. The Kesadharis are the ones who grow their hair and tie turban. However, in practice these are much more contentious issues and has often troubled scholars and the community.

6 Dr Ambedkar disposing before the Minorities Sub-Committee in the First Round Table Conference and in the Second Round Table Conference demanded special representation to the Depressed Classes. In the memorandum it was further demanded that under-representation and over-representation should be rectified. Dr B.R. Ambedkar. *Writings and Speeches. Vol. 2*. Education Department: Government of Maharashtra, 1982, pp. 400–401.

7 Pankhan incident in brief refers to the murderous assault carried out by the dominant Rajput castes in Pankhan in Gujarat in November 1999. For more details refer to Prakash Louis, The Political Sociology of Dalit Atrocities in Gujarat. In *State, Development and Identity in South Asia: A Search for Alternative Paradigm*. Edited by Vashum and Prakash Louis. Indian Social Institute, 2002, pp. 38–48.

8 Interview was conducted among the members of Shahid Baba Nihal Singh Shrine Committee who are mainly from Jat Sikh community by Surinder Singh Jodhka and Prakash Louis in the month of June 2003 when the news of the clash between Jat Sikhs and Ad-Dharmis was flashed in the national daily. Interview was conducted among the Ad-Dharmis too to ascertain their side of the story. Based on the field visit notes and also historical records available about the caste system, changes in caste practices, religious practices in Punjab and Jalandhar, this chapter was prepared.

References

Abbi, B. L. & Singh, K. (1997). *Post Green Revolution Rural Punjab: A Profile of Economic and Socio-Cultural Change (1965–1995)*, Chandigarh: Centre for Research in Rural & Industrial Development.

Datta, N. (1999). *Forming an Identity: A Social History of Jats*, New Delhi: Oxford University Press.

Gill, S. S. & Singh, G. R. (2001). "Land Reforms in Punjab and Haryana: Trends and Issues", in Sucha Singh Gill (ed.), *Land Reforms in India*, New Delhi: Sage Publications.

Hershman, P. (1981). *Punjabi Kinship and Marriage*, Delhi: Hindustan Publishing Company.

Jodhka, S. S. (2000). "Prejudice without "Pollution"? Scheduled Castes in Contemporary Punjab", *Journal of Indian School of Political Economy*, Vol. 12, No. 3&4, Pp 381–403.

———. (2001). "Caste in the Periphery", Seminar, No. 508.

———. (2002). "Caste and Untouchability in Rural Punjab", *Economic and Political Weekly*, Vol. 37, No. 19, Pp 1813–1823.

Juergensmeyer, M. (1982). *Religion as Social Vision: The Movement against Untouchability in 20th Century Punjab*, Berkeley: University of California Press.

Kaur, R. (2001). "The Eclipse or the Renaissance of 'Community'? The Career of the Concept", in Surinder S. Jodhka (ed.), *Community & Identities: Contemporary Discourses on Culture and Politics in India*, New Delhi: Sage Publication.

Louis, P. (2003). "Scheduled Castes and Tribes: The Reservation Debate", *Economic and Political Weekly*, Vol. 38, No. 25. Pp 2475–2478

Puri, H. K. (2003). "Scheduled Castes in Sikh Community: A Historical Perspective", *Economic and Political Weekly*, Vol. 38, No. 26.

Singh, H. (2001). *Green Revolutions Reconsidered: The Rural World of Contemporary Punjab*, New Delhi: Oxford University Press.

10 Globalisation[1]

Assessing Impact on the Dalits in India

Anand Teltumbde

Introduction

Globalisation is a euphemism for the imperialist strategy of capitalism in crisis. It is implemented through the programmes of the IMF and World Bank, viz., microeconomic stabilisation and structural adjustment programmes in the countries that needed the assistance of these institutions to get over their financial crisis which was invariably the results of the exploitative strategies of their imperialist patrons. In the unipolar world hegemonised by the USA, globalisation has become a ruling creed, a veritable religion of the elites. Right from its adoption as new economic reforms by India some 12 years ago, it has been wreaking havoc on peasants, workers, and middle-class people. However, sometimes with arguments like 'There Is No Alternative' (TINA), or sometimes by pointing at the glitter of "foreign goods" being freely available in shops or the spate of foreign cars running on the newly constructed flyovers as a proxy for development, or asking the counter questions like, 'what good did the forty years of 'Licence Raj' do to the poor?' the protagonists of globalisation confused the masses. Some people did present its gruesome impact, but either it was ignored as leftist prejudice or got drowned in the cacophonic din of the lies issued from Washington and amplified by the entire elite sponsored by the establishment in Delhi.

Even the well-meaning analyses of the impacts of globalisation expectedly either completely ignored or just passingly touched the Dalits who along with the Adivasis constitute more than one-fourth of the Indian population. And when inevitably even some Dalit intellectuals took up the analyses most of them just superficially hovered around its impact on reservations. Some even took a pro-establishment position supporting globalisation and spread confusion among the Dalit masses. They held that it was suicidal for the Dalits to oppose globalisation and even fraudulently invoked Ambedkar in support of their contention.

This chapter seeks to present a framework to assess the impact of globalisation on the Dalits. It is premised on the fact that while the Dalits are an integral part of the poor they are also an oppressed people unlike any other anywhere. The first section thus presents the devastation caused by globalisation to the poor in India using the latest available data while the second

DOI: 10.4324/9781003317173-14

section deals with them as socially oppressed people in two parts, viz., the first with their current mode of living and the second with their long-term project of emancipation. It concludes by summing up how badly globalisation has impacted Dalits in every aspect of their living and how if persisted with it will lead to their extinction. The remedy suggested is in terms of a broad-based anti-globalisation struggle which alone can shelter specific Dalit interests as well as accomplish their emancipation.

Impact on the Dalits as Poor

Since the entire argument of globalisation with respect to poor is based on the "trickle down" effect, it is admittedly not oriented to benefit the poor. But far from this trickle materialising, the trail of its operation has left behind calamitous consequences to poor people all over the world. Contrary to its fond claims about boosting economic growth, during its operation over the last two decades growth has been falling in about 100 countries, reducing incomes of about two billion people. The declines are unprecedented, exceeding in duration and depth of the Great Depression of the 1930s. One billion people, 30% of the world's workforce, are either jobless or unemployed. Even in the imperialist countries 100 million people live below the poverty line, 30 million are unemployed and more than 5 million are homeless.[2] One can see approximately a similar negative impact on the Indian economy during the globalisation decade. As shown in Table 10.1, except for the marginally positive growth in GDP on every other developmental parameter, the impact has been clearly negative.

In India the ill effects of globalisation surfaced soon after its launch through the results of the 53 rounds of the National Sample Survey (NSS).

Table 10.1 General comparison of pre- and post-globalization periods

	Decades of 1980s	*Decades of 1990s*
GDP growth rate	5.6%	5.9%
Growth rate of commodity production	5.0%	4.3%
Growth rate of agricultural production	3.84%	1.24%
Growth rate of food grain production	3.46%	1.22%
Increase in employment in organised sector over the decade	16.8%	5.8%
Growth rate of industry	7.7%	5.8%
Rate of capital formation	7.3%	4.2%
Growth of electricity generation	12.4%	3.5%
Growth of imports per annum	4.5%	8.0%
Growth of exports per annum	8.3%	8.4%
Drop in value of the rupee vis-à-vis US dollar	Rs. 10 drop	Rs. 30 drop

Source: Calculated from various figures in Economic Survey of various years.

Globalisation had reversed the decades-long declining trend of poverty (Teltumbde, 2000). Prof. S. P. Gupta estimated that the poverty figures for the rural area had gone up to 43.0% in 1998 from 34.39% in 1990 while that for the urban areas remained the same at around 35%[3] (Gupta, 2000). Many surveys and studies independently corroborated the significant rise in poverty figures after the launch of globalisation.[4] However, while releasing the results of the 55th round of the NSS the government suddenly started claiming a ridiculous fall in poverty figures ostensibly to counter the rising anti-globalisation sentiment prompted by this evidence. It fraudulently claimed a drop in the poverty figures to less than half from 37.09% in 1993/94 to 18% in 2001–2002. It took a while for the experts to know that the methodology of the survey was mysteriously changed (RUPE (30&31), 2001). The government may have succeeded in confounding the poverty issue among the experts, but the fact could not be hidden that poverty rose substantially during the globalisation decade. The government's own statistics on employment and food intake – the other indicators of poverty as well as the hard facts of starvation deaths reported from all over the country – cry out this truth. It is interesting to note that the World Bank puts the poverty figures at 44.2% on its criteria of income below $1 per day and 86.2% below $2 per day (World Bank, 2002)! Table 10.2 presents the comparative picture of the incidence of poverty among various categories of households of the SCs, STs, and others to highlight the miserable condition of the Dalits.

Poverty is the cumulative result of deprivation on many counts. As for the rural population, the declining public investment in agriculture, trade liberalisation in many agricultural products, declining rural employment, a sharp rise in prices of food items, and the government's abdication of the responsibility to provide food security to people by performing "funeral rites of the Public Distribution System" (PDS), all under the dictates of globalisation, have been mainly responsible for the increase in poverty.

Table 10.2 Persons below poverty lines, 1993–1994 – All India [%]

Sl. No.	Household type	ST	SC	OBC	All
1.	Self-employment in agriculture household	47.12	37.71	25.57	29.04
2.	Self-employment in non-agriculture household	44.70	33.14	29.49	31.95
3.	Agriculture labour household	63.83	60.00	52.64	56.78
4.	Other labour household	51.69	41.44	35.59	39.59
5.	Other household	31.39	29.65	20.19	22.47
6.	All household	52.17	48.14	31.29	37.09

Other: Non-Scheduled Tribes/Scheduled Castes
Source: National Sample Survey on Consumption Expenditure.

Agriculture growth has fluctuated touching deep troughs in recent years, from 5.0% in 1994–1995 to a negative 0.9% the following year and then to a positive growth of 9.6% in 1996–1997 and again a negative 1.9% in 1997–1998. It became positive in 1998–1999 at 7.2% but fell to 0.8% in 1999–2000. It can be mainly attributed to the sharp decline in investment in agriculture as shown in Table 10.3, from the level of 2.2% of GDP at the base year 1990–1991 to as low as 1.4% of GDP in 1998–1999. Food grain production is on the decline, and the IFPRI report warned that India could have cereal deficits of 36 to 64 million tonnes a year by 2020 (IFPR1, 2001). A recent study of Utsa Patnaik pointed out that the per capita availability of food grains for human consumption has fallen substantially during the last decade of reforms, and that the maximum decline has taken place during 1998–1999 to 2000-2001, because of the aggressive pursuits of the NDA government of income-deflating policies for masses as ordained by the globalisation package (Patnaik, 2001).

The price rise of food grains owing to cuts in food and fertiliser subsidies and consequent adjustments have particularly been harsh. In the preceding decade of the Reform the per annum price of rice had risen by 7% and that of wheat by 3.3%. But in the next four years of the Reform period, they registered a rise of 13.5% and 18.1% respectively. Other food grains also behaved approximately in a similar fashion. The price-rise for pulses has been 97.2%: that for vegetables 163.4%, for fruits 74%, and for eggs, meat, and fish group 102.5% (Teltumbde, 2000).

The free market ethos of globalisation also indirectly but significantly contributed to the price rise. In a single year between 1999 and 2000 the food prices doubled (Shiva, 2000). As a result, the per capita consumption of food grains has declined from 510 grams in 1991 to 458 grams in 2000. The National Family Health Survey (NFHS) (1998–1999) estimates that 47% of children below five were malnourished: similarly a study by the Indian Council for Medical Research and the Institute of Population Studies estimates that 53% of children in that age group are moderately or severely undernourished. The NFHS also estimates that anaemia affected 82.4% of pregnant women. It is under such conditions that the food subsidy is slashed! The Prime Minister almost did a Marie Antoinette advising peasants on 6 March 2001 that they should "Look beyond wheat and paddy and instead

Table 10.3 Investment in agriculture as a percentage of GDP

Year	Public	Private	Total
1990–1991	0.6	1.6	2.2
1996–1997	0.4	1.1	1.5
1997–1998	0.3	1.1	1.4
1998–1999	0.3	1.1	1.4

grow fruits, flowers, oilseeds and vegetables that offer remunerative production and have a good export potential".

In the name of global competitiveness, globalisation has directly impacted employment as reflected in the fall in employment elasticities in all the sectors of the economy as shown in Table 10.4. Scores of industrial workers have been thrown on roads due to downsizing and closures of industries. The latest report of the Union Commerce Ministry reveals that till the year 1999, in the public sector alone around 133,376 workers were retrenched in Voluntary Retirement Scheme (VRS). In the private sector the situation is still worse. The increasing incidence of industrial sickness and closures in both traditional and modern industries results in a massive loss of employment. Already over 250,000 sick or closed small-scale units in the country have thrown some 3 to 4 million workers on roads.

The flexible and lean firm is seen as best adapted to meet rapid changes in product markets. The trend is towards "variabalising' fixed costs and therefore increasingly resorting to casualisation, subcontracting, or body shopping of labour. The numbers of part-time workers, seasonal workers, home workers, and subcontracted workers are growing in leaps and bounds all over the world (Klerck, 1999). Table 10.5 presents the employment rates for males in various categories of employment, which clearly highlights the sharp decline in every category during the globalisation period.

The helplessness of the workers is reflected in the wage squeeze in recent years. In India during the 1990s, wages as a percentage of net sales of the private corporate sector declined from 6.0% in 1991–1992 to 5.2% in 1997–1998 (CMIE, 1999) The weakness of labour's bargaining power can be gauged from the ratio of man-days lost as a result of strikes to that due to lockouts. It has been consistently falling during the globalisation period,

Table 10.4 Sector-wide estimated employment elasticities[a] – All India

Period	1977/78–1983	1983–1993/94[b]	1993/94–1999/2000
Agriculture	0.45	0.50	0.00
Mining +quarrying	0.80	0.69	0.00
Manufacturing	0.67	0.33	0.26
Electricity, gas, water	0.73	0.52	0.00
Construction	1.00	1.00	1.00
Trade	0.78	0.63	0.55
Transport and storage	1.00	0.49	0.69
Financial services	1.00	0.92	0.73
Community, social, and personal services	0.83	0.50	0.07
Total	0.53	0.41	0.15

Sources: Planning Commission, 2001.
[a]Implicit elasticity based on 6.5% GDP growth.
[b]This period combines the two NSSO periods 1993 to 1987–1988 and 1987–1988 to 1993–1994.

Table 10.5 Employment rate for males (% of employed in total population) – All India

Years	Scheduled Caste				Others (non-SC/ST)			
	UPS	UPSS	CW	CD	UPS	UPSS	CW	CD
1977–1978	63.50	NA	56.15	52.50	56.05	NA	55.42	53.61
1983–1984	62.24	64	54.24	50.14	56.96	58.20	56.19	53.93
1993–1994	54.90	52.90	52.30	51.60	54.00	54.50	54.10	53.40
1999–2000	52.90	50.30	48.60	45.80	51.40	51.80	51.30	49.90

Source: National Sample Survey, 1977–1978, 1983–1984, 1993–1994, 1999–2000.
Abbreviations:
UPS: Usual principal status
UPSS: Usual principal and subsidiary status
CW: Current weekly status
CD: Current daily status

but in recent years the fall has been drastic. This ratio, which was 0.74 in 1998, fell to 0.65 in 1999 and further to 0.25 in the first nine months of 2000 (RUPE (30&31), 2001b). The rural employment growth fell to an alarming 0.67% during 1993–1994 to 1999–2000; urban employment growth fell equally sharply to 1.34% over the same period. These arcs are far below the annual growth of the population of the job seekers, thus causing huge unemployment year by year (RUPE (30&31), 2001a).

The pro-rich bias of globalisation has aggravated the existing inequality world over. In India, the data on consumption expenditure showed that the share of the bottom 30% people, which was growing consistently from 1987–1988 up to 1990–1991, both in rural and in urban areas, had a sudden reversal soon after the Reforms were launched. The share of the middle 40% population also dwindled in the same manner in both rural and urban areas. The loss of these 70% population appears to have benefitted the top 30% of the population. Their share for the pre-Reform period was on a consistent decline, which has suddenly jumped up in the Reform period.

Thus, each micro move of globalisation can be discerned to be directly hurting poor people. Dalits being the most vulnerable even among the poor, they are naturally being hit the hardest.

Impact on the Dalits as Socially Oppressed People

The impact of globalisation on Dalits as socially excluded people can be conceived in two domains: one, the constitutional space that signifies the current mode of their specific existence; and two, the long-term project of their emancipation.

The Constitutional Space for Dalits

The constitutional space for the Dalits comprises mainly the provision of reservations in the state-aided educational institutions and in the employment of government and public sector companies. Despite the dismal record of their implementation, there is no doubt that these provisions have played a crucial role in the advancement and progress of Dalits. Globalisation has variously constricted this space and as a result without any actual change in the Constitution has brought reservations to an end.

Reservation in Education

During the globalisation period the government appointed two committees: one, the Punnayya Committee (1993) that looked into funding of central universities to recommend how education, especially higher education, should be financed; and two, the Swaminathan Committee (1994) which looked into possibilities of resource mobilisation in technical education essentially through "cost recovery" from students. The latest in the series of policy recommendations is the Birla-Ambani report on the Policy Framework for Reforms in Education (April 2000) which, while casting the obligation of providing primary education on the government, advocated privatisation and total marketisation of higher education including the influx of foreign direct investment in it. It proposed the market for private credit under the alibi of providing financial assistance to needy students. It is interesting to see how the recommendations of these diverse committees confirm the World Bank document "Higher Education: The Lessons of Experience" (1994), which holds that eventually the role of government should be limited to providing primary education.

The thrust of the change can be discerned in terms confining the government's role to literacy so that people do not fall out of the market net (as illiterate they would not be able to read the advertisements!) and get higher education entirely in the private domain for a select few who can afford its "commercial" costs. The increasing cost of education, on one hand, and the drying up of the motivation for education because of no job prospects created by globalisation, on the other, are fast proving that reservation in education meaningless. In addition the generally pervading ethos of globalisation has marginalised the discourse of reservation. The recent court judgements removing the reservation to SCs and STs in minority-run educational institutions can be a good example of this trend. Globalisation has created a neo-caste divide in education which is pushing them back into the dark times. It is going to effectively shut the doors of education to Dalits as they were in the reign of Manu.

The impact of this trend is seen in an alarming rate of school dropouts among the Dalits. This may be explained by the need for Dalit children to supplement their falling family incomes as also by the erosion of the faith that education could be the instrument to change the pathetic course of their lives. With primary education itself becoming an insurmountable barrier and higher education becoming a virtual taboo, Dalits are getting literally left out of the educational arena. The impetus that privatisation and commercialisation of education received during the globalisation period is literally pushing education out of the public sphere and thereby neutralising the constitutional provisions for the Dalits. Left out of education, the only future that could be in wait for them is alienation, lumpenisation, and criminalisation.

Reservations in Services

The winds of privatisation within the globalisation package have already shaken the very foundations of reservations. Even without the actual privatisation of the PSUs, the kind of ethos it unleashed in the PSU managements under the plea to prepare themselves for competition in a free market regime has been grossly oppressive to the Dalit employees. Many of these companies have restructured themselves with the help of American consultancy firms whose half-baked wisdom would not care for the externality like positive discrimination in favour of the Dalits. This restructuring has given managements a field day in operating their pent-up prejudices against Dalit employees as evidenced by a sudden spurt in the cases of departmental actions against and dismissals of Dalit employees during this period,

Without resorting to the outright sale of the PSUs, the government initially tried out an indirect method of privatisation by allowing these PSUs to form joint venture companies in the private sector by offering its private partner 51% equity. As such, during the first half of the last decade, many profit-making PSUs had formed such joint venture companies (JVC) in the private sector. Theoretically, an existing PSU could hive off its business divisions into private JVCs and transform itself into a financial holding company with a Board of Directors and skeleton staff and effectively stave off the Dalit menace! Unfortunately for the companies this vile experiment of JVC has been a grand failure. It called the bluff of the management that the PSU framework shackled their "competence" and the infusion of Dalits weakened their "merit". It also conclusively proved the protagonists of the private sector wrong.

Having consolidated its fascist hold on the state, now the government has resorted to total sale of the PSUs through a separate ministry. Already Modern Bread, Balco, CMC, VSNL, IPCL, and ITDC Hotels have been privatised. The schedule for the sale of the balance saleable PSU companies is already announced. Notwithstanding the gross irrationality of the process and false arguments in favour of privatisation, it is certain that these companies shall be sold off and the Dalit employees there be got rid of in the course. In the government sector also a similar trend of downsizing by various means, outsourcing, and a freeze on recruitment is being followed in order to adhere to the "minimalist state" dictum of globalisation.

Reservations in services relate to the larger question of employment. If there is more employment than job seekers, there will not be any necessity for reservation. What does globalisation entail in terms of generating employment? Notwithstanding the protagonists' apologetic claims that globalisation will create huge job opportunities in the service sector (away from the traditional manufacturing sector), the answer is obviously dismal, as the vast empirical data all over the world would testify.

Project of Dalit Emancipation

The project of Dalit emancipation could be mapped for the purpose of assessment by the four empowerments: viz., economic empowerment_ personal empowerment, sociopolitical empowerment, and sociocultural empowerment, which in turn could be broadly linked to the issues of land reform, education, democracy, and modernity respectively.

Economic Empowerment – Land Reform

The economic dimension of the caste question is intimately connected with land reforms. Over 81% of Dalits still live in rural areas, of whom about 50% are landless labourers and about 25% are cultivators with marginal farms. The dependency relationship of Dalits with the upper caste has been a significant factor in shoring up the economic basis of caste. As only the land reforms could feasibly break this relationship, they constituted a progressive agenda all through the post-independence years. Globalisation has not only eclipsed this agenda of land reforms but also substituted it with the corporatisation of farming for the global agricultural market. Globalisation goes beyond the skewed distribution of land among people and rather takes advantage of it to consolidate farms for capitalist agriculture. Globalisation has undone the ceiling on land holdings in state after state to allow corporate super farms for luxury production for international markets (Shiva, 2000).

The policy thrust of the World bank–IMF–WTO combine has always been clear for the abolition of the land ceiling laws and for liberalising investment into agriculture. For example, Karnataka was one of the first states to amend its Land Reforms Act (1961) that aimed at removing the land ceiling for aquaculture in the Uttara Kannada and Dakshin Kannada districts and also for the horticulture, floriculture, and agro-based industries. Despite the massive protests it met from Karnataka Farmers Union – the Karnataka Rajya Ryota Sangha (KRSS) who have been spearheading the movement against the entry of multinational corporations in agriculture, one finds the corporatisation process going ahead unabatedly. A massive displacement of farmers from their land is taking place and creating an explosive situation, socially as well as politically. Food-growing land is being diverted to non-food crops such as flowers or luxury commodities such as shrimp.[5,6] Corporatisation of agriculture, which is being pushed under trade liberalisation as a successor of the Green Revolution, is leading to new poverty for small farmers as unequal and unfair contracts lock them into new forms of bondage

The globalisation agenda is systematically driving against family farming as in vogue today. It is driving towards the integration of Indian agriculture into the global agri-market and consequently towards its corporatisation. It has decidedly erased the agenda of land reforms and thereby removed the very basis of any radical movement against caste.

Personal Empowerment – Education

Education is another vital factor in the emancipation project of Dalits as reflected in all their movements. Mahatma Phule, for instance, had attributed the miserable plight of the Shudras and Ati-Shudras (Dalits) to the denial of education to them by Brahmins and had therefore opened schools for them. Every other leader who championed the cause of Dalits has stressed the importance of education. Babasaheb Ambedkar placed education foremost in his agenda, as his mantra – educate, organise, and agitate – reflects. As a result of these reform movements and particularly because of Ambedkar's role model, many Dalits took to education as a key to their emancipation and made some progress during the post-independence decades.

Education is a comprehensive instrumentality in the emancipation project: its role in providing individual and social competencies is much bigger than as a means of economic production. Fundamentally this paradigm is negated under globalisation, which has given impetus to "human capital" discourse that measures the education system exclusively in economic terms particularly in responding to market needs. This discourse is fraught with several implicit dangers not only to Dalits but also to the overall constitution of civil society. As for Dalits, it totally demolishes the extra-market rationale for giving them preferential access to and certain concessions in education.

As discussed above, the new Policy Framework for Reforms in Education, drafted by a committee convened by Mukesh Ambani with the likes of Kumarmangalam Birla as members, stands as a glaring example of globalisation in education. It seeks to drive privatisation and introduce rampant commercialisation of higher education along the lines of the USA. It envisages foreign direct investment in education, progressive reduction of government funding for universities and making them adopt the route of self-sufficiency, and concurrent development of a credit market for private finance to meet the cost of higher education. The latter is a clear smoke screen to diffuse its elitist intentions: as everyone knows that more than half the population of this country are just not creditworthy. Higher education, thus, is to be entirely market oriented and clearly (out of the bounds of the commoners. not to talk of Dalits. The framework has clearly advocated literacy' for the masses and education for the classes.

During the past decade of globalisation, we can clearly see the impact in terms of far more elitist orientation in education than ever before. In accordance with one of the globalisation virtues, the State in the attempt to contain its fiscal deficit has been throttling its funding to education. As a result, some elite institutions that had demand in the education market have increased their fees to be self-supporting. Many foreign universities have tied up their programmes with the Indian universities and denominated their fees in dollars: many new schools and colleges have opened up on a pay basis; new tribe of brokers that mediated in educational transactions have cropped up in this mega-business.

Already this trend has created a permanent divide between urban and rural areas, the latter having been totally excluded from education of any consequence. The commercial ethos that entered the education field through globalisation has further created a divide between haves and have-nots. The pay seats in educational institutions have fortified the class basis of education. Dalits who have been barely able to afford schooling with the aid of free ship and scholarship are squeezed out from both ends. Firstly, education has become increasingly inaccessible and unaffordable to them. Even if they persist with it, they have to face several hurdles on the way to get education that would get them gainful employment. The increasing opportunity cost of schooling is dissuading many Dalits from education resulting into increasing numbers of dropouts. Even if they crossed all the hurdles as an exception, they would face a far bigger hurdle in the job market that tended to value one's family background more than your scholastic performance. Economic globalisation has brought in a fundamental change in the composition of the job market. The manufacturing sector that valued formal educational inputs has been shrinking whereas the service sector that required such attributes as one's looks, mannerisms, "communication", connections, and relationships that could be summed up as one's class attributes did not value educational qualification. This class divide cannot be easily crossed by Dalits. Globalisation has thus raised a neo-caste barrier for Dalits that may be far more difficult to cross than that of even Manu!

Political Empowerment – Democracy

The importance of democracy as a value in the emancipation project of Dalits cannot be overemphasised. Whatever hue it comes with, democracy provides some space for weak people to voice their concerns. It is the framework within which the agitations can germinate, movements can be launched, and struggles can be waged. It may not be an exaggeration to say that the western liberal democratic ethos that pervaded the colonial rule has greatly facilitated the Dalit movement.

The consequences of globalisation to democracy are not far to seek: they are evident in the manner in which it was imposed on the people. Globalisation has never been a democratic choice of the people anywhere. The imperatives of globalisation have been business driven, by business strategies and for business ends. Governments have helped them by policy actions that were often taken in secret, without national debate and discussion (Herman, 1999). The manner in which globalisation was introduced in India in the garb of economic reforms, without any discussion in the parliament or with people, stands testimony to this fact. The intrinsic anti-democratic content of globalisation thus surfaces right from its birth.

The source philosophy of globalisation – neoliberalism – negates democracy in its advocacy of social Darwinism. Its "free market" grants more value to a moneyed person and thus is against the dictum of democracy of one person, one value. Democracy assumes community and existence of pluralist groups, but neoliberalism dismisses them and atomises population into discrete self-seeking individuals. This conception clearly favours business because it eliminates the concept of collective and thereby emasculates labour.

Democracy was built on the nation state. Globalisation seeks to remove power from the nation-state and puts it in the global arena thus crippling the nation-state in meeting the democratic aspirations of its people. Today we experience that year-by-year over the last couple of decades the reality of democracy is being weakened despite the loud talk of its glory.

The WTO, the IMF, and World Bank – the three most important international economic institutions that are the propellers of globalisation and are often described as "institutions of global governance" – are essentially unaccountable to any electorate, Indeed one does not need a conspiracy theory to notice the progressive removal of economic decision making from governments to unelected (and for most countries. foreign) officials. For much of the world, this is the face of globalisation that intrudes into civil society. The free market ethos of globalisation conceptually can neither confirm to the democratic spirit of the Indian Constitution nor can it coexist with the system of positive discrimination in favour of the Dalits.

The erosion of democracy under globalisation spells blockade of the very emancipation discourse of oppressed people like the Dalits. With powerful surveillance technologies at their disposal, they can nip any such attempts in the bud.

Sociocultural Empowerment-Modernity

Globalisation being the spread and intensification of capitalist relations, one expected that it would promote modernity, weaken the caste-feudalism, and thereby be beneficial to the Dalits in sociocultural terms. This argument pretending to possess theoretical propriety inevitably turns out as naïve in the context of historical experience with which capitalism not only did not dent the castes but also made skilful use of them in dividing the labour.

The phenomenon of the emergence of religious fundamentalism in many countries and particularly in our country in the era of globalisation is not a chance to happen. It is the imperative of globalisation that a large multitude of masses is held in conformist mode by whatever means. There are no potent and economical means as a religion for the purpose. The rise of Hindutva forces, demolition of Babri masjid, review of constitution, denigration and harassment of minorities, saffronisation of education, and generally communalisation of polity are not to be taken as unconnected events. They are very much complementary to globalisation. The events, if seen in totality, show the deeper linkage and chronological order between the decline of state-controlled economies, intensification of adverse effects of globalisation, the rise of America as the lone superpower of the world, decline of the authority of the United Nations, decline of the Non-Aligned Movement, and rise of fascist fundamentalist politics in our own country (Puniyani, 2001).

Not only in India but also all over the world neo-fascism and neo-Nazism are gaining ground. Glele-Ahanhanzo noted in a recent report to the U.N. General Assembly that the power of the extreme right-wing parties, which are thriving in an economic and social climate characterised by fear and despair, was on increase. Among the key factors fuelling the far-right reaction, according to the U.N. report, are "the combined effects of globalisation, identity crises and social exclusion. Where local traditions lose influence: individuals tend to become atomised psychologically and thus more susceptible to the lure of ultra-nationalists who manipulate deep-seated anxieties" (Lee, 1999). The upsurge of fundamentalist, obscurantist, and fascist tendencies world over is thus occasioned by globalisation.

There is no scope even to speculate that globalisation would entail the spread of modernity in society so as to bury castes. On the contrary, there is a good deal of evidence of caste discrimination getting accentuated during the globalisation period. The caste atrocities that best represent this menace show a significant rise during the globalisation period as compared to the pre-globalisation period as shown in Table 10.6.

The menace of Hindutva represents blatant anti-modernity and the worst kind of revivalism. It seeks to bring in the old obscurantist values that cannot exclude the code of Manu. Although the Hindutva project so far has not branded Dalits as their "other" like Muslims and rather co-opted them as their cannon fodder against these religious minorities as in the recent Gujarat carnage, it certainly expects them to abide by the "great" tenets of Hindu tradition. Insofar as there is an irreconcilable contradiction between the Hindu traditions and the Dalit aspirations, the Hindutva project shall mean the negation of the emancipation of the Dalits. Not only that it neutralises whatever progress Dalits made in challenging the system of caste exploitation but it also holds forth the horrific prospects of inhuman oppression that their ancestors lived. The "journey in reverse gear" that we observe in every field is going to be detrimental to Dalits and the minority community.

Table 10.6 Average number of atrocities per annum on the Dalits during the pre-Reform and the post-Reform years

Year	Murders Injury POA	Serious under	Rape	Arson	Others	Crime	Total
Pre-Reform Years 1981–1986	523.17	1416.8	666.3	1046.3	11530.1	10057.6	25237.3
Post-Reform Years 1995–1997	539.3	4197.0	929.3	449.3	12356.3	10458.7	28929.9
% increase during Reform-years over the pre-Reform Years	3.1	196.1	39.5	-57.1	7.2	4.0	14.6

Source: Computed from the figures from the reports of National Commission for SCs and STs.

Conclusion

Globalisation, an agenda of capitalism in crisis, driven by imperialist institutions like IMF, World Bank, and WTO along with the ideology of neo-liberalism, has essentially a pro-rich bias. Wherever they were implemented, they have worsened the situation of masses of poor people in absolute as well as in relative terms. Globalisation, contrary to the claims of its protagonists, has been a total failure even in generating growth or increasing productivity. It did not have anything to say about poor people except for its "trickle down" theory. Nowhere this trickle has materialised. On the contrary, it has created an unprecedented amount of inequality in every possible sphere. It has been a social disaster, an environmental disaster and a threat to the stability of the world. The claim of its proponents that free trade with private enterprise is the route to economic growth is also confuted by longer historic experience. No country, past or present, has taken off into sustained economic growth and moved from economic backwardness to modernity without large-scale government protection and subsidisation of infant industries and other modes of insulation from domination by powerful outsiders.

In India too all the ill effects of globalisation were experienced by the poor people in terms of inflation, deindustrialisation, casualisation of labour, unemployment, worsening food security, gnawing inequality, depeasantisation, destruction of environment and agriculture, suppression of democratic rights, pollution of culture, and, most importantly, its indigenous fallout in terms of fascist, fundamentalist, communalist, and obscurantist programme of Hindutva. Since the impact of all these is to be borne in direct proportion of the poverty and deprivation, the Dalits are naturally hit by globalisation the hardest. In addition to this impact they have to carry the burden of their identity as socially oppressed people. The Constitution of India had certain mitigating measures but globalisation has severally neutralised them and exposed the Dalits to brute market forces. It has similarly demolished their aspirations for emancipation.

Notwithstanding the contrary evidence even on the growth premise (compared to an overall average of 2.04% before reforms (1983–1994) the annual growth rate was a mere 0.98% in 1994–2000), the government has launched the second generation of reforms which are nothing but intensification of the globalisation-ordained policies. People have already experienced the back-breaking impact of its milder version; the devastation in store for them in future can only be imagined!

The government is sanguine with the grace of its global masters. It is totally oblivious to the people's plight. It does not understand that it is people who eventually constitute market, whether free or otherwise. And the market requires widespread purchasing power. It follows that the government should aim at empowering the masses and enhancing their capability. It should take effective measures for accelerated development of the disadvantaged sections like the Dalits. The pre-requisite for even the "free market"–oriented reforms comes out to be the radical land reforms, massive investments in rural areas into agriculture-related infrastructural projects, universalisation of primary education, primary health care system, reinforcement of positive discrimination in favour of the Dalits in all sectors of the economy, etc. The devil of casteism could be tamed only by freeing the general masses of the people from the anxieties and uncertainties about basic survival. The general condition of deprivation has rendered them vulnerable to be the preys to the frequent machinations of vested interests that make them see the enemy within their own class. The relative equality thus can be the bedrock for launching the sociocultural offensive in the form of mass-education programmes. But, surprisingly globalisation is opposed to every bit of this logical programme for sustainability.

What then could be the way out for the Dalits? At the beginning of this year, a group of Dalit intellectuals and activists, mediated by the government of Madhya Pradesh, worked out a charter called Bhopal Agenda demanding notably an all-encompassing reservation. Notwithstanding the political dynamics behind the move, this charter can well serve as a catalyst to germinate movements against globalisation. It will be naïve, however, to think that without such a movement, the demands in the charter can be won with mere political parleys. Globalisation did well to clearly show that the Dalit future is intertwined with that of general poor; the piecemeal and sectarian approach of any kind would not work. The Dalits had better learnt that castes can never be annihilated by caste organisations. Even for the positive discrimination in their favour, the Dalits will need to unite with others in a common struggle against imperialism. It is not the state but people who are their ultimate ally: it is only the united struggle that can conscentise people, cleanse society of the evils like caste, and accomplish Dalit project of emancipation.

Notes

1 Published in *Social Action: A Quarterly Review of Social Trends* (January–March 2003).
2 Figures are from the World Development Report. Oxford University Press. 1996 and The Human Development Report, Oxford University Report. 1996.
3 In addition to the reference to S. P. Gupta's estimates, the aggravation of poverty during globalisation period is well discussed by Mohan Guru Swamy in his "Life above poverty line: Rs. 264 per month is all you need", October 26, 2002.
4 http://www.tehelka.com/channelsicurrentaffairs/2001 ioct/30/cal030011ibl.htm. Also. see Alternative Economic Survey 2000-01.
5 A paper on 'Globalisation and Agriculture in India' by Dr Vandana Shiva. Ms Radha Holla and Ms Kusum Menon cited in "Globalisation of agriculture and rising food insecurity". Third World Network. http://www.twnside.org.sgititle! food -en.htm.
6 Same as 4 above.

References

Gupta, S. P. (2000). "Trickle Down Theory Revisited: The Role of Employment and Poverty", *Indian Journal of Labour Economics*, Vol. 43, No. 1, Pp 25–34.

Herman, E. S. (1999). "The Threat of Globalization", *New Politics*, Vol. 7, No. 2 (new series), whole No. 26, Winter 1999.

IIFPRI. (2001). "IFPRL: 2020: Gloomy Outlook for Malnourished Children", *New Report Projects Slowing Progress against World Hunger*. Washington, DC, 28 August 2001, littp:J',.srd.yahoo.coni/goo/%22International+Food+Poliey+Research+Institute%22°''02b2020%2bindia/4/T=1011371526/F=d9d141a12ede609f2 7e794ec5e2a603th* http://www.futureharvestorg/health/impact_release.shtml

Klerck, O. (1999). Casual Labour (draft paper) cited in Iauch. Herbert. Globalisation and Employment: New Opportunities or Continued Marginalization? Labour Resource and Research Institute. Presentation at a Panel Discussion of the Namibia Economic society, Windhoek, 7 March 2000.

Lee, A. Martin. (1999). "Fascism and Globalization: The World/Europe; The Fascist Response to Globalization", *Los Angeles Times*, November 28, 1999, Sunday, Home Edition.

Patnaik, U. (2001). "Falling Per Capita Availability of Food Grains for Human Consumption in the Reform Period in India", *ilklibar*, No. 2. October 2001 also available on http://www.ercwilcom.nett-indowindowrakhhar/2001-02/global.htm

Puniyani, R. (2001). "Globalisation and Politics of Identity", *Akhbar*, No. 3. November 2001 available on littp://www.ercwilcommet/-indowindow/akhbar72001-03/leature.htm

RUPE (30&31). (2001a). "Fraudulent Fall in Poverty", *Aspects of India's Economy*, Nos. 30 & 31, Research Unit for Political Economy.

RUPE (30&31). (2001b). "Depression of Wage Levels and Employment", *Aspects of India's Economy*, Nos. 30 & 31, Research Unit for Political Economy.

Shiva, V. (2000). "Poverty & Globalisation", available on http://news.bbc.co.uk/hi/English"staticicventsireith_2000/lecture5.stin

Teltumbde, A. (2000). "Impact of New Economic Reforms on Dalits in India", in P. G. Jogdand (ed.), *New Economic Policy and Dalits*, New Delhi: Rawat Publishers.

World Bank. (2002). "World Development Report, 2000–2001", Table 4, http://www.worldbank.org/povertyiwdrpoverty/report/tab4.pdf

11 Panchayati Raj Institutions and Social Inclusion of Dalits[1]

Karunakar Singh

The independence of the country and the republican form of polity with universal adult franchise has initiated the process of political modernisation and democratisation in the country. However, political modernisation has been confined only to state- and national-level politics. When India emerged as a republic, rural society was mostly feudal in nature. Dalits (constitutionally categorised as "Scheduled Caste") were, since time immemorial, socially excluded from the mainstream of society in every aspect, i.e., cultural, social, political, and economic. They were the tragic victims of the rigid and immobile Hindu caste system. Dalits had no place in social and political decision-making. The ideas and orders were imposed on them by the dominant upper castes, and this was the main hindrance in the nation building process after independence.

Social exclusion involves the process through which individuals or groups are wholly or partially excluded from full participation in the society within which they live – on the basis of perceived group attributes like social origin, ethnicity, and religious conviction. It is the denial of equal opportunities imposed by certain groups of society upon others which leads to inability of an individual to participate in the basic political, economic, and social functioning of the society (Chinna Rao, 2010). In the Indian scenario, social exclusion is not a new phenomenon. History bears witness to exclusion of social groups on the bases of caste, class, gender, and religion. Most notable is the category of Dalits. Denial of access to and control over economic and social opportunities has relegated them to the category of excluded groups.

Dalits constitute one of the largest social groups and account for about a fifth of India's population. Over the centuries, they have suffered extensively from caste and untouchability-based exclusion and discrimination. Traditionally, they were excluded from access to property rights as well as economic, civil, religious, and other rights. Disabilities of untouchables become more severe as they are also physically and socially segregated from the rest of the Hindu society through the institution of untouchability. It is this institutionalised, comprehensive, and multiple exclusion of the low castes that has severe consequences on their deprivation, and hence differentiates them from their poor counterparts in the upper castes.

DOI: 10.4324/9781003317173-15

In recognition of the problems of the excluded, the state enacted anti-discriminatory laws and policies to foster their social inclusion and empowerment. The Anti- Untouchability Act of 1955 (later renamed as Protection of Civil Rights Act in 1976) and the Scheduled Castes (SC) and Scheduled Tribes (ST) Prevention of Atrocities Act of 1989 figure among some of the legal steps taken by the government for the welfare of these communities. In addition to legal protection, the state also used affirmative action of reservation policy to provide due share in education, employment, and other services.

Despite these provisions for equal participation and empowerment, exclusion and discrimination of these excluded groups continued; so, there was a need to address issues of "inclusion" in a more direct manner. To broaden this inclusion, the Parliament provided reservations for these disadvantaged sections in the local bodies through the 73rd Constitution Amendment Act, 1993. The 73rd Amendment has greatly contributed to the political empowerment of Dalits in rural society. It has thrown open political opportunities in the panchayats as well as resulted in the overall transformation of these disadvantaged sections.

As this chapter primarily looks at panchayats from the perspective of Dalits, at the onset, it is imperative to discuss the Gandhi–Ambedkar debate for the incorporation of Panchayati Raj Institutions (PRIs) in the Constitution. Therefore, the debate in the Constituent Assembly was much more fundamental.

Village swaraj was the alternative to Gandhi's vision of an independent India. This was due to his fundamental opposition to parliamentary democracy which he saw as perpetuating domination and his belief in an economy of limited wants based on local production, resources, consumption, and technologies (De Souza, 2002). Dr. Ambedkar opposed this suggestion, viewing village India differently and believing that the path of the future lay in a constitutional parliamentary democracy. For him, the village represented a regressive India, a source of oppression. The modern state hence had to build safeguards against such social oppression and the only way it could be effected was through the adoption of a parliamentary model of politics (De Souza, 2002).

A compromise was reached, and establishment of panchayats at the village level as one of the goals was incorporated into the Constitution. The constitutional provision states: "the state shall take steps to organise village Panchayats and endow them with such powers and authority as may be necessary to enable them to function as units of local self-government" (Article 40, in Part-IV-Directive Principles of State Policy). So, efforts were made to set up panchayats at the village level through various legislations in all states and Union Territories in the early years of independence.

The formal beginning of Panchayati Raj in post-independence era can be traced to the launching of the nation-wide Community Development Programme (CDP), when the need was felt for an effective institutional mechanism to involve the local communities in the process of development. The policy on Panchayati Raj emerged from the recommendations of the Balwantrai Mehta Committee which stated that one of the least success- ful aspects of Community Development Programme (CDP) and National Extension Council (NEC) work was its attempt to evoke people's initiative. This view of the committee provides a broad perspective of contextual ante- cedents ground in which the concept of democratic decentralisation is devel- oped to strengthen the rural local administration. However, these programmes failed to enthuse the local population to participate actively. Therefore, the concern for economic development was emphasised in the recommendations of the Mehta Committee, calling for entrusting the administration of rural development programmes to the elected representatives at the local level. The political and economic objectives behind the introduction of these institutions may become clear from the statements of political leadership, which were used at the time of the inauguration of the scheme. Jawaharlal Nehru, when he launched Panchayati Raj in Rajasthan on Gandhi Jayanti in 1959 said,

> To uplift lakhs of villages is not an ordinary task.... The reason for the slow progress is our dependence on official machinery. An officer is probably necessary because he is an expert. But this work can be done only if the people take up the responsibility in their own hands. The people are not merely to be consulted. Effective power has to be entrusted to them.
>
> (Narayana, 1996)

Jai Prakash Narayan, one of the well-known leaders of Indian democracy, observed that "it is a matter of great satisfaction that in our country a begin- ning has already been made in laying the foundation of participatory democ- racy in the shape of Panchayati Raj or what was called at first, democratic decentralization" (Narayana, 1996).

Panchayati Raj, launched on 2 October 1959 (Rajasthan), was conceptu- alised as a vehicle through which people, from all sections of rural society, would be able to work collectively to solve their problems. Jawaharlal Nehru, the first Prime Minister of India, while inaugurating the Panchayati Raj in Rajasthan, said, "Everybody should be considered equal in our Panchayats and there should be no discrimination between men/women and high/low" (Tyagi and Sinha, 2001). Thus, Panchayati Raj was considered a political and administrative innovation of far-reaching importance when it was intro- duced in 1959. It was depicted as a mechanism for popular participation. The Panchayati Raj bodies were expected to awaken political consciousness in the countryside and to engender the democratic process in rural India.

However, Panchayati Raj has experienced several ups and downs since its inception. Subsequent to 1965, panchayats underwent a period of stagnation and decline till the late 1970s. Therefore, a few states took active steps to

rejuvenate and strengthen the institutions based on their own political ideologies. But, in most others, a condition of degeneration continued to prevail.
The bane of the problem lay in the fact that regular elections were not held
in most states for decades. States like Bihar, Tamil Nadu, Karnataka, and
Uttar Pradesh (where the last elections in the pre-notification period were
held in 1978, 1986, 1987, and 1988, respectively) are glaring examples of
this inconsistency. The absence of elections was not the only anomaly. The
functioning of Panchayati Raj has depended more on the whims of the state
governments and less on the mandate of the people. The Panchayati Raj bodies have been further crippled by either lack of finances and resources, greater
centralisation, limited rights and jurisdiction, or by the creation of parallel
structures of authority at the local level. In such a context, far from emerging
as instruments of self-governance and decentralised democracy, Panchayats
could not even effectively undertake the wider developmental role prescribed
for those bodies in a number of areas like agriculture, forestry, cottage industries, and welfare. This was so because they were denied any meaningful integration with development programmes and administrative structures. Thus,
the past experience of many states shows that these institutions have not
played their envisaged role and have not been associated with the planning
and implementation processes at the lower levels.

It is also an undisputed fact that the PRIs have not been beneficial to the
poor and the weaker sections of rural society. Power has remained in the
hands of the rural elites, and the poor and weaker sections have been largely
marginalised. These sections have not been associated with the decision-
making process in the Panchayats even in states where the system has been
working well – states like Karnataka, Gujarat, Maharashtra, and Andhra
Pradesh. The system has mainly been working to the advantage of the dominant groups.

The Seventh Five-Year Plan document corroborated this sad state of affairs
of the panchayats and admitted that the PRIs have been reduced to an extremely
peripheral status mainly due to untimely elections in the states and inadequate
technical and financial resources. Thus, the PRIs have not been able to acquire
the status and dignity of viable and responsible people's bodies due to a number of reasons including the absence of regular elections, prolonged super-
session, insufficient representation of the weaker sections including women,
inadequate devolution of powers, and lack of financial resources. The main
reason for this state of affairs is stated to be the absence of constitutional obligation for the state governments towards Panchayati Raj bodies. The PRIs had
no existence of their own, and they formed part of the state list. Hence, there
was a demand for constitutional status of PRIs (Narayana, 1996).

It was in this context that the foundation for the 73rd Constitutional
Amendment Act was laid by the then Prime Minister of India, Rajiv Gandhi.
He suggested introducing an amendment to the Constitution to accord constitutional status to the third level of governance. Although the amendment
could not come about during his lifetime, his successor P.V. Narasimha Rao

drew up a fresh constitutional amendment for the PRIs. This emerged as the Constitution (73rd Amendment) Act 1992 and came into force from April 1993.

The Constitutional 73rd Amendment Act, 1992, is a significant step in the political history of independent India. The Act, which provides the much-required constitutional recognition to the long-standing need of developing the power of people at the grassroots level, promises not only decentralising administration and local self-government, but also the participation of those groups of persons hitherto considered as weaker sections, namely, SCs, STs, and women. Article 243 (D) makes provision for the reservation of SCs and STs, in every panchayat in proportion to the population of that area. Such seats will be filled by direct election and shall be allotted by rotation to different constituencies. Not less than one-third of the total number of seats so reserved shall be reserved for women belonging to SC/ST. Besides, not less than one-third of the total number of seats (including the seats reserved for SC/ST women) to be filled by direct election shall also be reserved for women and allotted by rotation. The office of the chairpersons in panchayats at the village level or any other level shall be reserved for the SC/ST categories and women in such manner as the legislature of the state by law may provide (Bohra, 1997).

The experiment of Panchayati Raj has been made to provide firm and deep roots to democracy and a broad base to the democratic structure so as to make the common man a real partner in the conduct of his own civic and political affairs. The PRIs have been considered an important aspect of socio-economic structures. PRIs are expected to serve the interests and meet the aspirations of various sections of the Indian rural society. Democratic decentralisation is not merely the devolution of powers. It must also comprise devolution of responsibility (Desai, 1990).

Political Participation of the Weaker Sections

Generally, the power structure in gram panchayats is in favour of the upper castes and locally dominant castes in the society. The emergence of such type of power structure not only defeats the basic implications of democratic decentralisation but also the aim of rural development with social justice. In this context, reservation provides scope for women and for the members of SC/ST communities to participate in panchayats. Before the 73rd Constitutional Amendment Act came into operation there was no effective participation for the weaker sections. In earlier state Acts there was no reservation of seats for SCs and STs. In states like Andhra Pradesh, Bihar, Haryana, Himachal Pradesh, Karnataka, Orissa, Punjab, Rajasthan, and Tamil Nadu, the reservation was based on their population. In Uttar Pradesh, there was a provision in the Act to specify the minimum of SC and ST members in the panchayats. The Acts of Goa and West Bengal did not provide for the reservation of seats for SC/ST candidates. Most of the states did not provide reservations for the post of chairpersons at any level. Very few states had provided such reservations. Madhya Pradesh, for instance, provided reservations for the post of chairperson at the block level. Andhra Pradesh provided reservations for SCs, STs, and BCs for the post of chairpersons at all levels, including district levels. There is now significant reservation in panchayats at all levels. The Amendment Act has a clear provision for providing reservations for SCs and STs for not only the seats but also for positions/chairpersons (243D (4)). The local depressed groups have a better chance of organising themselves and resisting the elite in Panchayati Raj elections because of increasing reservations. As the panchayat elections are being regulated by the state election commission, booth capturing and similar strong-arm tactics would be minimised. This would enable the weaker sections to mobilise freely during elections and exercise their franchise without hindrances (Narayana, 1996).

Dalit Leadership in PRIs

One of the studies conducted in Gujarat found that the panchayats serve the interest of mainly one group, namely, the group of big farmers and rich traders usually belonging to upper castes. The SC/ST members of the Panchayat are selected by the elite group, and they do not really represent the interests of the poor in the panchayat and therefore the masses have practically little say in the decision-making process in the panchayat, with the result that the activities of the panchayat do not serve the interests of the poor in the developmental activities, including the special programmes for the poor (Hirway, 1986). Another study conducted in Karnataka also made similar observations. It shows that the village masses are neither fully aware of the functioning of the Panchayats nor are they able to participate in their activities (Gurumurthy, 1987).

B.R. Ambedkar was apprehensive of the aforesaid state of affairs with reference to the potential of PRIs in the emancipation of the marginalised sections. He was opposed to the introduction of PRIs. Speaking at the meeting of the Constituent Assembly on the Draft Constitution, he strongly criticised those who romanticised the villages as republics and argued that a village is nothing but "a sink of localism, a den of ignorance, narrow-mindedness and communalism. I am glad that the Draft Constitution discarded the village and adopted the individual as its unit" (Ambedkar, 1995).

But in contrast to this, there are studies that prove that because of PRIs there has been a change in the rural power structure in favour of the weaker sections. It is observed that in West Bengal, Andhra Pradesh, Rajasthan, and Gujarat, the Panchayati Raj leadership pattern, as well as the authority structure, in rural India has registered a major shift. Gradually, people belonging to lower socio-economic backgrounds have joined the Panchayati Raj institutions. Irrespective of the charge that dominant sections of the society misutilised the reservation provisions, it cannot be denied that the PRIs have made it possible for the weaker sections to get into elective offices and get into the pace of further development (Shiviah, 1986). In his study of West Bengal, he concluded that the village elite were confined to upper castes now it is widely diffused.

The Panchayati Raj institutions would help the lower castes to move up in governing their own affairs in villages (Gangrade, 1991). So, it is necessary to give more importance to the awareness of the common people about this system (Palanithurai, 1996). Ajit Kumar (2004), in his study of Nagpur, found that village politics has undergone considerable changes since the 1960s when the Panchayati Raj system was introduced. In the early years, caste considerations strongly influenced most decisions, but now institutional politics has a broader base including many caste categories. Regarding the political empowerment of Dalits at grassroots level, a study of Scheduled Caste panchayat *pradhans* (heads of the village council) in Western Uttar Pradesh has analysed the impact of political socialisation on their political outlook, the pattern of their recruitment and their performance (Vijay, 1989). Based on the analysis of the village panchayat elections of 1982 in Uttar Pradesh, the study suggests that the election had brought a major change in the "political socialisation", "recruitment", and "performance" of the Dalit leaders at the grassroots level of democracy in the rural setting. Earlier, most pradhans from the upper castes had held the offices of the panchayats. However, in one block of Ghaziabad district, seven pradhans were elected from amongst the Dalits, even without reservation, which was not a small achievement. Their performance was also said to be far more satisfactory in comparison to the upper-caste pradhans of these areas. Thus, the presence of the Dalit leaders in the PRIs has proved to be helpful to the Dalits in solving their day-to-day problems.

Dalit among Dalits: Dalit Women Scenario

The 73rd Amendment, while granting reservation to Dalits, has made it compulsory that one-third of the seats reserved for them be filled by Dalit women. The conformity legislations in the states have also reiterated this provision. Existing studies suggest that the impact of reservation has been differential. In states where the social status of women has traditionally been better and levels of literacy, status in society and participation in the workforce are higher, women have been able to take advantage of this measure. Quite a few studies had pointed out the difference those women members made to the nature of the decisions and the process by which they are formulated. Power meant giving priority to issues like drinking water supply, installation of hand pumps, construction of toilets, village wells and roads, appointment of teachers, closing of liquor shops, etc. There were instances, as in Vitner village in Jalgao district (Maharashtra), where women got playgrounds built, land was transferred to 127 women from their husband's share, and toilets were constructed in the Dalit areas. Women in Pidghara (MP) went for a 27-point action plan that took up the building of educational and other community-based infrastructure. The experience and action agenda of the seven-member pan-chayat of Brahmanghar of Pune was also similar (Kaushik, 1995). In such states, reservations have helped strengthen the position of Dalit women.

In other parts of the country, where women's position in the family and society and participation in public affairs has traditionally been low as in the states in the northern plains, the reservation measure has not caused much change. The impact of this measure has been much slower. A study argues that reservation alone cannot change the status of women and enable their participation in local bodies. The position of women and the perception that they have little knowledge about, and are incapable of taking part in pub-lic affairs, even of independent voting, remain strong. The pradhanis in the study were mere namesake representatives of the male members of the house-hold (Pai, 2000).

In some states, there has been little or no acceptance of reservation for the lower castes by the upper castes in the village. This has resulted in atroci-ties against panchayat members, including women. Four case studies from Madhya Pradesh reveal that the power structure in villages in this state remains oppressive. Dalit women who stood for election were beaten, raped, and ill-treated and their land was grabbed by members of the higher castes who were not prepared to relinquish power to the lower castes. An easier method to retain power is to put up proxy candidates but keep the control in the hands of the dominant castes, always men. The incapacity of women, particularly Dalit women, to assert their rights is at the root of the prob-lem. The study showed that reservation for Dalits, particularly for women, is accepted in form but seldom in substance. Any change in the status quo is resisted, sometimes violently (Mathew and Nayak, 1996). This points to the limitations as well as the possibilities of state intervention without the neces-sary social support systems. Similar experiences have been reported in Tamil Nadu, Rajasthan, and Bihar (Mathew, 2004).

Dalit women have also faced many problems in performing their duties due to illiteracy, lack of information, and dependency on the male members of their families. An important obstacle is no-confidence motions against Dalit women pradhans by the dominant sections who are unable to accept that power is in the hands of the poor and disadvantaged women (Mahi Pal, 1998).

Social Inclusion of Dalits and PRIs

One of the distinct changes that has come out as a result of democratic decentral-isation is the emergence of Dalit leadership in the panchayats. The traditional caste panchayats which were decision-making bodies of the villages denied access to the Dalits. The rural sociopolitical life was upper caste–dominated, and Dalits were mere voiceless spectators. It is believed that the long-standing tradition of democratic demonstration and radical provisions of reservation for Dalits has drastically changed the sociopolitical scenario in rural India.

However, the problem is that it is observed that most of the members of the panchayats from reserved constituencies are illiterates and inexperienced and are controlled either by their relations or by vested interests, so the very purpose of reservation is defeated. In the panchayats there are two major means of discrimination. One is that the Dalits are kept away from the panchayat proceedings, development work, schemes, etc., and another is that wherever Dalits are in power by virtue of reservation they are targeted, and their posts are declared null and void after a certain period of time. Secondly, the Dalits who are in positions like sarpanch or panch are toppled within a short period by bringing in a no-confidence motion. This has barred many Dalits from exercising their rights in the panchayat institutions. Those who had survived have complied with the norms set by the caste masters or have applied corrupt politics. The 73rd Amendment to the Constitution was viewed as a powerful instrument of social inclusion in the country and one expected that the hitherto excluded communities would get justice after its due implementation.

Conclusion

The 73rd Amendment has emerged as an effective instrument to unleash the tremendous energies for social transformation in Indian society. Strong political institutions at the grassroots level are a necessary condition for carrying out the new possibilities of the post-73rd Amendment PRIs. The 73rd Amendment has aided the process of inclusion by providing reservations to Dalits and other weaker sections. However, reservations alone cannot carry forward this democratic process; the provisions for education and employment by the state will help raise capabilities and awareness among Dalits, together with political mobilisation through civil society and political parties. Indian society with thousands of years of its oppressive, anti-human, and status quoist history could be changed through democracy, practised through vibrant self-governing institutions at the village level. However, it is not a quantum jump but a painfully slow process.

Note

1 Published in *Social Action: A Quarterly Review of Social Trends* (January–March 2012)

References

Ambedkar, B. R. (1995). *Writings and Speeches*, Vol. 13, Bombay: Education Dept., Govt. of Maharashtra, p. 62.
Bohra, O. P. (1997). "Women in Decentralized Democracy", *Journal of Rural Development*, Vol. 16, No. 4, pp. 672–673.
Chinna Rao, Y. (2010). "Social Exclusion in India: Concepts and Context", in Yagati Chinna Rao and Sudhakara Karakoti (eds.), *Exclusion and Discrimination: Concepts, Perspectives and Challenges*, New Delhi: Kanishka Publishers.

De Souza, P. R. (2002). "Decentralization and Local Government: The "Second Wind" of Democracy in India", in Zoya Hasan, E. Sridharan and R. Sudharshan (eds.), *India's Living Constitution: Ideas, Practices, Controversies*, Delhi: Permanent Black, p. 372.

Desai, V. (1990). *Panchayti Raj: Power to the People*, Bombay: Himalaya Publication.

Gangrade, K. D. (1991). "Power to the Powerless: Dawn of Participatory Democracy", *Kurukshetra*, April.

Gurumurthy, U. (1987). *Panchayati Raj and the Weaker Section*, New Delhi: Ashish Publishing House, p. 168.

Hirway, I. (1986). "Panchayati Raj at Crossroads", *Economic and Political Weekly*, July 22, pp. 1663–1667.

Kaushik, S. (1995). *Panchayati Raj in Action: Challenges to Women's Role*, New Delhi: Friedrich Ebert Stifting.

Kumar, A. (2004). "Politics in Three Villages: A Study in Nagpur District", *Economic and Political Weekly*, January 17.

Kumar, V. (1989). *Scheduled Caste Panchayat Pradhans in India, A Study of Western Uttar Pradesh*, New Delhi: Ajanta Publications.

Pal Mahi. (1998). "Women in Panchayats: Experiences of a Training Camp", *Economic and Political Weekly*, Vol. XXIII, No. 4, January 24–30, pp. 150–152.

Mathew, G. (2004). "Local Self- Government and Dalits", in Bibek Debroy and D. Shyam Babu (eds.), *The Dalit Question: Reforms and Social Justice*, New Delhi: Globus Books with Rajiv Gandhi Institute for Contemporary Studies, pp. 255–262.

Mathew, G. & Nayak, Ramesh C. (1996). "Panchayats at Work: What it Means for the Oppressed?" *Economic and Political Weekly*, Vol. XXXI, No. 27, July 6, pp. 1765–1771.

Narayana, E. A. (1996). "Panchayati Raj and Scheduled Castes, Scheduled Tribes and Other Backward Classes", in M. Wadhawani and S. N. Mishra (eds.), *Dreams and Realities*, New Delhi: Indian Journal of Public Administration, p. 103.

Pai, S. (2000). "Pradhanis in the New Panchayats: A Study from Meerut District", in Kiran Saxena (ed.), *Women and Politics*, New Delhi: Gyan Publishing House.

Palanithurai, G. (1996). *New Panchayati Raj System: Status and Prospects*, New Delhi: Kanishka Publication.

Shiviah, M. (1986). *Panchayati Raj: An Analytical Survey*, Hyderabad: NIRD.

Tyagi, L. K. & Sinha, B. P. (2001). "Empowerment of Weaker Section through Panchyats: A Diagnosis", *IASSI Quarterly*, Vol. 19, No. 3, p. 134.

12 Discrimination and Exclusion in Education[1]

A Perspective from Below

Paul D'Souza and Teena Anil

Based on an empirical study of the children of households associated with "Unclean" occupations in urban India, this chapter highlights that educating the future generation is still a struggle for Dalit masses located at the bottom of the social hierarchy, especially those most marginalised and excluded among Dalits. The chapter examines discrimination and exclusion in the educational system for marginalised children with the 4A scheme of Accessibility, Availability, Acceptability, and Adaptability and further critically contextualises how national flagship programmes of Swachh Bharat Abhiyan can complement the educational programmes in general and special educational initiatives for the children associated with households engaged in "Unclean" occupations.

The Problematic and Its Empirical Investigation

Attainment in education is deemed to be one of the key indicators of the development of a marginalised community. As per Census 2011, out of a total of 208 million children between 6 and 13 years, 18.3 per cent were not attending any educational institution. Realising the importance of education, Parliament amended the Constitution of India through the 86th Amendment in 2002. Article 21A was inserted which reads as follows: "The State shall provide free and compulsory education to all children of the age of six to fourteen years in such manner as the State may, by law, determine". Moreover, Article 46 highlights the importance of education for the weaker sections. The Article reads as:

> Promotion of educational and economic interests of Scheduled Castes, Scheduled Tribes and other weaker sections – The State shall promote with special care the educational and economic interests of the weaker sections of the people, and, in particular, of the Scheduled Castes and the Scheduled Tribes, and shall protect them from social injustice and all forms of exploitation.

DOI: 10.4324/9781003317173-16

The Government of India's commitment towards a hundred per cent enrolment of children was further strengthened by the enactment of the Right of Children to Free and Compulsory Education (RTE) Act, 2009. Several schemes have been launched by the Government of India to enrol every child in the education system. However, various studies show that caste-based discrimination and exclusion continues to be an influential factor in the low educational mobility of the Scheduled Castes despite various government programmes aimed at the development of the community (Secada, 1989). On the other hand, movements to abolish the caste system and end discrimination have always proposed education as the primary means to overcome caste oppression (Omvedt, 1995). Educational institutions, particularly schools, are considered to be places in which integration across caste communities could take place devoid of prejudices and set mind-sets. But in reality, prejudices against the Scheduled Castes persist in various forms in the classrooms, playgrounds, mid-day meal schemes, and in common activities of the school.

Over the last few decades, the change in the status of the Scheduled Castes in general and their educational status in particular has become part of a discourse in academic institutions as well as in social and political spheres. On the one hand, the resistance to the inclusion of Dalits is becoming more and more visible in the process of socio-economic development under the liberalisation, privatisation, and globalisation regime. There is a continuous assertion from the deprived castes and classes demanding their rights, especially in education. In the growing developmental paradigm, the Dalits are visibly shifting towards a greater need for the education of their children seeking better opportunities and avenues. Nevertheless, social prejudice and exclusion accumulated over the centuries are hard to deal with still; the resistance by private schools to admit students from the lower rungs of society under the Right to Education Act is a living example. Analysing the impact of affirmative action, various studies (Parvathamma, 1984; Oommen, 1990; Sachchidanand, 1974) have invariably revealed that the undemocratic institution of caste and the resultant inequalities have not only survived but have also become a matter of conflict and hatred, especially after the implementation of socio-economic and political privileges granted to them under the Constitution of India.

With this background an empirical study was undertaken to gather evidences of discrimination in education and its causes and consequences on the attainment of education of the children, especially of those belonging to households associated with "Unclean" occupations in urban India. For the purpose of the study, the association of households with "Unclean" occupations was broadly premised not on the basis of hygiene; but more of a religious prescription. *The households irrespective of caste or creed of which the members either presently engaged or were engaged in the past in occupations that "involve physical contact with blood, excrement, and other bodily defilements" were principally considered impure and polluting.* The "Unclean" occupations are classified into two broad categories. The first deals with direct service to the community that involves cleaning of human excreta, disposal of human wastes, sweeping, garbage collection and its disposal, and cleaning clothes with stains of human wastes, including marks of blood such as during menses or birth. The second one deals with individual community occupations like, domestication of "impure" animals such as rearing of pigs, and involvement in leather works such as tanning, flaying, and washing of stained cloths. These occupations are profoundly being carried out by various Dalit castes, mainly the Valmiki, Mehtar, Dhanuk, Chamar, and Dhobi. The study covered households engaged in a range of occupations, traditionally as well as in present times considered "Unclean" which are largely associated with death or human wastes.

For the empirical investigation residential localities with a higher concentration of households associated or engaged in "Unclean" occupations were identified in order to examine the educational status of their children. The localities represented eight cities in four states, i.e., Faridabad and Panipat in Haryana, Jaipur, and Alwar in Rajasthan, Ghaziabad and Mathura in Uttar Pradesh and Shimla and Solan in Himachal Pradesh. Depending on the size of the city and the population engaged in "Unclean" occupations the number of households surveyed varied state-wise. The survey covered a total of 5,665 households and further qualitative data was gathered from 40 schools in respective cities, in-depth profiling of 40 parents, teachers, and other stakeholders and around 150 students were interviewed for gaining a detailed understanding of their perspectives on various issues related to exclusion in education. Similarly, 40 focus group meetings were held with students and community members for qualitative data gathering.

For education to be meaningful 4As scheme was developed by the Committee of Economic, Social and Cultural Rights (CESCR),[2] which also adopted 4As to understand the marginalised children and their right to education within the context of formal education. The 4As were: *Availability* of free and government-funded education,[3] *Accessibility* to all irrespective of gender, race, or caste,[4] *Acceptability* which explains the content to be relevant, non-discriminatory, and culturally appropriate,[5] *Adaptability* which involves evolving with the changing needs of society and contribute to challenging inequalities.[6] In order to document and assess the multidimensional factors hindering the education of the children at the empirical level, the study adopts a framework of the 4A scheme model to analyse and interpret the empirical data gathered from the fields on the status of education among children of marginalised communities.

Based on the findings of the study, the chapter identifies the processes of exclusion and discriminatory practices meted out to the children in schools from the households associated with "Unclean" occupations and how they influence their lived experiences of education. The chapter looks at their educational status and reasons for such status, the situation of discriminatory practices at school, and the impact of such discrimination; and finally in the light of the measures initiated by the governments the chapter further proposes a list of policy recommendations to promote comprehensive poli-cies by the state and central governments. The chapter also examines how the national flagship programmes of Swachh Bharat Abhiyan can complement the educational programmes in general and special educational initiatives for the children associated with households engaged in "Unclean" occupations.

Thus, an assessment of the educational status of the children will help us to look beyond just quantitative aspects of exclusion and discrimination to the qualitative dimensions operative within and outside the educational sys-tem. Both the instrumental and structural dimensions within and outside the educational system are crucial in generating and sustaining social exclusion, and, therefore, need to be attended to on an equal footing for a better future for the children of marginalised communities in India.

The Reality at the Bottom: Factors Hindering the Education

The household survey covering a total of 5,665 households listed 12,348 children in four categories of educational status, i.e., those who completed education at a higher level, are continuing education at some level, discon-tinued schooling at some level (dropouts), and never attended school. The overall educational status of children shows that 73 per cent of them are continuing education presently at one or the other level; nearly 19 per cent of them are dropouts and 7 per cent of them never attended school. However, only 0.6 per cent of the children identified claim to have completed some level of education.

The educational institutions where the children study and the socio-eco-nomic backgrounds of the households they come from have very close cor-relations. Thus, the educational status of children is swayed by the structural factors within the educational system as well as outside. Further examination of the "educational level" (level implies the educational class among those continuing education) shows that the number of children pursuing higher levels of education declines drastically. Among those continuing education 42 per cent of the children are pursuing education at the primary level, only 13 per cent of the children are continuing their education at the level of higher secondary and above (see Chart 12.1).[7]

An analysis of the above data reveals that in general there is a good ratio of enrolment of children till the primary level of education. Nevertheless, when it comes to higher levels of education there is poor educational representation of children from households associated with "Unclean" occupations. Similarly, it also points toward two major dimensions, i.e., there is a lack of instrumen-tal support at higher levels of education and the government's insensitivity to understanding how the structure of caste and its socio-economic effects on children affects their access to higher levels of education. Correspondingly, the absence of government policies and schemes reinforces the exclusion of children from households associated with "Unclean" occupations, restricting access to higher education. Surprisingly, despite considering education as the

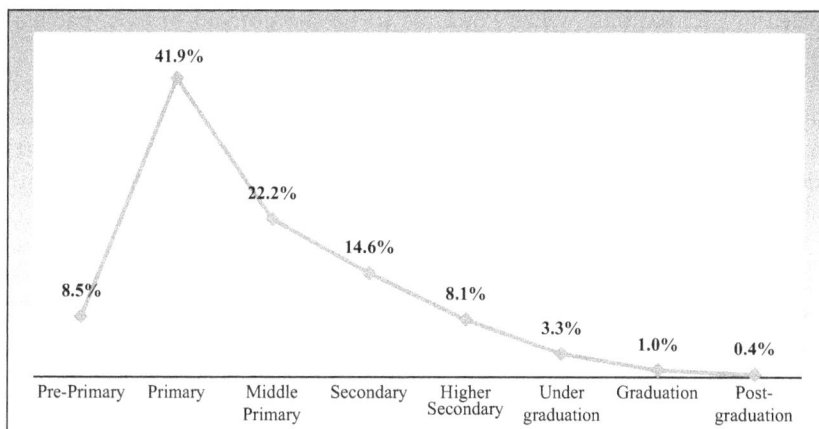

Chart 12.1 The educational class among those continuing education The data
presented in the chart is from - "Discrimination and Exclusion in
Education: A study of the Children of Households Associated with
Unclean Occupations of Uttar Pradesh, Rajasthan, Himachal Pradesh
and Haryana", conducted by Indian Social Institute, submitted to the
Indian Council of Social Science Research (ICSSR).

ninth pillar for the country's development, in the Union Budget of 2017–2018
about 6 per cent of the GDP was allocated to the education sector.[8]

The perspective from below reveals that the exclusion in education is a
multi-dimensional process and the children of the households associated with
"Unclean" occupations are impacted by both the instrumental dimensions
within the educational institutions and the structural dimensions outside the
educational system. The multiple dimensions create lasting negative impacts
on children at both academic performance and psychological life. The chapter highlights a few of the factors hindering the education of children from
marginalised caste communities.

Caste in Education: Classroom as Site for Reinforcing Caste Identities

The major caste category-wise distribution of the total surveyed households
shows that nearly 81 per cent of them belong to different caste groups in the
Scheduled Caste category; 12.2 per cent belong to Other Backward Caste
groups and 4.3 per cent are from General Castes. Only 2.6 per cent households are listed under the Muslim category as not mentioned under any other
specific caste category. A descriptive account of the social status of children
associated with "Unclean" occupations explores that 93 per cent of them are
from the Scheduled Castes[9] and among the Scheduled Castes the majority of
the households belong to Valmikis (86 per cent) and Chamars (5 per cent).
An analysis of the above data further advocates that in urban smart cities,

the hierarchy of caste-based occupations continues to persist in the case of "Unclean" occupations, which continue to be the domain of SCs, particularly of the Valmiki caste.

A narrative discussed below clearly indicates that the stigma is attached to the occupation and is ascribed to the Valmiki caste, nor will untouchables be assimilated or accepted in the society which often resent any such efforts made by the Scheduled Castes. As the president of the Dr. Ambedkar Welfare Society from Himachal Pradesh reveals,

> Who says there is no caste problem in Shimla, it is there in this city. Our children were denied admission in the prominent schools[10] ... but it is true that there is no open form of discrimination that exists in Shimla which is very much in the hill region. There is a caste issue, despite completing college education there is no job available for us in the state government.

Thus, the social stigma of caste derived from one's caste identity is not only rooted in the social milieu but has further established its dominance in the secular domain like the educational system. For a Dalit child, access to school is as much a cultural question as it is one of a school being available in the neighbourhood. There are accounts of Dalit children being alienated and humiliated in a formal educational set up and this is equally true in gender discrimination. In such circumstances children are pushed out rather than being dropping out of school.

In spite of many measures to eliminate caste from sociopolitical spheres, caste continues to impact all relations. Its prominent presence is felt by Dalit students in classrooms which remain a site for reinforcing caste identities. A large number of the children respondents coming from households associated with "Unclean" occupations narrate that there is segregation in seating arrangements in classrooms. The children from the Valmiki community are made to sit separately in both private as well as in government schools. In a private school in Faridabad, the sitting arrangement is made according to caste communities, and it was on the instruction of a teacher.

One of the dropout students from Jaipur's 80 Quarter area narrated the abhorrent practice of making Valmikis sit in the corner of the class in one of the government schools of the area. During his explanation, it was observed that this segregation has detrimental effects on Valmiki students' interest in their studies. He narrates,

> When I was in class VI, then "Harijans" were made to sit in the corner of the classroom. Therefore, they don't come to study. The children of the general caste and OBC look down upon them. If there was a Harijan boy then he used to sit behind.

A humiliation of this kind discourages them further leading to an increasing number of dropout children.

Sharing their experiences regarding the treatment by the teachers and the relationship with their peer groups, a majority of the students from all the selected states said the discriminatory treatment by the teachers, especially those from the upper castes is a common experience. On the other hand, interactions with peer groups are often restricted to their own caste groups. The students from households associated with "Unclean" occupations feel comfortable with their friends who are usually from their own caste groups. The lack of intermingling of students from different caste groups has long-term implications for their studies and children's future scope. Therefore, caste in education becomes a key structural factor that shapes and guides the instrumental factors leading to multiple forms of exclusion in education as experienced by the children of households associated with "Unclean" occupations.

Exclusionary Practices and Denying Quality Education in Schools

Governments have initiated several programmes, policies, and rules to protect and empower Dalit students. But at the level of implementation, the policies, programmes, and rules get subverted by unofficial norms, prejudices, and values that are structured by the caste-based society. The most important spheres within the school where exclusionary practices continue to flourish are the issues concerned with water and food, which have been traditionally potent sites of caste-based discrimination. The practice of drawing drinking water from common sources has witnessed discrimination against the students from Dalit communities.

As observed in a secondary school in Alwar, it was found that Valmiki caste children were thrown out of the school for drinking water from an earthen pot meant for the Savarna caste students. Some of the teachers also objected and stopped children of Dalit communities from drinking water from a common source. Pooja, a student of class XI from Himachal Pradesh, reported that her upper-caste friends avoid taking home-cooked food from her as their parents have forbidden them from having food from Dalit children. On similar lines a student from a prestigious private school reported that sharing of food with teachers is a common practice. However, since his mother worked as a *safaikaramchari* the teachers would never taste his food. He says, "I just stopped asking my teachers and would just sit in one corner and have my own food alone".

The participation of children in "co-curricular" activities is an important sphere of school life for developing personality and confidence of the students, strengthening peer relations, and building secular identities in school. Many children said that they are interested in cultural programs but are rarely given the opportunity to perform and had been often told by teachers that they are "good for nothing". Such discriminative attitudes have impacted students adversely making them apathetic towards cultural activities.

Some of the students have expressed that children from the marginalised communities are pushed to disciplines like humanities and home science and are not allocated subjects like science and computers which they are not happy doing and thus resulting in high dropouts at a later stage.

Gendering Education: Patriarchal Practices

Studies have shown that Dalit girl students are the most vulnerable in comparison to other students. They are subject to multiple exclusions generated by poverty, caste, and gender. Another reason for their high rate of non-attendance might be the fact that most parents are reluctant to send their girl children to distant schools for a number of cultural and practical reasons (Nambissan, 2006: 230–231). According to the survey data, a higher percentage of boys than girls attend private schools amongst households associated with "Unclean" occupations. The parents' preference for English medium school for boys is evident where 49 per cent of the female children are enrolled in government schools and 51 per cent in private schools whereas 45 per cent of boys are in government schools and 55 per cent in private schools. The state-level data shows significant gender discrimination in Haryana where 56 per cent boys are in private schools as against only 50 per cent girls and in Rajasthan where 63.4 per cent boys are in private schools against the 58 per cent girls.

Reflecting on the patriarchal system, Usha, a 39-year-old from Haryana, mother of two daughters, reveals that the patriarchal setup gives all decision-making power to men, making both women and girls helpless and dependent and having access to only government schools. The foremost reason given was the tradition of a heavy dowry causing the parent to cost-cut in the schooling of girls. Many girls shared that parents start saving for dowry early, leading to the poor quality of accessibility in education. In this context, it is apt to say that gender as a structural factor reinforces the exclusion in education, situating the barriers to inclusion in the quality of education in particular.

Occupational Compulsion Leading to Educational Marginalisation

Caste system is one of the unique features of the Indian social structure and social life. The system not only assigns a definite occupation to each individual but also imposes certain restrictions on the change of occupation. The persistency of bonded labour ties Dalits to specific occupations and does not give them independence or freedom. Similarly, cities continue to perpetuate the hierarchy of the caste rather than enable them to pursue new opportunities.

The age-old association of some of the traditional caste occupations and the practice of untouchability derived from the principle of purity and pollution has not lost its sheen in the secular democratic urban mind-set.

The engagement of parents in the disdainful "Unclean" occupations as a structural dimension gets reinforced and reciprocated within the microsystem of education, at times directly in visible form and at times in subtle ways, obstructing the quality of accessibility, availability, and acceptability in education.

> Sagar, 12 year old, son of Raj Kumar, Mohan Nagar Rajiv Colony, Ghaziabad belongs to Valmiki community, is presently studying in class IX. Both his parents work as private sweepers as wage earners on a monthly basis. The poor financial conditions of his family do not enable him to purchase education related materials like books, uniforms etc. in order to improve the quality of education. His parents are unable to provide him with extra coaching. All this makes him lag behind in his study. Since his parents work as sweeper so other caste people abuse them by using the term "*Bhangi, Gandgi saafkarnewala*".

Spatial Segregation and Lack of Educational Environment at Home

It is well documented that Dalit parents who migrate from villages to urban cities look for better educational opportunities for their children. However, they get segregated in urban spaces finding accommodation in urban slums. The settlements in which the communities engaged in "Unclean" occupations reside do not have proper roads and basic civic amenities like water, electricity, and toilets. The homes are small, dilapidated with no repair, and without proper ventilation. The surroundings are full of filth and slush flowing from open drains that make the living conditions, most unhygienic and create several health hazards for all especially children.

   The educational backwardness of the Dalit communities is generally attributed to poverty and illiterate home environment prevailing among them. The empirical evidences observed in almost all the selected settlements show that the pathetic conditions in which the households associated with "Unclean" occupations live are not only un-conducive for a dignified living but also therein one cannot expect much from the children in pursuing educational goals. Thus, for the well-being of families, especially the educational well-being of children it becomes imperative that those who keep our cities clean also get a better environment to live in.

Measures Promoting Inclusive Education

Incidents of discrimination and exclusionary practices in educational institutions experienced by children from marginalised communities are regularly reported from across India. In spite of positive measures in the form of policies and programs undertaken by central and state governments, these have not brought an end to caste-based dehumanising treatment meted out by

teachers, peer groups, and the educational system at large, to children especially those from the Scheduled Castes and among them those belonging to
the households associated with "Unclean" occupations.

Considering the empirical situation of continuing discrimination and
exclusion in education at the grassroots it is obligatory for the state and
policymakers to adopt a holistic approach to inclusive education. There is
a need to go beyond initiating positive measures to a positive attitude of
"cleaning-up" systems more comprehensively. The government at various
levels must systematically conceive a social program of complementing inclusive education with flagship government programme of modernising India's
sanitation, i.e., Swachh Bharat Abhiyan. This would not only make our
country clean but will bring drastic structural and cultural changes in the life
of the students belonging to the household associated with "Unclean" occupations. The holistic approach of collaborating Swachh Bharat Abhiyan with
the Right to Education will enable inclusive education by providing greater
accessibility of education to the children associated with households associated with "Unclean" occupations. The following measures need to be seen
from this broader perspective:

Need of Conscientising Teachers

To reduce the psychological and physical impacts of exclusionary and discriminative practices in the school that discourage and demoralise students
from marginalised communities, teachers have to be effectively organised
and motivated more empathetically, with training to develop skills to manage classrooms that have children from diverse backgrounds, especially children from marginalised communities. They should be trained to empathise
with Dalit students and taught about the impact of social prejudices and
attitudes.

Creating Empathetic Learning Environment

The central characteristic of the school, and the classroom in particular, is
that meaningful access to school education is sustained through the active
participation of the children in the learning process and classroom activities.
For this important function of the educational system, the schools should
have qualified teachers that are sufficient in proportion to the number of students. The teachers should be accountable for their professional duties and
not engage or be employed for other administrative duties.

Educational Accessibility and the Role of the State

One of the major problems that marginalised communities face is that
physical access to school is compounded by the problem of social access to
schooling. The implementation of various measures undertaken has not been
adequate enough in reducing the historical disabilities that were enforced

upon by the age-old caste structure. Therefore, the state should consider the educational vulnerabilities of the Scheduled Caste children in general, and children from households associated with "Unclean" occupations in particular, while formulating policies and their implementation.

Enabling Accessibility with Quality Information

The provisions made in the Right to Free and Compulsory Education (RTE) Act, 2009, i.e., a minimum of 25 per cent free seats for children belonging to weaker sections and disadvantaged groups (EWS) in all private unaided primary schools, must be mandatory. Many of the households from marginalised communities are unaware of such schemes. Therefore, efforts must be made to publicise this legislation by making people aware of the provisions and ensuring implementation of it.

Establishing Common School System

Establish only one type of school, i.e., funded by the government, where students from all sections of the society study together. The government should ensure a common school system for the rich and the marginalised with equality and quality. Governments should monitor schools for de facto discrimination, and identify and address the issues in terms of policies, institutions, programmes, spending patterns, etc.

Improving Infrastructure Facilities in Schools, Ensuring the Social Security

The basic infrastructure, facilities, and services must be available in the school in order to improve the performance of the students. Special attention must be given to basic services like water, electricity, sewerage; didactic facilities like sports, libraries, and computers; a standard classroom with chairs, blackboard, etc. to keep the retention rate higher. In order to ensure social security, attention must be given to make the toilet facilities available in schools, especially for girls. Similarly, preventive measures must be kept in place against any kind of harassment especially of girl children or disadvantaged children in travelling to and from schools.

Extending Economic Accessibility in Partnership with Other Stakeholders

The provision of scholarships and other mandatory contingencies should be implemented at various types of schools – government schools, private schools, and aided and unaided schools. Nevertheless, an emphasis should also be given, where scholarships should be need-based, adequate, and timely. Children should be provided with *good quality* mid-day meals. The quality of economic accessibility should be improved further by setting up a monitoring committee having adequate representatives.

Widening Economic Accessibility with Reference to Target Group

Understanding the intensity of marginalisation that has been observed by the different social groups presently engaged/associated with "Unclean" occupations, it is pertinent to have the provision of separate scholarships for special categories of students whose parents are currently involved in "Unclean" occupations apart from Scheduled Caste category in general.

Improve the Economic Accessibility of Those Associated with "Unclean" Occupations

The state needs to pay special attention, going beyond manual scavengers to the households associated with "Unclean" occupations to improve their economic status. It has been observed that a majority of the families have income below Rs. 5,000 and that the poor economic conditions affect the education of children. A number of children drop out of school to support home and take up sanitation work that they are most familiar with, and many children have not attended school at all due to the poor economic conditions of the household. The state therefore should pay special attention to the accessibility of quality education by providing economic resources within the educational system that will take care of the socially marginalised groups at large.

Making Schools Available for the Marginalised

The expectations of aspirational parents for enrolling their children in private schools for better and quality education are not being realised as mushrooming private schools are as good as the government schools in and around the selected localities in the cities. Government must ensure that there are schools closer to the residential localities of marginalised communities informed by analysis of disaggregated data and school mapping exercises in collaboration with private–public partnership (PPP). However, without shirking its responsibility as the welfare state, the government should intervene in monitoring the facilities and infrastructure in the mushrooming private schools in the city.

Policies to Promote Higher Levels of Education

The state must make concerted efforts in making quality education available and in promoting a higher level of education among the students from marginalised communities. Attainment of the aim of universalisation of primary education requires the creation of additional proficiencies by introducing new secondary schools and institutions of higher learning vital to manage the increasing outflows from the lower levels.

Need to Review Syllabus and Make It More Inclusive

The school syllabus generally ignores Dalit literature and issues related to caste and discrimination. In the overall environment, whether private or government school, there is no space for Dalit culture, ideology, and icons in the schools. In such cases, students from marginalised communities find it extremely difficult to be in tune and empathetic with the school system. The syllabus should be more neutral and all-encompassing; must be more inclusive of all points of views and not be a monopologized majoritarian point of view.

Abolition of Contract Jobs and Regularisation of Sanitation Workers

In order to break the vicious circle of poverty, the state must change the policy of recruitment and the contract job system should be abolished. Without regularisation of services, proper safety net available to the employee, and social security, there is no scope for a better future for the children of sanitation workers. The regularisation of sanitation workers will give them job security and better wages. After a minimum term of service, they may be regularised. The contracts of sanitation should be given to sanitation workers' cooperatives and self-help groups that would also look at the welfare of the workers.

Improving Adaptability Measures by Consultations with Stakeholders

In order to improve adaptability measures it is mandatory to hold broad consultations with the respective communities, rights-holder groups, and other stakeholders in educational processes. Efforts should be made so that the parents actively participate in parent–teacher associations and in general body meetings to know what is happening in the school, with the ward, and the children of their community. The community leaders and local civil society organisations should be encouraged to be involved in the affairs of the schools through school management committees (SMCs) to create community ownership of the school rather than mere participation.

Enlisting Children's Participation in Monitoring and Developing Schools

The Right to Education Rules should include provisions for children's participation in the monitoring and developing of schools. Understanding the needs of disparate social groups, inclusive standards, and indicators for monitoring equity and inclusion provisions of the Right to Education should be developed in every school and mechanisms should be put in place for its implementation.

Locating Education in Broader Perspective of *Swachh Bharat*

The data on the overall educational status and the enrolment and continuing higher levels of education of children from households associated with

"Unclean" occupations raise three important and fundamental questions among many others, i.e.: (1) do all children from marginalised communities associated with "Unclean" occupations have access to primary education as guaranteed in the Right to Education Act (2009)? (2) Beyond elementary education, are children from marginalised communities able to access, avail and afford higher levels of education? (3) Are the children from the households associated with "Unclean" occupations deprived of quality education due to structural discrimination owing to lack of adaptability and acceptability of their specific context?

The search for answers does not get restricted only to physical or material/quantitative dimensions of accessibility, availability, acceptability, and adaptability of education but also looks into quality dimensions of education for the children of marginalised communities. As discussed earlier, 4A scheme has provided a better understanding about the factors that impinge on the educational exclusion of children from households associated with "Unclean" occupations. Since the launch of the Clean India mission to make the country open-defecation free, more than four million individual toilets and about 223,000 community toilets have been built. Yet, there is also no discussion of caste, when nearly all sanitation workers are Dalits, and no recognition of the abuse they suffer and the stigma that their children suffer affecting their access to education.

Corroborating empirical data from four selected states – Haryana, Rajasthan, Uttar Pradesh, and Himachal Pradesh – suggests that the association of households with "Unclean" occupations reinforces the poor quality of accessibility, availability, acceptability, and adaptability affecting the educational status of the children of these households. The multiple dimensions of exclusion in education, both within the educational institutions and outside the educational system, create lasting negative impacts on children, not only in the academic domain – the performance in the school, but also in the personal domain – the psychological life as a person. The immediate- and long-term impacts of discrimination and exclusion of children of communities engaged in "Unclean" occupations are visible among children which were identified and observed during qualitative investigation in the selected cities, such as lower self-esteem and self-worth, self-denial among children, lower levels of interest and motivation in studies, poor performance, high rate of absenteeism and discontinuation of studies, and low aspirational levels to pursue higher studies.

What emerges from the study are diverse spheres of school life where social relations and pedagogic processes fail to ensure the full participation of Dalit children and they are in fact subject to discriminatory and unequal treatment in relation to their peers and teachers. While on the one hand, these experiences are detrimental to children's self-esteem and self-worth, on the other hand, they are likely to have serious implications for their interest and motivation in studies. It is not surprising that a majority of Dalit children who enter and are formally 'included' in schools often fail/perform poorly and discontinue their studies.

The study reflects that the households engaged in "Unclean" occupations live in the most deplorable conditions of economic backwardness and social discrimination. In such situations education of their children which is a paramount factor in bringing individual and societal levels to social and economic transformation remains elusive. The Swachh Bharat Abhiyan, or Clean India Mission, brings those engaged in "Unclean" occupations to the forefront, but will it ensure that their children get educated and would these children also get access to dignified occupations promised by modern India – "skill India", "Digital India", and "Start-up India" or will these communities be permanently trapped in the mission of cleaning India because of their traditional occupation and discrimination associated with caste identity? The study also reveals that 'caste in education' is being continuously perpetuated by structural dimensions both within the educational system and outside that excludes and discriminates children from marginalised communities leading to discontinuation of education and from pursuing higher levels of quality education.

Making education available, accessible, acceptable, and adaptable remains the obligation of the state. The state owes greater responsibility not only in formulating appropriate policies and programs for inclusiveness in education but also to implement such policies and programs in its spirit to bring desired results so that the right to education becomes an instrument of social transformation, especially for the children from the marginalised communities left at the margins of our society.

Notes

1 Published in *Social Action: A Quarterly Review of Social Trends* (October–December 2018).
2 4As scheme was developed by the former UN Special Rapporteur on the Right to Education, Katarina Tomasevski, to assess inclusiveness in education (http://r2e.gn .apc.org/node/226).
3 Availability: Making the school available is not sufficient. The system should locate and address the exclusionary practices of caste system and structural forces that discriminate or discourage children to continue education.
4 Accessibility: The accessibility is understood at two levels, physical access, and social access. While the former focuses more about physical proximity the latter focuses more on social dynamics such as caste.
5 Acceptability: "Acceptability" of education has been highlighted by considering quality as an important facet to acceptability. Thus, urging governments to ensure quality education is provided, to stimulate a welfare programme towards multiple forms of discrimination, to identify the participation of the marginalized groups in and outside the classroom and parents' freedom to educate their children in whichever school they would choose to.
6 Adaptability: In education strategies, policies, and programmes should be flexible and relevant so as to respond to the needs of changing societies and communities. Those have to be addressing the needs of different students within their diverse social and cultural contexts.

7 The data presented in the chart is from "Discrimination and Exclusion in Education: A study of the Children of Households Associated with Unclean Occupations of Uttar Pradesh, Rajasthan, Himachal Pradesh and Haryana", conducted by Indian Social Institute, submitted to the Indian Council of Social Science Research (ICSSR).

8 http://indianexpress.com/article/business/budget/union-budget-2017-five-things-education-sector-expects/.

9 The present study also found some cases where individuals of other castes such as OBCs and even a few general castes are also found engaged in "Unclean" occupations. The involvement of these individuals is mainly because of their unemployment and poverty.

10 Some of the parents who moved out of caste professions echoed the same information, but there were cases where in children of parents engaged in "Unclean" occupations are admitted in to cities' most prominent convent schools. One such case is Dalit Christian girl whose father is working as a sweeper in a corporation. She was admitted in this school at the behest of a local priest.

References

Nambissan, G. B. (2006). "Terms of Inclusion: Dalits and the Right to Education", in Ravi Kumar (ed.), *The Crisis of Elementary Education in India*, New Delhi: Sage Publications, pp. 225–265.

Omvedt, Gail. (1995). *Dalit Visions: The Anti (?) Caste Movement and the Construction of an Indian Identity*, New Delhi: Orient Longman.

Oommen, T. K. (1990). *Protest and Change: Studies in Social Movements*, New Delhi: Sage Publications, 309 pp.

Parvathamma, C. (1984). *Scheduled Castes and Tribes: A Socio-Economic Survey*, Delhi: Ashish Publications.

Sachichidananda. (1974). *Education among the Scheduled Castes and Scheduled Tribes in Bihar*, Vol. 1, Patna: A.N Institute of Social Studies.

Secada, W. G. (ed.). (1989). *Equity in Education*, New York: The Falmer Press.

13 Dalit Merit and Institutional Injustice

A Case Study[1]

N. Sukumar and Shailaja Menon

Access to Education

The colonial rule inadvertently created spaces for the marginalised communities to access educational opportunities. The missionaries had a commendable role to play in this process. Radical thinkers like Phule, Jyoti Das, to Periyar and Ambedkar argued and worked tirelessly to empower the downtrodden groups. They made use of every avenue to press for educational opportunities for the excluded groups. Representing the cause of the Scheduled Castes before the Simon Commission, Ambedkar demanded special provisions for education. Based on this, the Hunter Commission recommended compulsory primary education for deprived communities. During the anti-colonial struggle, Tagore and Gandhi too identified the fundamental cause of many of India's social and economic afflictions as being rooted in the lack of education. In their view, the imposing tome of misery which rests on the heart of India has its sole origin in the absence of education. Caste divisions, religious conflicts, aversion to work, and precarious economic conditions all centre on this single factor.

There were intense debates on the nature of education. The Radhakrishnan Committee on University Education observed in 1949 that the most important and urgent reform needed in education is to make it freely accessible and inclusive, to endeavour to relate it to life, needs, and aspirations of the people and thereby make it a powerful instrument of social, economic and cultural transformation necessary for the realisation of national goals. For this purpose, education should be developed so as to increase productivity, achieve social and national integration, accelerate the process of modernisation, and cultivate social, moral and spiritual values within the society and among individuals.

In continuation of the emancipatory tradition, the Constitution of independent India created an egalitarian road map for the country, emphasising the values of liberty, equality, fraternity, and justice. Ambedkar consistently argued for a uniform national education policy to ensure quality education for all. However, education became a state subject with every state pursuing its own agenda and policy on education. Further, the Directive Principles of State Policy highlights that every child be provided with free and compulsory

DOI: 10.4324/9781003317173-17

education till the age of 14 years. Even this measure is scuttled by the lack of political will and administrative inefficiency.

Any individual from the historically and socially oppressed communities who entered the threshold of an educational institution experienced an enhanced sense of awareness of the world, an improved sense of social worth. The lack of educational opportunities crippled individual thinking, thereby creating a room for subjugation. Thus, education is a vital instrument of social mobility to realise multiple freedoms.

Poverty is simply not just poor living. Aristotle linked the richness of human life by first ascertaining the function of man and then exploring life in the sense of activity. He observed an impoverished life to be one without the freedom to undertake important activities that a person would choose.[2] Being excluded from social relations can limit our living opportunities. Social exclusion can, thus, be constitutively a part of capability deprivation as well as instrumentally a cause of diverse capability failures.[3] One form of dispossession from social interaction is the inability to appear in public freely and participate in the life of the community. It is a loss on its own, in addition to whatever further deprivation it may indirectly generate both actively and passively. Among the multiplicity of exclusions, what is relevant for us is the sharing of social opportunities. It was precisely the lack of social opportunities, sanctioned by law and custom, which pushed vast sections of Indians to live a life of penury, denied of both cultural and social capital. In order to bridge the gap, affirmative action was made constitutionally mandatory so as to enable the deprived populace to regain their dignity.

However, the reality is diametrically opposed to the perceived vision. Though affirmative action has made it possible for marginalised groups to take the first step towards education, the end result is far from satisfactory. Numerous reports, by official bodies, international agencies, and non-governmental institutions, testify to the dismal statistics where the education of the former is concerned.

The Strange Case of Krishna Mohan

In May 2007, Krishna Mohan[4] landed in Delhi from a non-descript village in Chengalpattu district in Tamil Nadu. Hailing from a Dalit background he received neither financial nor academic support from his family which subsisted on daily wages. However, he was confident of his academic abilities as he had scored first class throughout his student life. He joined the post-graduate course in Mathematics Department at Delhi University after clearing the entrance examination. It is essential to include a caveat here. The sciences programme in any Indian university operates with a Brahmanical mindset. The assumption is that as the science subjects are very serious and tough unlike the "frivolous" humanities and liberal arts programme, only the cream of brains can access it. No wonder the departments balk at any idea of implementing affirmative action and campaign vociferously that the idea of merit will be diluted if students from the marginalised groups enter the won-drous world of science. There are numerous cases of Dalit students dropping out of science programmes unable to cope with the humiliation that they experience.[5] To illustrate, a university professor and a Pro-Vice Chancellor (from the Mathematics Department, Hyderabad Central University) got a well dug in his official quarters as the municipal water supply would smear his "Brahmanical purity". When public resources are sullied by such antics, one can imagine the helpless plight of Dalit students in negotiating the insti-tutional power structure.

Krishna Mohan wrote the internal exam for eight papers, with the weight-age of 25 marks. However, he scored in single digits in all the papers. Similarly, in the annual examination, his highest was 24 in two papers out of a maximum of 75 marks. The end result showed a grand total of 147 marks out of a total of 800 marks. Needless to say, he had been failed deliber-ately. Ironically, Krishna Mohan secured 69 per cent in his Secondary School Examination, 77 per cent in Senior Secondary, and 63 per cent in his gradu-ation. All these percentages of marks were scored in Mathematics. It is dif-ficult to imagine how suddenly his percentage will register a sharp decline in his first-year Master of Science course.[6] Determined to fight this blatant discrimination, he spoke privately to a few sympathetic teachers, but to no avail. He approached student groups ranging from the radical left organisa-tions to Dalit groups who were unable to extend their support both morally and financially. They could not bargain either with the department or with university authorities to amicably resolve the issue.

Thus began his journey of running from pillar to post, from the University Vice-Chancellor and the Registrar, Dean Students Welfare, the National Commission for Scheduled Castes, the Ministries such as Social Justice and Empowerment, Human Resource Development, and the University Grants Commission in his quest for justice. He even approached the Chairperson, Parliamentary Committee on Welfare for SC/ST Matters. However, his pleas for redressal got buried under the maze of bureaucratic tangles. His was a lonesome struggle. No organisation took out a candle light procession in his support nor was any financial help forthcoming. The entire edifice of the grievance redressal mechanism failed to deliver. Or maybe Krishna Mohan was too inconsequential for the system to respond.

Institutional Responses/Failures

Initially, Krishna Mohan approached the faculty concerned of the Department of Mathematics, Delhi University, and they derisively informed him that the evaluation process was appropriate and that there was no discrimination. On 1 September 2008, he registered a written complaint to the Chairperson, Scheduled Caste Commission, New Delhi, about the ongoing harassment of Scheduled Caste students, including himself, in the evaluation process of the above-mentioned department.

This year I had to appear for M.Sc (Previous) examination due to the denial of marks which I actually deserved in the last year's examination (2007). But things have not changed and again this year, I am denied the deserving marks. This is posing a threat to my career; I cannot even appear for CSIR exam for further studies.[7]

In response to the above complaint, the Commission directed the institution to submit a status report and comments on the complaint received, within 15 days of the notice, either by post or in person, or by any other means of communication, failing which the Commission may exercise the powers of the Civil Courts.[8] Taking cognisance of similar complaints filed by Krishna Mohan, the Ministry of Social Justice and Empowerment also requested the university authorities to examine the matter and take necessary action in the interests of the student(s) concerned.[9] The university Registrar was also requested to expedite a solution to Krishna Mohan's problem. An identical letter was dispatched by the University Grants Commission to the Deputy Registrar, SC/ST Cell, with a special request to pursue the matter of SC/ST candidates with the university for appropriate action.[10] In addition, in responding to Krishna Mohan's plea, the Private Secretary to the Minister of State for Human Resource Development (GOI) communicated to the Vice-Chancellor, Delhi University, to examine and appropriately consider the matter.[11]

Interestingly, the university authorities thought it apt to respond to only the communication from the Scheduled Caste Commission since the Constitution of India has conferred upon it the powers of the Civil Court under Article 338. Hence, if no reply is forthcoming within the stipulated time (15 days) of the receipt of the notice, summons can be issued to appear in person or by a representative of the institution concerned, before the Commission. As the other bodies are merely advisory in nature, without any statutory obligations it is easy to ignore their appeals. The university authorities simply quoted the rules of the examination procedure, without even verifying the marks or discussing with the aggrieved parties.

> Since the candidate could not secure the requisite percentage of marks, i.e., 40% marks, in at least half of the courses, his result of the above examination taken by him has been *correctly declared as "Failed"*. It is requested that the position explained above may be taken on *record and the matter closed*. (Researchers' Emphasis)[12]

As the university failed to respond in a positive manner, the SC Commission further directed the former to place a comprehensive report on the actual performance of Krishna Mohan within five days of the receipt of the letter.[13] The university provided a complete account of the marks obtained in the Master of Science (Mathematics) both Part I (Eight Papers 2007) and Part I (Re-appeared in 2008). In Part I, the score was 66 out of a total of 600, the internal assessment component comprising 200 marks, out of which he attained 41. The grand total was 107 out of 800 marks. Out of the total of eight papers, the candidate achieved minimum pass marks only in one paper (40 marks). He again appeared for the same examination as an ex-student in 2008 and was able to notch up 106 out of 600, and in internal assessment, 41 out of 200. The grand total was 147 out of 800. The astonishing feature is that in the paper (No. VIII), which he had cleared as a regular with minimum 40 per cent marks, he was not able to reflect comparable merit and he flunked the same paper as an ex-student (31 marks).[14]

The SC Commission flagged the issue as "Denial of Marks of qualifying in the Exam" and directed the University Vice-Chancellor and the Registrar to discuss in person with full facts accompanied by all the original documents of the case. The petitioner was also directed to be present at the time of discussion in the commission.[15] The university, in a lackadaisical manner, curtly informed the SC Commission that the candidate's answer scripts have been checked and no discrepancy has been found in the process of evaluation.[16] Krishna Mohan's was not an isolated case as another student of the same department had approached the SC Commission on 10 November 2008 complaining of harassment in the department. He too had found fault with the evaluation process.[17]

Deeming the university's response as too apathetic, yet again the SC Commission directed the Registrar and the Senior Deputy Registrar (SC/ST) to respond to the complaints of both candidates with full facts and all relevant original records of the cases.[18] Likewise, the University Grants Commission reminded the university of its failure to take action regarding its earlier communications. This letter also included a copy of the representation received from the Ministry of Human Resource Development (No.F.7-1/2008 (SC/ST) 16/9/2008) to the University Grants Commission to take necessary action in this matter.[19] A copy of this letter was marked to the complainant, the Deputy Registrar, SC/ST Cell Delhi University with a request to pursue the matter of SC/ST candidates, and the Under Secretary, GOI, SC/ST Cell, Department of Higher Education, Ministry of Human Resource Development.

The entire case of Krishna Mohan was dealt with by junior officials of the SC Commission. Perceiving that the university authorities are not taking serious note of the problem, the Director of the SC Commission intervened in the matter. In a communication to the Vice-Chancellor and the Registrar, he mentioned the complete case details and rejoinders and urged the university to place before the Honourable Chairperson, SC Commission, all the original answer sheets and question papers in a sealed cover within three days of the receipt of the letter.[20] Despite receiving such an urgent notice from the SC Commission, the university authorities remained unfazed, upon which a reminder was sent to the Vice-Chancellor and the Registrar to appear in person within two days of the receipt of this letter for the information of the Honourable Chairperson. Any failure to comply with this order would make the institution liable for judicial action.[21]

A meeting was scheduled with the consent of all the parties (the complainant and the university authorities) on 23 February 2009[22] at the office of the Honourable Chairperson, SC Commission. However, the same was postponed and re-convened on 5 March 2009. All pending cases of Delhi University were taken up for discussion.[23] The university failed in submitting Krishna Mohan's answer scripts during this meeting.[24] A decision was taken that the faculty of another university will evaluate the answer scripts to verify Krishna Mohan's "merit".

While pursuing his battle for justice, Krishna Mohan was in frequent contact with the researchers. His apprehension was that even if the external evaluators mark him correctly, he would be further victimised in his department, since he had the temerity to question their judgement. At the most, the university would only offer him pass marks which will hamper his career prospects. In order to salvage his professional life, he appeared for the entrance examinations for different premier institutions, including the Indian Institute of Science, Bangalore, and again Delhi University. He proved his "merit" by securing a direct PhD seat at the Indian Institute of Science, Bangalore, which he could not avail of as he had to clear his master's first. Despite receiving an offer to join an internationally renowned institute to again pursue his master's, Krishna Mohan was in a dilemma as the admission fees were unaffordable. He conveyed to the researchers that he would like to continue his relentless efforts to secure justice. On further probing, he admitted that though he will avail fellowship, it was impossible for him to pay the admission fees. This was the reason that he was gambling with his career, knowing fully well the "hostility that comes with being a reserved category student".[25] At this juncture, some concerned teachers came forward to pay his admission fees.

Conclusion

On a personal level, Krishna Mohan proved his "merit" by continuing his studies despite the efforts of modern Dronacharyas to thrust him out of their sacred space. He displayed courage in taking on the entire institutional structures in his relentless struggle to get justice. Unfortunately, the system set in place to minimise discrimination and ensure equity miserably failed to uphold their constitutional obligations. Even the most definitive constitutional body, the National Commission for Scheduled Castes, merely wrote letters despite its mandate to prosecute the violators of Dalit "merit". It is incongruous that when the civil society is debating the Right to Education Act, the university authorities, the University Grants Commission, and the Ministries of Social Justice and Empowerment and Human Resource Development could not guarantee that a single Dalit student, who proved his "merit" through entrance examination, could successfully complete his course. The tale is more tragic that even student organisations of whichever ideology failed to support Krishna Mohan. It is a sheer fortune of destiny that he received timely assistance from some concerned teachers that the story had a happy ending.

There are many more unfortunate victims who are sacrificed at the altar of spurious "merit". How can we forget Senthil Kumar,[26] a doctoral scholar in the Physics Department of Hyderabad Central University? He committed suicide as he was deliberately not promoted. As a result, his fellowship was curtailed. His family survived by rearing pigs, and his scholarship money was a major source for them. One can only ponder at the evaluation system that Senthil Kumar successfully completed MPhil, acquired the required grades, cleared the entrance exam, and enrolled for PhD. Suddenly, his teachers at Hyderabad Central University found him unfit for research. He was not provided a supervisor even after a year of study. Unable to withstand this humiliation he took his life.

These two case studies reveal the diverse forms of protest. However, Krishna Mohan succeeded in challenging the system and thereby reaffirming the "politics of presence". His exemplary valour should be a reference for anyone fighting for equality and justice. The institutions funded by public resources should be more accountable for upholding due procedures and norms. Giving admissions is the first step. Providing an enabling and inclusive environment will enhance the students' potential and nurture their development as responsible citizens and lead a meaningful life.

Notes

1 Published in *Social Action: A Quarterly Review of Social Trends* (January–March 2011).
2 Aristotle, *Nicomachean Ethics*, Tr. By D. Ross, 1980, pp. 12–14.
3 Amartya Sen, *Social Exclusion: Concept, Application, Scrutiny*, Critical Quest, New Delhi, 2007, p. 3.
4 Name and Place Changed to Ensure Privacy.
5 Thorat Committee Report: Caste Discrimination in AIIMS, 24/08/2008, http://endcampuscasteism.wordpress.com/2008/08/24/thorat-committee-report-caste-discrimination-in-aiims/ Accessed on 5/12/2010.
6 The Candidate's Statement of Marks of Different Institutions.
7 Correspondence Between Krishna Mohan and the Chairperson, Scheduled Caste Commission, New Delhi, 1/09/2008.
8 Ibid.
9 Correspondence between the Deputy Director SC Commission, New Delhi, GOI and the Vice Chancellor and Registrar, University of Delhi, File No. 16/47/2008/DELHI/ESDW, 15/09/2008.
10 Correspondence between the Additional Secretary, Ministry of Social Justice and Empowerment, GOI and the Vice Chancellor, Delhi University, 16/09/2008.
11 Correspondence between the Under Secretary, University Grants Commission and the Registrar, Delhi University, File No. 7-3/2007 (SCT), 25/09/2008.
12 Correspondence between the Private Secretary, Minister of State (HRD, GOI) to the Vice Chancellor, Delhi University, File No. 2570, 15/10/2008.
13 Correspondence between the Registrar, University of Delhi and the Deputy Director, National Commission for Scheduled Castes, GOI, Ref. No. Exam. III (i)/2008/1495, 6/10/2008.
14 Correspondence between the Assistant Director, National Commission for Scheduled Castes, GOI, Ref No. 16/47/08/ DELHI/ ESDW, 20/10/2008.

15 Correspondence between the Registrar, Delhi University, and the Assistant Director, National Commission for Scheduled Castes, GOI, Ref No. Exam III (i) 1532 24/10/2008.
16 Communication through Fax between the Assistant Director, National Commission for Scheduled Castes, GOI and the Vice-Chancellor (Fax No. 27667049) and Registrar (Fax No. 27666350) Delhi University Ref No. 16/47/08/Delhi/ESDW, 4/11/2008.
17 Correspondence between the Deputy Registrar (Results) University of Delhi and the Assistant Director, National Commission for Scheduled Castes, GOI, Ref No. Exam III (i) /2008/1570, 15/11/2008.
18 Correspondence between the Deputy Director, National Commission for Scheduled Castes, GOI, and Vice-Chancellor and Registrar, Delhi University, File No. 16/60/08/Delhi ESDW 17/11/2008.
19 Correspondence between the Assistant Director, National Commission for Scheduled Castes, GOI, and Registrar, and the Senior Deputy Registrar, Delhi University, No. 16/47/08/ Delhi ESDW 26/11/2008.
20 Correspondence between the Section Officer, University Grants Commission and the Registrar Delhi University, No. F 7-3/2007 (SCT) 2/12/2008.
21 Correspondence between the Director, National Commission for Scheduled Castes, GOI, and the Vice- Chancellor and the Registrar, Delhi University, No. 16/47/08, 16-60-08/Delhi/ ESDW 16/1/2009.
22 Communication between the Assistant Director, National Commission for Scheduled Castes, GOI and the Vice-Chancellor and Registrar Delhi University, Ref No. No. 16/47/08, 16-60-08/Delhi/ ESDW 3/2/2009.
23 Communication between the Assistant Director, National Commission for Scheduled Castes, GOI and the Vice-Chancellor and Registrar, Delhi University, Ref No. No. 16/47/08, 16-60-08/Delhi/ ESDW 20/2/2009. Communication between the Registrar, Delhi University Assistant Director, National Commission for Scheduled Castes, GOI No. SPA/R/2009, 20/2/2009.
24 Communication between the Assistant Director, National Commission for Scheduled Castes, GOI and the Vice-Chancellor and Registrar, Delhi University, Ref No.16/56-A/08/Delhi/ESDW 3/3/2009.
25 One of the Researchers was part of the meeting.
26 Thorat Committee Report, op.cit.

Index

.

For Product Safety Concerns and Information please contact our EU
representative GPSR@taylorandfrancis.com
Taylor & Francis Verlag GmbH, Kaufingerstraße 24, 80331 München, Germany

www.ingramcontent.com/pod-product-compliance
Lightning Source LLC
Chambersburg PA
CBHW070711280326
41926CB00089B/3775